Hugh Hood

Hugh Hood was born and raised in Toronto. He received his Ph.D. from the University of Toronto, and later settled in Montréal where he teaches English at l'Université de Montréal. *The New Age/Le nouveau siècle* unites his encyclopedic knowledge of art with a keen sense of Canadian culture and style. Hood has created a group of novels that capture what he calls "historical mythology, the articulation of the past, the articulation of the meaning of our society in terms of the way we live our lives, in terms of the institutions we're so intensely aware of that we don't even think we're thinking about them."

Louis de Niverville

Louis de Niverville was born in Andover, England, and was raised in Ottawa and Montreal. He moved to Toronto in 1957, and it is in that year that he began to paint. His works are in numerous public and private collections in Canada and the United States.

New Press Canadian Classics

Distinguished by the use of Canadian fine art on its covers, New Press Canadian Classics is an innovative series of high-quality, reasonably priced editions of the very best Canadian fiction, nonfiction, and poetry.

New Press Canadian Classics

Hubert Aquin *The Antiphonary*, Alan Brown (trans.)

Margaret Atwood *Surfacing*

Sandra Birdsell *Night Travellers*

Constance Beresford-Howe *The Marriage Bed*

Marie-Claire Blais *Nights in the Underground*, Ray Ellenwood (trans.)

Clark Blaise *A North American Education, Tribal Justice*

Matt Cohen *The Expatriate*

George Elliott *The Kissing Man*

Mavis Gallant *My Heart Is Broken*

Anne Hébert *Héloise*, Sheila Fischman (trans.), *In the Shadow of the Wind*, Sheila Fischman (trans.) *Kamouraska*, Norman Shapiro (trans.)

David Helwig *The Glass Knight, Jennifer, It Is Always Summer*

Hugh Hood *White Figure, White Ground, You Can't Get There from Here, A New Athens, Reservoir Ravine, Black and White Keys*

M.T. Kelly *I Do Remember the Fall*

Martin Kevan *Racing Tides*

Robert Kroetsch *Alibi, Badlands*

Félix Leclerc *The Madman, the Kite & the Island*, Philip Stratford (trans.)

Hugh MacLennan *Voices in Time, Each Man's Son, The Watch That Ends the Night, Two Solitudes*

Keith Maillard *Alex Driving South, Cutting Through, The Knife in My Hands*

Antonine Maillet *Pélagie*, Philip Stratford (trans.)

Gwendolyn MacEwen *Noman*

Brian Moore *An Answer from Limbo*

Ken Norris (Ed.) *Canadian Poetry Now*

Leon Rooke *Fat Woman, Shakespeare's Dog*

Reorge Ryga *The Ecstasy of Rita Joe and Other Plays*

Carol Shields *Various Miracles*

Audrey Thomas *Intertidal Life*

Helen Weinzweig *Basic Black with Pearls*

new press CANADIAN CLASSICS

Hugh Hood

The Swing in the Garden
The New Age: Volume One

Stoddart

Published in 1993 by
Stoddart Publishing Co. Limited
34 Lesmill Road
Toronto, Canada
M3B 2T6
(416) 445-3333

Canadian Cataloguing in Publication Data

Hood, Hugh, 1928–
The swing in the garden

(New Press Canadian classics)
ISBN 0-7736-7414-4

I. Title.   II. Series.

PS8515.049S8 1993   C813′.54   C93-095312-6
PR9199.3.H66S8 1993

Originally published in 1975 by Oberon

ECW Press edition published in 1980

General Paperbacks edition published in 1984
Reprinted in 1983, 1986

Printed and bound in the United States of America

For Sarah Hood, with my best love

1

In those days we used to have a red-and-white garden swing set up in the backyard beside the garage, a noisy outbuilding of rusty corrugated metal stamped in shivering, wave-like sheets, which rumbled with theatrical thunder when the wind blew hard. We would pretend a thunderstorm was at hand, Amanda Louise and I, making the swing oscillate faster and faster in anticipation of a brisk blow. There was a seafaring tradition behind both sides of the family; my mother's grandfather had been a sea captain and my father's people had vaguely naval connections, so we might pretend to be aloft in the rigging, clambering up the swing supports to lie along the crosspieces at the top of the frame, able seamen on an exposed yardarm, something along that line.

That swing suffered many imaginary metamorphoses, being alternately sailing vessel, locomotive, racing auto, bedroom for Amanda Louise's nomadic, ever-varying tribe of dolls and animals—most often some means of transport, a comparison that suggested itself very naturally from the shape of the swing and its members. It was a design which, I suppose, originated in Québec or along the Ontario-Québec border, possibly because of the abundance of cheap lumber in hinterlands still imperfectly cleared. Parts of the swing were painted a very grateful red, almost a cherry colour, and the remainder were finished in a hard, clear, faintly yellow varnish which resisted all weathers. The swing was never taken in during the winter. We made up stories about who

1

was living in it while it lay buried in snow, but discernible as a blocky hump with perhaps four nubbins of wood projecting through a sheath of ice, the top corners of the wooden skeleton, sodden bleeding red ends. Amanda would insinuate the presence of goblins inside the hump, snow elves like those in the terrifying story of the snow queen in the third volume of *Journeys through Bookland*. Elves, or maybe trolls, she would profess, older than I was by not quite three years, sharply aware of my infant addiction to realities and facts.

After she went away to play with her large family, in late afternoon with darkness drawing in at four o'clock, I would stand at the dining-room window and stare out into the darkness, trying to make out the parts and movements of the swing under the crusted ice, imagining how it would be when spring came and we could make it go again. It was built in two principal parts, a frame comprised of four sturdy red wooden uprights joined at the top by crosspieces of a striking scissor-like shape, and the moveable body of the swing itself, with slatted benches facing one another across a floor or footrest, also slatted. This floor could be removed by enterprising children so that the bench seats hung loosely, suspended from above; they could then be made to swing independently of each other, and unwary neighbour kids could be trapped and sometimes nearly decapitated by benches swinging out of phase. This manoeuvre was theoretically forbidden, but I remember Adam Sinclair running all the way to the end of the street, crying bitterly that we had inveigled him into this dangerous situation, then almost killed him. A witness to the attempt, my mother compressed her lips—I wasn't sure why—and ordered us to put the floorboards back immediately. She turned to my grandmother, then staying in the house, and murmured something about destroying evidence.

They returned to the house while Amanda Louise and I hefted the platform and wrestled it into place. At each corner it had little bite-sized slots which fitted over the wooden rod that supported the bench seats; when the apparatus was in motion the rods rolled in their slots, making a musical sound of wood on wood almost like the tone of a violin. This music could not be banished by successive lubrications. I believe the rods swelled and contracted from alternate damp and dryness because it was often very hard to fit the floorboards back in place after a session of "executioner," our name for our game of playmate-entrapment.

Amanda named the game. I was far too young to know such a word, much less pronounce it. But I got the sense of it from playing the game. Amanda had invented "executioner" and played it first on me before trying it on Adam and later on Mildred and Marigold Smith, daughters of Mr. Busdriver Smith who lived two houses down the street. Their wails over badly barked shins seemed as loud to me as their mother's voice when she used to call them at mealtimes.

"Mildred . . . Marigold. . . ." Her voice had a swanlike, elegiac, floating quality. She used to end her call on a rising inflection, as though asking a question of the greater part of north Rosedale.

". . . Mildred . . . dred . . . dred . . . Marigold . . . oollllldd." Echo upon echo.

Her girls' voices had something of this floating airy carry to them. When we swung the swing seats at them from behind, chopping them off at the knees and executing them like the executioner in *Alice* (which is where Amanda Louise found the word), their wails of pain may have drifted halfway up the Bridle Path across the tracks, or southward to mysterious St. Andrew's Gardens, trackless and inviolate.

Not all swinging games involved aggression and execution; most invoked processes of transport, I guess because of the CPR main line which ran immediately behind our backyard at the foot of the hill, below the range of overgrown vacant lots that lay along the hillside separating north Rosedale from Moore Park.

Rosedale Heights Drive. Sighthill. Ridge Drive. These names swam naturally to the surface in the imaginations of real-estate developers of the nineteen-twenties to demarcate with sturdy gentility the prospect southward from Moore Park. The heights, hill, ridge so marked were of course that same hill found all the way across Toronto, of sharper or gentler incline depending where you take it, on Christie Street, on Bathurst, on Avenue Road and Yonge Street, up MacLennan Hill, declining only across the Don Valley where other ridges and spurs break the pattern of escarpment.

The Hill! Cursed roundly all winter by streetcar motormen. Cause of terrible breakdowns in traffic flow at every rush hour, then and now. Our promised land as we gazed at the hillside across the tracks from seats in the swing on bench or floor. We thought the Bridle Path was the Bridal Path, associating it not so much with horses as with the wedding march.

We found early on—before Amanda Louise went to baby class—that you could lift the bench seats and fold them back like a windshield against the seatbacks; then you could climb down inside the bench and pretend to be any of half a dozen things: operator of one of the handcars we saw daily along the tracks; locomotive engineer; oarsman because of the rowing motion which made the swing go. One of us could pump, slowly at first as the other called out "Boooaaarr-rddd," and then faster and faster as the brakeman, usually Amanda, chose the right moment to hop aboard.

A few years later we used to play this game with real boxcars along the train tracks, but we wouldn't let the girls come along, too scary. There were other things we did when the time came, which would have made my mother purse her lips more forcibly. I don't know how much she ever heard about them. Tricks played on top of boxcars and under their wheels along the rods, learned from swinging I suppose, but more grown-up or at least more like later childhood, demonstrations of feelings of growing independence, which evolved slowly in me. I was happy for long to stay in the backyard where I'd been told to stay, lifting the bench seats and squeezing into the open space below, the cockpit—a word I learned early from stories of flying aces read to me out of *Collins' Aircraft Annual* by one or another of the leisured adults who inhabited our six-room house: my maternal grandparents during longer or shorter periods of financial instability and recapitalization; my father's parents for a brief time until they went to live across the ravine on Summerhill Gardens where, one cold morning in February at the beginning of the nineteen-thirties, my father's mother died rather young, very easily in her sleep, the absence of any breath detected by the ancient device of holding a mirror before her mouth, the sudden desperate act of her youngest son.

After that my father's much younger brother Philip might stay with us from time to time, burning bedclothes with cigarettes and generally distressing his older brother. My uncle Philip had been "hit hard" by his mother's death, and never seemed completely repaired in later life. Such a father, such an elder brother, must have seemed a heavy burden to him, growing up in Toronto in the early thirties, uprooted from genial Maritime home to observe his father's adventures and misfortunes in Upper Canada, his mother's sudden death in this distant country.

Our house had strangers in it at all times, when not relatives then maids or indigents and unfortunates whom my parents would find here and there. I speak of it as a six-room house and so it was at first: living-room, dining-room, kitchen, three bedrooms and a bathroom upstairs, enormous uneconomical clinker-laden coal furnace lurking in cavernous cellar. It had been built at the tag-end of the twenties by a small builder, not a real-estate developer, named Faucett, who had lived in it himself for a short period, perhaps testing his own design for future modification elsewhere. Then he had rented it to my parents for $40 a month, rather a steep price in those days. They had been married for almost four years. Amanda existed—her existence has always been unquestionable—and I was giving evidence of imminent arrival. Houseroom became mandatory.

"What we have is a six-room house." My father had

many small turns of phrase, easily parodied and remembered, with which my mother, and eventually his children, used to tease him by choral, almost antiphonal repetition. "What we have is a six-room house." "Put the cap on good and tight." "The peaceful evolution of Socialism." He sometimes referred to Adam Sinclair, though never to the child's face or in front of his parents, as "yon wee Scotch farrrrtttt," rolling the *r* in caricatured Scotticism. This was not meant in any way to ridicule or diminish Adam; it was a complicated criticism of verbal style, a kind of humour almost impossible to explain or defend before people with no ear for it. My mother would be shaking with silent laughter, and her mother would be unmoved, incapable of detecting a joke of this kind.

"What we have is a six-room house," my father would maintain, for some years after Mr. Faucett built the addition at the back, which might justifiably be denied the status of room proper. It was an insulated frame sunporch, just useable in winter, looking out on the swing and the garage and the weeds, where successive familial squatters, grandparents or uncle, might be lodged for longer or shorter terms and where "the maid" lived when space was available. I don't remember the construction of this addition and surmise that it was done during my mother's pregnancy before my birth. Mr. Faucett, an easygoing, accommodating landlord in those days, must have tacked on the sunporch as an improvement on his investment, perhaps also as a gesture in honour of the pending arrival of the infant Matthew Goderich.

"It's actually your room," my mother would say to me as we sat next to the hot window glass in March. "It was built because of you, that's the same thing."

"How did you know I was coming? And when?"

"Oh I knew, my friend. I could tell."

If staying in the house, my grandmother would call from the kitchen, "You spoil that child, Isabelle," and my mother would stiffen slightly, then give me a squeeze. In moments my grandmother Archambault would appear in the door from the kitchen which fascinated me because it had been the door to the outside, and you could still see the marks around the aperture where the outside steps had gone down.

"*Va-t-en, lapin,*" she would say. A determined woman, not to be deflected from her purposes by charm, something I learned early and one of the most valuable lessons anybody ever taught me. We had a set of heavy velvet curtains hanging from a brass rod in the double doorway between living-room and dining-room. They were ordinarily drawn right back to either side of the frame and hung in musty, deep-piled folds, dark red on one side, dark blue on the other; to me they were immensely ancient robes or tents or tapestries or some other thickly covering object. I used to wrap one of the curtains around me, then turn on my heels and wind myself up inside the twisting narrowing folds, sometimes to the point where my hair was twined into the velvet. The air would be dark red, dark blue.

I would begin to spin the other way. The tightly twisted material would roll suddenly open all the way down its length and I'd fall out on the floor where the dining-room and living-room met, staring at the tiny brass plate let into the floor, housing for the latch of double doors which had been removed. Above me the curtain would swirl and sussurate, and my grandmother, arms akimbo, would stand glaring at me.

"*Enfant gaté!*"

One day while I was playing this ostensibly innocent game, my parents away from the house and my grandmother in charge of me, I wound the curtain one or two turns too far and all at once the heavy brass rod jerked loose from its supports, fell and conked me on the head, then rolled harmlessly away along the floor.

Sometimes you see characters in animated cartoons who have sustained a severe accidental blow. Their eyes are made to roll like marbles in their sockets, round and round with the sound of stones rolling in glass. I felt as though my eyes were rolling like that, stunned and deeply pained at the same time. My legs went rubbery, though the falling rod had been partly cushioned by velvet. My grandmother looked up vindictively from her sewing basket.

"Dieu t'as puni," she exclaimed with succinct force. I've never forgotten that moment. It seemed to me then, and does now, strangely disproportionate to invoke the dreadful engine of Divine Wrath to correct the obstinacy of a three-year-old. A scolding would have been appropriate or even no punishment at all but the dazed feeling and the hope that no permanent injury had been self-inflicted.

"God punished you." At this date I can't blame my grandmother's idle exclamation for feelings of oncoming retribution grown up through five decades, more, more. That God will indeed punish repeated wrong has always seemed to me a reasonable expectation, even before the brass rod fell on my head in, I figure, the year 1933. Before that certainly; how long before? Does one suspect this in the womb? Seems a hard fate. That first expulsion, psychiatry to the contrary, is nothing to what follows, successive expulsions outward toward larger, larger, less enclosed spaces. My grandmother liked to get me out of the house as much as possible, not because she disliked me—on the whole I doubt if she did—but because she had a deep faith in the cautionary power of existence out of doors. I never remember a time when, meeting her in the sunporch or kitchen, she didn't say, "Run outside and play, *petit*." She said it to Amanda Louise, quite clearly her darling, as often as to me, so I have no complaint, and I owe to Mme. Archambault my fascination with the backyard, the train tracks and the hill lying above the tracks, and what I could see or guess at along the tracks to east and west.

Before I was allowed to go out of the backyard, I knew pretty well what I could expect to find toward the west end of our street. The tracks ran straight in that direction and if I pressed right tight against the network of tough wire fencing with barbed wire on top, right over in the corner of our yard,

I could see quite a long way west. Not as far as the ravine, or what was then called North Toronto Station, but certainly as far as the level crossing at the foot of MacLennan Hill. There was a watchtower at the crossing which I could easily see from the backyard, and a set of gates, in my infancy operated by hand by the watchman, later on mechanically. I could see cars bumping over the crossing and proceeding gingerly up the steep hill, cars with folding canvas tops and mica side-curtains that snap-fastened into place.

Perhaps most of the practical *va-et-vient* of living can be abstracted into patterns of the conquest of space. I can remember how strongly I felt that I was moving outward into bigger and bigger rooms and perimeters: there was the first blankness, not forgetfulness because of there being nothing recollected. I mean the womb. Was nothing recollected? I won't dispute the question, but supposing that the womb was an insensate blankness, I came first into a wooden rocking cradle, painted white, with clusters of small blue and red flowers and bows traced on the head and foot boards. We still have that cradle; my children use it. Afterward I was strapped into a wicker go-cart and taken for rides up and down the verandah. The first tool or instrument I ever learned to control was the brake on that go-cart, a little switch on a spring which pressed a plate against the right front wheel. Traditional in the Goderich annals is the tale of how at eleven months I put out my infant hand and put the brake on, when the go-cart rolled away from my mother toward the verandah steps. First episode in the epic cycle. I don't quite remember having done that, but I vividly remember resenting the chest strap that held me in place. Spaces. Ever widening spaces. When I first played in the backyard, I was on a lead, a length of cord attached to a ring which slid along the clothesline and gave me perhaps more range of movement than my parents had in mind. When on the lead I could work in around behind the garage, wedged up against the railway fence, where I made enchanting discoveries well before the age of three. There was a two-foot space between the garage and the fence in which was deposited considerable junk: at least three old tires, the narrow high tires of 1925, an auto battery, some rusty pieces of iron whose use I couldn't guess, broken window glass, greenish sharded. Orange Crush bottles. Large chunky tufts of coarse grass rooted in hard mud. Ancient licence plates, two enormous pieces of glazed pottery in a shiny deep brown—beautiful objects I thought them at the time. Now they've become collectors' pieces. They were insulators fallen from the Hydro line which hummed overhead along spindly towers. And in that squeezed-in cockpit were also short lengths of eavestroughing, a paint can with skinned-over green paint at the bottom, a hardened misshapen paintbrush, an old rubber boot which made me laugh when I spied it. I knew whose it was. There were big worms. And King Billies in the summer. And along the tracks went older boys of the neighbourhood whose names I gradually came to recognize by an inner osmotic process that nobody can explain.

The Silcox boys, the Levys, Jerry Forbes from Jean Street and later on his little brother Jakie, Georgie-Balls Bannon, occasionally Howard, Dick and Harold Lyall. The kingly Mostyn McNally.

"Let him off his leash and bring him along."

"Don't be a dilly, Silcox. He's too little. He'd get hurt."

"Who's got a big cent? Here, lay it on the track."

I stood with my nose pressed through an aperture in the weave of the wire fencing and watched, fascinated. David Silcox put his ear to the track and listened. "She's coming." He looked in his pockets and found another big cent and laid it flat on the rail.

"Come on, Silcox, you'll get cut off."

Now you could hear the train.

"A double-header, I bet you." Bells clanged at the level crossing and the boys scampered across the tracks and rolled into the drainage ditch on the other side as the train came by. It was a double-header, which meant seventy cars or more. That's how I learned to count, long before I went to school, counting the cars on passing freight trains. I learned the alphabet the same way, all out of order. I thought R followed P and P followed C. It took me a couple of years in the lower grades to stop saying A,B,C,P,R, when asked to recite the alphabet. My father used to chortle about this and even boast about it to colleagues from the university, around the house for an evening.

"A striking instance of auto-didacticism," he would say. "Come here, Matt, say the alphabet."

My father and I understood each other pretty well, and I used to play up to him shamelessly, working the initials of half-a-dozen railroads into this calling-over of the infrastructure of literacy. T,H and B, would go in, C,P,R, quite naturally, N,Y,N,H and H was harder to embroider into the fabric of the joke, and very seldom seen along the tracks anyway, but at two and a half I had learned by sight the Delaware and Lackawanna (romantic name), Lehigh Valley, Chesapeake and Ohio, Boston and Maine, and once perhaps (or did I imagine this much later in life) I saw a box-car with Stoverville, Westport and Lake Superior written on it.

A double-header travelling at the speed permissible along that right of way, which approached a bridge a mile or so to the east, would take a while to pass, certainly five minutes, perhaps more. In wintertime the transit of such a train would cause a long backup of cars at the level crossing, then trouble in the ascent of the notoriously difficult incline. There were large hoppers full of sand and gravel at bottom and top of the hill for motorists to use. After a train passed during rush hour in January, there would be confusion at the level crossing for as long as half an hour. Curious how the train tracks used to dominate the life of Canadian cities; that stretch of CPR mainline caused heavy stone overpasses to be built and rebuilt over and over again in Toronto on all main north-south roadways, at immense trouble and expense to departments of public works. It's the same in Montréal, where train tracks used to cut the city virtually in half at certain times of day—cold slow late afternoons in deep winter.

Flatcars, gondola cars, hopper cars, refrigerator cars, cattle cars, tank cars, box cars, automobile carriers, all known to me and identifiable at three years; when they had passed the boys would reappear along the tracks creeping like Indians from a pampas concealment, from overgrown embankment or culvert or just ditch, to recover the copper coins which the train had pressed flat. Sometimes a thin smear of copper colouring could be peeled back from the shining rail; otherwise it might be run and rolled out so fine as to merge in alloy with the steel. Could that really have happened? Had the weight of those many wheels so heated the copper and liquefied it as to have bonded it to the rails? The Silcox boys, their father a mining engineer and company promoter, claimed expert understanding of all metals, and asserted largely that an alloy had indeed been formed by the pressure. "My father said so, that's why, Bannon, you want to fight about it? You want to call my father a liar? My father knows more about metals that you'll ever know or your father either. . . ."

This was a low blow and warning looks would pass among the boys because Georgie-Balls Bannon had no visible father on the record.

"Shut up Silcox," said Mostyn McNally, "let's go down along to the bridge and fool around." I never remember hearing those boys using the common obscenities, certainly not Mostyn McNally. That day I couldn't talk perfectly, but I could understand their talk and when I saw that they were going away from me I began to cry. I knew I would not be allowed off my lead for years to come.

"I come too. I come too."

Mostyn stopped and came back. He seemed as old as my parents, but must really have been only eleven or twelve at the time, the natural leader of this group though from the poorest family.

"Don't cry, Matthew." He got down on his knees and

smiled at me through the fence, goldenrod tickling his chin and mine, some small blue flower flicking against buttercups. "I'll show you a secret but you have to promise not to use it, right?"

"All right, Mostyn."

He lay almost flat on his stomach and dug around with both hands in the grass and mud beneath the fence, clearing away stalks of weeds. All at once I perceived a hole under the fence plenty deep enough for a boy to wriggle through. This was how they got onto the tracks, when they didn't want to go through the tiresome business of being shouted at, cursed warmly, sometimes even chased by the crossing guard, or warned away from the tracks by Constable Kelly, who guarded the crossing before and after school hours. Later on I discovered a chain of these holes along the bottoms of wire fences which must extend across Canada. They are everywhere you look for them, dug by boys to get onto the tracks.

"Don't you come through here, Matt, you could get hurt by the trains. Do you understand?" He had slithered under the fence on his back and was sitting beside me with his arm around me. Then he jumped up and kicked one of the abandoned tires over the hole and sat on that and my mother appeared at the corner of the garage holding her camera, one of those old Kodaks with a lens that folded into the case, in an arrangement like an accordion in black leatherette. I used to think that this camera resembled the front end of a locomotive—everything was trains to me till I was four, and then everything was cars. The camera had an eye in front like the headlight on an engine; the viewfinder sat on top of it like a stubby smokestack and then it popped out of its flat case on a spring just like an engine coming out of a tunnel, I thought. In the *Book of Knowledge* there was a highly-coloured picture of a locomotive emerging from the guts of the Alps, perhaps from the Simplon tunnel, which looked to me exactly like my mother's Kodak.

She levelled this instrument at the two of us. "I didn't know you were around in back, Mostyn. I didn't notice you go up the driveway." She loved him. We all did.

"I just came to say hello to Matt, Mrs. Goderich," he said, smiling happily.

And so she took his picture that day in, say, 1932, sitting on top of an old tire, hiding the entryway to freedom with his legs and worn sneakers. Old Mostyn. With me looking up at him worshipfully, wanting to be just like him. Mostyn had a brother Monty, much closer to my age, in fact the same age as Amanda Louise and the first boy who ever had a crush on her, or so she began to maintain when they had gone through three grades together. I never felt as close to Monty as to Mostyn. They lived down the street on the other side of the stoneyard in a frame house which might have been a farmhouse long before the district was opened up and urbanized. Mostyn and Monty McNally. The first time I was ever allowed in their house I was stunned by the sudden sharp stink of poverty and dirt.

A few minutes later, after taking two or three snapshots, which turned out magnificently—my mother had a natural gift for photography—she left us alone, and I laughed and smiled as Mostyn worked his way back under the fence. "Goodbye, goodbye," I said, enjoying the shared secret of his arrival and departure, already able to sense the uses I might make of such a means of egress, if I could ever solve the problem of the knotted rope that attached me to the clothesline. I never did manage to untie those knots by myself; they were weirdly complicated, especially those of my grandmother's creation. She might have wanted me out of the house, but she also wanted me safe, and not off somewhere wandering along the tracks.

"Blowing his fingers off with percussion caps," she would say. One of the great succubi of my grandmother's fantasy life was percussion caps, their image constantly on her lips. Afterward when she and my grandfather used to have us to stay for part of the summer in their house in Sturgeon Falls, her apprehension of these objects was intensified because in that remote place the railroad tracks were not simply double and a main line, but a whole ramified arrangement of station, sidings, spurs, the shipping railhead for the town's sole product, wood pulp. When we used to go and stay for the summer in Sturgeon Falls, I was old enough to wander free, and my grandmother's warnings about percussion caps grew high in key.

And to this day, though I have seen many and many a piece of railwayman's paraphernalia, a percussion cap I have never seen. I wonder what they are, or were. Mme. Archambault's theory was that you picked them up on the tracks and they blew your fingers off, but I have no notion why this should be so, or what percussion was involved, what object percussed.

I began to sniffle privately after Mostyn had loped away along the tracks, but was soon distracted from the novel experience of grief by the appearance of a handcar from the west, two thin men in overalls laboriously working the handles up and down, and a fat man, doubtless a foreman, sitting on the edge of the platform dangling his legs; he smoked a pipe quite peacefully while his underlings sweated above and behind him. As they passed, he took his pipe from his mouth and smiled at me. I had often seen him before.

"Hello sonny."

One of the pumpers craned his neck around at a difficult angle and gave me a grin. Soon they moved around the wide graceful curve of the tracks, going away eastward toward the bridge over the belt-line ravine, the foot of Bayview Avenue, the bluffs below Leaside, and the Don Valley. I could hear the slow clickety-click of the flanged wheels long after they were out of sight.

There were other little cars like this, along that stretch of track, some operated by small gasoline engines, some with rudimentary cowcatchers. The roadbed must have required constant expert attention because of the volume of traffic that passed along it. My education—such as it is—was grounded in what I saw going along the tracks. I estimated the arrival of new seasons by shipments of canoes or cars or coal. Every November I got a great thrill when I saw flatcar after flatcar of Christmas trees go by from east to west. I suppose they were unloaded at some midtown siding and trucked away to vacant lots all over Toronto.

Cabooses.

I used to think how wonderful it would be to live in a caboose, to light the little lights to either side of the rear platform and entryway. To sit in the little tower and wave to children as our train passed through city or countryside—trainmen always waved to me, and I swore that given the chance I'd do likewise. I would climb up into that tower in my overalls of that peculiar seersucker-like striped blue-and-white material. There must be some kind of staircase or ladder, I thought. I would perch there and watch the front of the train. Sometimes I'd climb on top of the caboose and walk along the tops of the cars by the flattened runway I could see from the backyard, spiked to the roof of each car. I would now and then stand on the narrow steps at the very end of the caboose, lean way out to one side swinging a lantern and bellow commands to inferior members of the train crew. I was always the conductor. I'd learned from my father that every train carried a conductor, that every conductor carried a pocket chronometer adjusted to Greenwich Mean Time.

Every afternoon exactly at 5:30 a freight train passed the house, which meant that I would shortly be unleashed and brought into the house for my supper. By October it would already be getting dark, and I'd see the lights of the caboose move slowly away from me to the east as the train proceeded out of town—it was the most romantic image of my infant fantasy life, that pair of lights, red, green, curving off to the left in the growing dusk. Sometimes the door to the caboose would open suddenly and I'd see a trainman's figure silhouetted in weak yellow light, and I wanted to get off my restraining line and travel with him. Then I would be cross and close to tears when my mother came for me.

"Next year, next year," she would croon, picking at the knots in the rope, "you can run away from home next year." But I never ran away from home, never wanted to, don't want to now, just want to be free to travel hither and yon as I choose. It wasn't the railroad tracks that gave me freedom though, nor the garden swing. Sitting low down in the swing, working my arms and legs the way the handcar men pumped up and down, I early recognized that their activity, seemingly aimless and repetitive, had the effect of propelling them forward to some purpose, whereas my pumping, no matter how tireless and energetic, merely moved me back and forth in the same place, so that playing in the swing eventually began to tire me out and make me cranky and badly behaved. I could not admit the idea of so much action issuing in so little progress, and I might even have generalized this view at the age of four. I saw then that one has three choices about his course of life: progress, regress, or preservation of the status quo. I didn't have the vocabulary to make the point quite so precisely to my father, but I made it in some sense or other, because I can remember the delighted look of shared experience that crossed his face when I made the observation.

"You can go ahead, or go in reverse, or stay in the same spot," I said, "and that's all you can do." Perhaps the words "go in reverse" seem precocious for a four-year-old. Perhaps I didn't say exactly that, but I suspect that I did, because I was a mighty verbal type from babyhood and "go in reverse" was precisely the sort of phrase I'd have learned from the motoring enthusiasts of the early thirties. When my father heard these words, he took one of those instant decisions so characteristic of him. "Like Napoleon before Toulon," he used to say, and years later I understood that instinctive decisions of this sort formed a principal part of my father's myth of himself as great captain or leader of industry or baseball player. In fact he was a teacher of ethics and social philosophy at University College and lived a peculiarly retired life, making decisions mainly of the kind I now relate.

"He's too old to be kept in the backyard any more. I never liked keeping him on a string anyway."

"Oh Andrew!"

"We ought to let him go free."

My mother might have squeezed out a token tear. "I'd worry so much . . . and then there's this one. . . ," patting her abdomen. She was almost at the term of a third and final pregnancy.

"Yes, there is that. I don't want you worried. Suppose we say in the spring."

"In the spring, yes. I wouldn't mind that. There'll be his little sister to think about."

"We're going to have another son, Isabelle," said my father positively, one of the first of his speeches that I can remember word for word, likely because of the accuracy of its prediction. My brother Tony was born almost immediately thereafter—it might have been the next afternoon—and I was released from the backyard the following April, with ceremony, on my birthday.

I was in and out of our garage, the noisy shaking whistling thundering shack next the swing, dozens of times daily. I especially admired the complex patterns of oil in tarry dirt which adorned the earth floor, oil fallen from the crankcase of our ramshackle Durant. And I cherished the collection of Ontairo Motor League Highway Guides which lay piled on top of one another on an orange crate at the rear of the building. The special adornment of this automotive museum, though, was my father's collection of Ontairo licence plates dating as far back as 1922, several years before his marriage. Not in those days of uniform size and annually alternating colour scheme as they are now, they varied in shape and in the typography of the numerals, and were so muddled and bent that it was difficult to guess their original appearance.

Free access to the garage was my first taste of liberty, away from the backyard and the humiliating clothesline. From the garage I could look down the length of the driveway we shared with the Buttermeres next door, old Mr. Buttermere the landscape-gardener, his sons Roland and Leonard, and his daughter Mabelle, an oddly assorted trio.

Mr. Buttermere himself was an ancient gentleman, in family legend treated as an expert in his trade, possibly a leading practitioner. I used to suspect that my parents cried up his expertise to minimise the humbler aspect of his work; he had been an underservant in "the Old Country." As a youth he had been under-gardener on some well-connected squire's small country property in the north of England, which made him out to be a feudal appendage of the upper classes, not perhaps our equals in the by-no-means democratic society of English-speaking Canada in the twenties and thirties. My father was a professor, his father a lawyer, a KC, at one point almost a judge. This made them professional persons; lawyers and professors have done much to direct the evolution of life in our country, for good or ill. I think for ill. They, and above all their classy wives, have insinuated at every chance the natural inequality of human beings. For me to describe Mr. Buttermere as "an ancient gentleman" involves a repudiation of attitudes acquired fatally early.

I started to read books—sometimes surprisingly grown-up books—when I was four years old. I don't put this forward as an attestation of my moral superiority to anybody. God, no! I have found progressively as time passes that dexterity in reading and writing in no way guarantees mental power or good conduct—sometimes takes away from them. Too great readiness of self-expression inhibits and finally dissipates delicacy of feeling.

I can remember countless instances experienced in my own life or witnessed in others' lives—and multitudes heard of in passing—of persons who could so readily tell what they felt that they began to invent feelings to keep pace with their sentences; in the end they felt little more than that they were talking well, or at least at a consistent rate of speed. Thinking does no harm to feeling; idle chatter violates it. I remember hearing it said in front of me that Mr. Buttermere's name had been assumed by our elderly neighbour in youth because he knew nothing of his origins, was in short an orphan, possibly a foundling.

"You mean a little bastard," said my father, looking keenly at my mother.

"Something like that."

She was probably right; the name certainly suggests the poetry of Wordsworth and the geography of Cumberland. Mr. Buttermere may have been a bastard, and was certainly an under-servant of a Cumberland family of small gentry. In Canada in 1930, how did this obtain? Of what use was it in fixing him? He used to go to his work on an old Planet bicycle, with a spade, a rake and I think a hoe, bundled together with brown twine and somehow attached to his wheel. Rarely, yet often enough to be recalled in memory, he towed behind him a sweetly oiled, silent running lawnmower. He had funny hair, extremely grey and tightly kinked and grizzled, cut very close to the skull, and rheumy eyes, and the cough one gets from being out in all weathers. His was the first corpse I ever saw, laid out in a Yonge Street funeral chapel that is now a unisex boutique. He was never really well when I knew him.

I see that my parents really rather disdained the family and were uncomfortable with these plebeian associations right next door. My mother retained well into my childhood those motives, whatever they were, which led her to anglicise herself to the point where she almost resented her mother's frequent, flowing and ready French. My mother would read class-conscious, bad English novelists: Galsworthy and worse, E.M. Delafield, Angela Thirkell and their Canadian surrogate, Miss de la Roche, and once in a while perhaps an "emergent" Canadian novelist of slightly higher pretensions, Murray Sansfoy or someone similar, Hennepin or MacCrimmon, or a new poet. She would not read Québec writers. Somehow or other she managed to identify herself with the English class of service families, not very high-ranking generals, barristers, small baronets, judges, whom

Galsworthy wrote about till he died, I suppose because my father taught in a provincial university, and his father was a lawyer from a smaller province. These positions recall Balzac rather than John Galsworthy; to my mother they were the guerdon of the upper-upper-middle class, at least.

I wonder about it. One of the most, as it were, *derailing* accidents that has happened to me was my picking up from a casual perusal of such books (having found them around the house in random, brown-varnished bookcases) of the really silly notion that I was in some way or other a member manqué of the English service or small proprietor class. An aristocrat in a tiny, stupid way. A gentleman!

There are no gentlemen in Canadian life, never have been of a native growth, though a few poor exiles with some sort of claim to that status, often a forfeited or counterfeit claim, may have found their way here in the fragmented retinue of a Simcoe or a Bagot. Perhaps the closest thing to a native gentleman in this country was a *seigneur* of the second generation, and even he could only with grave difficulty maintain the claim. In any case his property was hopelessly divided among his heirs in the succeeding generations. We have never allowed the entail or primogeniture in Canada, bloody good thing too.

This dream of gentility to a boy off Summerhill Avenue in north Rosedale was destructive to the imagination, or at the least corrosive; it made me think all kinds of things about myself that simply were not the case—that I was some sort of natural aristocrat, better than Jerry and Jakie Forbes because I could read better. Better than Monty and Mostyn because they were what my father called bog-Irish. Superior to Georgie and Molly Bannon because their father had left their mother at some prehistoric period, so that she had to go out to work as a secretary at certain mysterious intervals. I had presumptions and illusions that now seem to me utterly preposterous, but they caused real feelings, sometimes sharp and hurtful, sometimes ignobly pleasing.

I understand now that though there are existential divisions in Canadian society, there are no rooted classes in the traditional sense; it is just that some of us have more money than others. There are no gentlemen in Canada; there is no squirearchy, no aristocracy. The poor are just poor, and not an ostracized caste of untouchables. If you are very, very lucky, it is possible to escape from the primordial condition of poverty; you aren't locked into it by eternal law. You may eventually acquire the same collection of wooden and metal objects as higher earners and you will have made it into the other group that lives in Canada.

Later on, when my father gave up his university appointment on conscientious grounds, I had to bear the lash of poverty for a time that seemed endless and was actually long enough to leave tiny marks. This belt-tightening retrenchment went on for about five years; after that I learned to make money for myself. But it stung. It stung to have to admit to being poor in a way it wouldn't have done if I'd been dead certain about my place in life, its classlessness and corollary freedom to come and go, rise or fall, and if I hadn't thought that, really, the Buttermeres weren't much, though they shared our driveway and their home was if anything more commodious and slightly less densely populated than our own.

Roland and Leonard. And Mabelle. How had the Buttermere boys come by those heroic names, what had their mother been thinking of when she chose them, who had she been? Why did she spell her only daughter's name as a compound French word instead of plain "Mabel"? I've met a Mabel or two in my time, and they were innocent folk, but Mabelle, *ma belle*! We never knew Mrs. Buttermere. She must have been a generation older than my father and mother, and it isn't certain whether she had emigrated with her grizzled husband, or died faced with the prospect of removal from the Cumberland estate on which their family had sheltered from before the turn of the century. She must have been a great reader of some species of delusive romance, suffering, as I did, from a mitigated *folie de grandeur*.

We accepted favours from the Buttermeres. I recollect stretches of weeks in a row when my father would put his head out of the bathroom window in response to a honk in the driveway to shout, "Be right with you, Len." And he would finish shaving unhurriedly, then go downstairs and out the side door, entering Len Buttermere's Chrysler coupé to be driven down to the university. The Chrysler was an infinitely better automobile than our decrepit Durant; our family was reputedly above caring about such comparisons, but we would take rides in Chryslers when offered, as well as other tribute.

For example: the day I was four years old, a dry, clear, almost warm day in very early spring, around ten o'clock in the morning, Mabelle Buttermere came to the side door with the air of a co-conspirator and said to my mother with a toothy smile (she had fearsomely protrusive incisors) that there was something in their garage.

My mother replied in a tone that meant she was falsifying something. "In your garage, in your *garage*? What do you suppose it could be?" She turned to me, where I sat on the kitchen floor playing with a garage and two cars, a set, a gift from my uncle Philip. "There's something in the garage."

I held up my small metal toy and tried to see inside.

"No no, not in there, in the Buttermere's garage. Shouldn't we go and investigate?" This last sentence gave me an intense thrill of pleasure. I loved my mother most when she used words to me like "investigate," "proboscis" or "superannuated."

We walked up the cindery drive, crystalline black shapes crackling underfoot. The Buttermere garage was undeniably a more impressive structure than our galvanized shack. Wooden, with folding doors in which you could pinch yourself, it would hold two cars. The Buttermeres did not own two cars, and the second space was usually crowded with the implements of old Mr. Buttermere's profession or trade; but Roland talked continually of owning a car and had once brought home a small blue Plymouth two-door sedan, one of the very first model year of the Plymouth marque, on an overnight demonstration. Automotive opinion on our part of Summerhill Avenue tended to be be dominated by the Chrysler-Dodge-De Soto-Plymouth lines, for various arcane reasons.

I now began to feel obscurely, then consciously, then intensely excited. "There's something inside," I said irrefutably. "It's for me."

"We've been keeping it for you," said Mabelle Buttermere, her eyeglasses shining with goodwill. She seemed incredibly old to me that morning, and was probably in her late twenties, still hoping to be married at some time or other. She went to the folding doors and began to waggle the hasp of the latch. I shot past her as soon as there was room enough and flung myself on my knees beside my big birthday present. On its blunt nose there was a small painted crest with the word "Dodge" minutely lettered below. There were hubcaps—HUBCAPS—on each wheel, and they had the little monogrammed intertwined DB that meant Dodge Brothers. The wheels were discs of curved metal with thick solid rubber tires; the discs were painted an infinitely beguiling leaf-green, and a thin line of red trim had been drawn around their inner circumference. It now seems to me that the trim had been done by hand; it wasn't shaky or irregular but it didn't seem machined.

The body of this dazzling gift was likewise leaf-green with red trim. The steering wheel was an oak rim with metal spokes. On the dashboard were painted a speedometer, an ammeter, a gas gauge and a clock. There was a throttle on the steering column. I could reach the pedals. I got in, saying no word to the two women who stood looking at me.

"Brrrruummmmmmmummmmm," I said, warming her up, "brrruummmm, brruummm."

I saw that there was a hand lever for the brake of much the same design as that on my wicker go-cart. I worked it back and forth, making sure it was in the OFF position indicated by an arrowhead, then pedalled at all possible speed out of

the garage and down the driveway, which was steeply inclined, down and out onto the sidewalk in front of the house,
making a skidding, exhilarating turn at the bottom of the incline, burning rubber, then accelerating in top gear along
Summerhill Avenue toward Hollingshead's Grocery where
the display of one-cent candy was. I had never been to Hollingshead's alone, but I'd been there with my father and had
seen the showcase full of treats. Behind me, my mother and
Miss Buttermere debouched from the driveway, calling me
to return and laughing about the extreme speed of my departure.

"You never saw such a thing," my mother said that night
over supper. "He'd obviously been planning a getaway for
months."

Thinking it over later, I saw that I had in fact been planning it all winter; but I hadn't expected to escape by car.

"So you liked your present?" said my father.

"Yes I did, but I wonder who it's from."

"It's from us."

"Oh, I thought it was from the Buttermeres."

"No, it's from us. Miss Buttermere kindly consented. . ."
and my father began to grin, ". . . kindly consented to conceal it for us. We weren't certain we could hide it in the
house."

"He'd have smelled it out," said my grandmother, turning to me and smiling. "Did you like the golf sticks?" She
and Grandpa Archambault had made me a present of a toy
golf bag, quite an elaborate green plaid affair, with three
rubber golf balls in a pocket, some wooden tees in various
colours, which bled their paint dreadfully when wet—all over
my first pair of white duck shorts—and four accurately
modelled clubs, a driver, a mashie, a niblick and a putter.
Nobody uses those names for the clubs any more, and hasn't
for decades, but the cast heads of my clubs had these names
and the maker's insignia, moulded into the metal.

Mashie, niblick, cleek, baffy, driver, spoon, mid-iron,
mashie-niblick, names out of the P.G. Wodehouse stories

about golf redolent of the atmosphere of English countryside
farce, inadequately translated to the Toronto of the early
thirties and the play-for-pay courses, around which my
father and one or two colleagues who were free in the mornings and liked to walk used to circulate: St. Andrew's, Glen
Mawr. I forgot brassie. And driving iron.

Mulling over these names I see that almost every one of
the dozen basic clubs in modern use—four woods and eight
irons, give or take an iron—had its own authentic and personal name rather than a number, deriving one imagines
from Scotch golfers' slang. Thus a baffy is a club used for
baffing, and to baff is to hit the ground with the club head
before it meets the ball. A golfer once killed his wife, apparently inadvertently, by hitting her on the head with his
backswing in a sandtrap, with an iron. When the club professional was apprised of this fatality, he said, "What club?"

"His niblick."

"That's the club," said the pro.

This joke has much more point when the club is called a
niblick than when it is simply an eight iron; why is that?
There seems to be a fascination in the special languages of
sports and crafts and trades; certainly the phenomenon was
familiar enough to writers like, say, Kipling or John
O'Hara. There is a kind of mind among writers of fiction
which feeds on fact, on the precisely accurate choice of name,
the skirt-length observed to the millimetre, the strange word
"niblick." Such a mind has an element of the hysterical and
compulsive—this seems clear when we think of Kipling,
O'Hara, perhaps Dreiser. The neurotic need to get the fact
straight, the name correct, which has a flavour of the quiz-
contestant or the person who reads dictionaries and en-
cyclopaedias for pleasure, or who corrects film-makers on the
technical details of their décor, never seems to become sufficiently intense to issue in art of the highest order. For we do
not find this breed of exactitude in Tolstoy or Proust, and the
interest of the minutely particular to James Joyce, which
made that writer check his facts again and again, sometimes

in what seems to us compulsive gesture, lies not in the facts themselves but in the exactions of the *a priori* form into which they had to be made to fit—a condition not found in the work of Dreiser or O'Hara. In this way Proust will present his character, and the factual model for that character— Swann and Charles Haas—in the same scene, caught perhaps in characteristic poses at the Jockey Club, and this instancing, this alliance of doubled realities, may, and often does, issue in art of extraordinary richness.

A niblick then may be seen as "a niblick" with the quaintness and Scotticism working in it, but it is also a real kind of golf club, swung by golfers in the sandtraps of the nineteenthirties, an object at once of faintly neurotic whimsy and of vital historical imagination. The toy clubs in the green plaid bag my grandmother gave me were mashie and niblick, not "mashie" and "niblick."

She and my mother would chortle as I got my car out of the garage, shoved bag and clubs in the back, then pedalled away down the driveway, giving a turn signal with my arm at the sidewalk and driving westward toward the Kniblock's front lawn, four houses up the street, which the very indulgent Mrs. Kniblock allowed me to use as a simulation of the fairways of Glen Mawr. The Kniblocks were an elderly couple whose only child, their daughter Jean, had married and moved away several years before; she had a little boy about my age, Herbie, who used to visit his grandparents now and then, when my nose would be put drastically out of joint.

Herbie's grandparents petted him in exactly the way they petted me when he was not there and I saw readily enough that most of the time I functioned in the old couple's life as a kind of Herbie-substitute. At four I had learned to be canny enough to avoid the issue and enjoy their green lawn. If a Herbie-substitute was wanted, I would accept the role as a greens-fee. This seems cynical; perhaps children can be more cynical than we suppose or are prepared to admit. I saw that I was accepting a fictive, even a spurious affection from Mr. and Mrs. Kniblock as I knocked clean white rubber balls about on their lawn ("He's so sweet. Isn't he sweet, Edgar?") And I felt that I was doing something in return for favours received. I allowed them to pet me in the full expectation of there being no petting when Herbie was around.

Don't use your niblick on the Kniblocks,
Use your niblick on the Kniblocks' lawn.

My dad used to sing that on Saturday mornings as I drove off up the street to that pleasant small square of grass that I secretly called Glen Herbie on the analogy of Glen Mawr, the name of the course my father and his friends used to carve up with their inexpert flailings. Sometimes he would come onto the verandah with one of his collection of museum-piece clubs, to take a comical practice swing, perhaps to put heart into me, perhaps to exercise his arms and shoulders. I associate this period with days when my father, his habitual good humour and perfect manners toward the rest of us momentarily undermined, would roam around the house hollering, "It's King or chaos," then grinding his teeth in a really frightening way and repeating over and over, "I'm for chaos," though he was actually deeply involved in the founding of the League for Social Reconstruction with his friends, Mr. Underhill at the university and Mr. Scott and Mr. Gordon down in Montréal.

I had no idea what he was going on about, what had upset him so, why society needed reconstruction, not that year anyway, but this strange behavior persisted for what seemed ages. It couldn't really have lasted much longer than the length of an election campaign, maybe three dismal months, but it seemed ages. I'd pedal off to play golf and behind me, in early morning, home from school during the long university vacation, my dad would be standing in shirtsleeves, hair sticking up, far from ready for the business of the day, if there were to be business, swinging an antediluvian brassie and mumbling about the Regina Manifesto, in a distracted style that I found distinctly alarming. This lasted until the Liberal administration under the extraordinary Mr. King was lodged in the secure position it maintained for a generation. King or chaos!

I thought the King in question was the old gentleman with the pointed beard and spiky moustache who expired in December of that year after the tranquil newspaper message, "The King's Life is Drawing Peacefully to a Close." A gentle, decent way of expressing a hard fact, more characteristic of the press in the thirties than later. That king and our King were to me the same, a distant source of lawful behaviour with a beard, very old. Like my father's father in fact, that dreadful Maritimer whose quarrels with the Liberal party enjoyed an epic status in our home. A decade before, when he had risen to the highest eminence afforded by the Nova Scotia villages of his day, mayor, magistrate, owner of the weekly newspaper, highly successful member of the bar, this more irascible of my grandfathers, a bizarre polar opposite to silent and ruminative Papa Archambault, had conducted negotiations with various discreet Liberal bagmen about a judgeship which was clearly going to be up for disposal at almost any time, the incumbent being certainly on his deathbed. An election impended—this was 1926—and there was no time to be lost. The expiring judge must breathe his last and my grandfather be appointed before the fortunes of politics changed and the federal Liberal party's leverage in the province was reduced or reinforced. He tried to sew up his appointment by making a substantial contribution to the campaign fund—in the accounting of 1926 an immense contribution for a village lawyer and would-be member of the judiciary. The election came too soon and was won and the village lawyer's support was not longer mandatory; the campaign contribution went silently into the bag, the incumbent died, the appointment was given elsewhere and my grandfather became a KC, a petty distinction that irritated him for the remainder of his life. It was some time after this grave misadventure that he chose, in very late middle life, for he

was born in the year 1870, to uproot himself and his family
and move to Toronto. It was sheer pique, trivial disappointment, that impelled the decision, which he lived to regret
bitterly.

"King and country," king and country, I couldn't tell the
phrases apart, but I knew they had something to do with
England and the Empire, and I wasn't much disturbed by
the evidences of colonialism around us. Getting out and
about along Summerhill Avenue in those summer afternoons
of deep 1935 with King and/or chaos abounding around, I
saw as soon as I motored to the end of the block that
Englishry was everywhere there; a whole family of household
servants dwelt in a row of houses at the end of the block by
the level crossing: Sinclairs, Cloughs, Farquhars, intercon-
nected by a labyrinthine web of marriages, who were not
long from the old country and who were the paid dependen-
cies of the Lowther family who had an enormous house in
south Rosedale—the rich part of the district. When I told
people later on that I'd grown up in Rosedale, they were
always impressed and ready to concede me a class distinction
that I'd never thought of asserting. If I identified the location
as "north Rosedale" the mistaken identification didn't occur, because north Rosedale was in some degree the dormitory of the servants of the south.

Perhaps I seem to be identifying myself with a servant
class, by definition an exploited class, without sociological
warrant. My father was a professor, his father "almost a
judge," and in my teens I thought I was a gentleman. But as
the great bloody old Depression really came down icy and
hard on us in the mid-thirties, two or three years after it got
terrible in the States, when their banks closed (we're always
a few years behind the States, even in misfortune), when the
phrase "salary cut" began to be heard, when hamburger
was 8¢ a pound—if you had the 8¢—there were intimations
all around us, along the railroad tracks where out-of-work
men often stalked past our backyard, were often fed through
the fence but not encouraged to climb over it and join us,

where Mostyn and Monty wore threadbare knickerbockers
to school and their house smelled dirty and poor, that poverty, even desperation, were not too far off. My father took
two salary cuts at the university, in 1934 and 1936, and was
told by a department chairman that he was lucky indeed to
be reappointed; it may have been the shock of this friendly
communication that turned him even further away from
either King or king, toward the alternative "peaceful evolution of socialism."

The Sinclairs, Cloughs, Farquhars, were all related and
had all come from England, *not* from Scotland, though the
names suggest it, and had all found employment as servants
of the very rich Lowthers, who settled them in row housing
much as they might have been housed on some gentleman's
country estate in England a decade or two earlier, perhaps
before the first Great War, in a system of life that must have
been reaching extinction in Britain just as the Lowthers were
instituting it in Toronto. The Sinclairs and Cloughs and Farquhars were *cottagers*, by gum, that one might have found in
the delusive pages of Galsworthy, already obsolete in
England with the coming of the council estates and other
forms of cheap housing, but recreated in paler image along
our fringe street, a kind of attic of Rosedale, no attar of roses
during hard times in the Dominion.

In the trough of the thirties, no salad days but salary-cut
days, Adam Sinclair's maternal uncle, Mr. Clough, was the
Lowthers' chauffeur. He used to bring their town car home
with him most evenings in order to polish it, clean the interior, wash the extensive expanses of window glass inside
and out. It was a 1924 Rolls-Royce Phantom II limousine,
with the chauffeur's compartment roofed over and enclosed—humanitarian gesture—and showing a vast spread
of passenger compartment with a pair of strapontins, which
folded into the back of the chauffeur's seat when not in use.
In this limousine were a fold-down writing desk in rosewood,
which Mr. Clough used to caress with furniture polish the
way a lesser man might stroke his girl friend, and a nest of

crystal glasses and decanters in leather containers, which
were stowed in a drawer when not in use, and little recessed
side-lights, scrolled and voluted, curtains and window-
blinds, footrests, footwarmers, driving robes in deep-piled
mohair, the lot. The vehicle itself did not possess an all-metal
body, strangely enough. The roof was of some peculiar com-
position, black fabric stretched over a wooden frame
perhaps, seamed and lined all over and painted with varnish
or preservative. The fenders were painted a glossy black, the
rest of the body and hood a dark millionaire's green, the colour of money, and then there was the magnificent radiator.
And the UK licence plates, the RAC badges, the silver lady
on the radiator cap. I would stand silently beside Mr.
Clough the whole of a Sunday afternoon while he soaped the
car, rinsed it, rubbed it gently with chamois, then repeated
the entire operation; two washings were routine, three not
uncommon. I see now that Mr. Clough, a little stooped, not
a talkative person, with a faint smell hanging about his neat
dark uniform and black gleaming boots of polish and motor
oil, was acting out the role of coachman or undergroom on
some vanished noble estate, or possibly the mews of some
noble town house. A coachman. He treated the Rolls—I
thought rightly—as a living thing, some splendid embodi-
ment of equinity. Thinking it over I see that the functions of
the servitors of the horse were bequeathed in my own day to
chauffeurs and mechanics, finally to operators of filling stations, where now some redolences, traces of horsiness are
still dimly to be descried. It is clear that the relation between
used-car salesman and buyer is exactly that which obtained
between horse trader and countryman in the last century.
One deals for a used car expecting to be cheated, distinctly
on one's guard. In my childhood, automobiles were called
things like: landaulette, brougham, cabriolet, coupé, phaeton, sedan de ville, wagonette, runabout, roadster. Does
anybody remember these evocations?

Of course they were names from the great age of coach-
building, still just not extinct in my childhood, much like the

great age of sailing ships in which my forebears were deeply immersed until the coming of the Great War, and even briefly thereafter.

The Studebaker brothers were wagon builders, continuing to make automobiles through the middle of the twentieth century. In 1935, sitting on my front sidewalk steps playing with a garage and two tin toy cars, opening the garage doors and making them go in and out, I could have told you the precise coach-builder's distinction between a cabriolet and a landaulette, and identified at a glance every make of automobile then extant in Toronto: Gray Dort, Star, Oakland, Durant, Frontenac, Franklin, Willys-Knight, Hupmobile, Reo, Graham-Paige, where are they now? They have gone where the brougham and phaeton have gone and the barouche-landau. In *Emma* Jane Austen makes a horrid lady boast of her friends' barouche-landau, glamorous vehicle, and the rotundity of the name makes us long to behold the chariot *in se*. With these eyes I have seen a barouche-landau, for along Summerhill Avenue every Sunday in spring or summer when the weather was fine, in those feudal days, would drive the Lieutenant-Governor of the Province of Ontario with a party of ladies, in an open carriage drawn by four horses, two coachmen seated on the box and mark you, friends, *footmen* up behind the passengers on a rear platform, wearing curly little tall hats with brushes stuck in their bands. And this immensely evocative, sounding and ringing and jingling, richly-caparisoned circus wagon was exactly a barouche-landau. They would be returning from church after an infra-royal progress through wealthier Rosedale, via this northern, almost hyperborean, route to Chorley Park, the vice-vice-regal residence at the east end of Summerhill.

A year or two afterward, which seemed a long age to me at six, seven, eight, Chorley Park was closed down by order of the then Premier of Ontario, the rumbustious Mitchell Hepburn, the most graceless and odious of politicians, and the house became the haunted mansion of all subsequent

Goderich recollections. I was getting almost . . . almost . . . able to take excursions toward that end of the street by myself. By 1937 I was sneaking away from the house, at first to go into Mostyn and Monty McNally's home just long enough to be perplexed by the smell of unaired bed linen and dirt—not their fault, I said to myself, in what I thought was magnanimity. Then to tag along after Mildred and Marigold Smith, or to stand at the bus stop right outside their house till their father drove up in his red and yellow TTC streamliner—the Rosedale · line was early equipped with the new Twin Coach buses with modern streamlining, which came in on passenger automobiles only in 1936 with the celebrated Chrysler Airflow, a design conservative by European standards and in retrospect awkward, ill-lit and cumbersome but to the romantic vision of a child obsessed with automobiles a voyage into the future. Mr. Busdriver Smith's Twin Coach had *rubber mudguards*, a stroke of ingenuity which seemed to me to lie at the top and head of the designer's art.

I would sit and wait for a couple of hours on an afternoon in spring when all the older kids were up at school, Whitney or OLPH, and down by Glen Road the bus would heave into view around the corner, stopping in front of Letty Millen's house, then proceeding toward me, past the rear of the Lyalls' house on St. Andrew's Gardens, past George and Molly Bannon's backyard where they had the hockey rink in winter, to halt quietly and precisely in front of the Smiths' house.

I wondered how Mr. Smith had arranged matters so that his home life and his work were so intimately associated. He would very occasionally leave the bus and enter his house, if there were no passengers, or one or two whom he knew, ladies returning from a midday shopping tour on Bloor Street. I believe he drank a cup of tea in the house; then he would reappear, wiping his little pencil-line moustache. He had a lean, very brown face and the nattiness of a jockey. He would give me the glued-together books of transfers from

which the ends had been torn for distribution to passengers.
I got to know the colours of the transfers for different streetcar lines all across Toronto and contemplated making a collection of them, but always rejected the idea because the set
would have contained at most 30 members. Instead I might
collect Big Little Books or hockey cards, or another set of
gum cards depicting the kings and queens of England which
is responsible for the sad fact that I can recite them and their
lineage to this hour, beginning with the last of the Saxon
monarchs, Edward (the Confessor, why, what?) and Harold,
and continuing through two Williams, a Stephen and
Matilda (whom I never got straight and still wonder about;
Matilda?) and a covey of Plantagenets beginning with the
first Henry. Plantagenet derives from the Latin *planta gensta*
or *genesta*, meaning the common broom-plant. Does anybody
care about that now? Does anybody know that the transfers
for the Glen Road/Summerhill bus line were a rich buff colour with red lettering, that the King Street car line had
chastely simple black on just-off-white transfers? I care. I
care so passionately about these matters that I am sometimes
shaken by the power of the feeling. I was early fascinated by
the fineness of the type face on these slips of paper, and by
the way the coarse weave of the paper accepted colouring, in
childhood, almost in infancy.

I remember the walkway from sidewalk to verandah in
front of our six-room house, now and for many years since
buried under the storefront of a dry cleaners. I remember sitting out there that first spring of my liberation, staring at the
cement of the main sidewalk where the men of the City of
Toronto Works Department had imprinted their mark and
the date on sidewalk recently repaired. I looked around
behind me at the shaley cement of our front walk, traced out
with lines and in parts superficially scarred and eroded. I
then stared across the street at the mute silent closed back
end of the Levys' garage. All the houses across the street
fronted on St. Andrew's Gardens and presented only their
backyards and garages to my inspection, except at the ends

of the block where a few houses faced onto Summerhill. The length of that block became one of the liberating categories of childhood, but I wasn't considering exploration then, or the secrets of the stoneyard, or what lay around the corner on Jean Street, home of feared Jakie Forbes, who had beaten up on Amanda Lousie though much younger than she and would certainly clean up on me if he caught me; he was known to be "after me."

A brand-new 1934 Ford phaeton V-8 came silently along the street from the direction of Jean Street. I regarded it with the profound concentration of a practitioner of Yoga or Zen. Almost the first of the V-8 series, these 1934 models were enormously peppy, hot little cars, figuring for years afterward as police vehicles in an ongoing cycle of gangster movies of which I was as yet unaware. This four-door automobile, which would a few years before have been referred to as a "touring car," this classification implicit in its taut canvas roof, which folded neatly into a well behind the rear seat, was in the 1934 advertising described as a "phaeton," a designation which entranced me. It was one of the very first words whose pronunciation aloud, purely accidentally, by my mother, reading an advertisement over my shoulder, astounded me at how far off I had been, guessing at its sound from the look of the word on the page. I had been sounding it mentally to myself as something like "pah-thigh-on" but she made it "fay-eton." I suppose my childish confusion is clear. Most of us growing up have taken a printed word—or printed musical notes—to sound in one way, then found that everybody else pronounced the words, or played the music, quite differently. My brother Tony thought that the word "misled" meaning to have been confused or led astray was sounded as though it rhymed with "wise-eld." Can you tie that? I remember how he said, "I've been mize-eld," one night at dinner, whereupon my parents did simultaneous double-takes and corrected him very gently. My parents, on the whole, displayed beautiful manners toward us in such situations, never laughing at our misconceptions.

"Fay-eton," my mother said, looking at the ad in the paper.

"What?"

"Fay-eton."

"Is that how you pronouce that?" I said, saying nothing about how I'd have tried to say it.

"It's the name of the unlucky son of Apollo," said my mother. She started to tell me some tale or other of the Greeks and their gods, but I was wholly given up to contemplation of the picture of the new model, and did not hear a word. Fayeton. Phaeton, touring car. Canvas top.

When I saw one roll toward me in the flesh, perhaps I should say in the living metal, I started to feel and think and vibrate in a way that nobody else I knew did. Nobody I knew cared about shapes and sounds and colours and lettering and the sound of motors, not as motors but as rhythms, the way I did, not even my father. It's funny how these things are clear to a child who is obscurely conscious of not behaving like everybody else. I took in everything about that damned car, how quiet its engine was, and yet how different it sounded from the engine of a Model T or a Model A. You could hear the eight cylinders and from their sound alone could sense how smooth and powerful the supply of power to the crankshaft, differential, rear axle, would be, and also how light the body was in relation to the amount of power available, how the car would move around a curve, swaying over to one side. Before ever I saw a Ford Phaeton enacting the role of a police car in some Warner Brothers program picture three years later, I knew how one would look as it cornered at speed, from hearing the engine and studying the springing and bounce of the coachwork. I saw the delicate, narrow wing windows, which were hinged on the corner posts of the windshield, and rejoiced at their placement, so just and neat. They and the windshield were the only glass; the car still was equipped with canvas and mica side-curtains. I knew this because I could see the metal circlets that housed the snap fasteners. I was keenly aware of the tan hue of the canvas roof, wondering if the side-curtains were in a matching tone. I loved the idea of how cosy it would be inside, like a tent on wheels, when the side-curtains were affixed. A womb image. I had not been long from the womb and on a bad day would ache to be back inside, figuring this to myself as the inside of a tent or touring car, sleeping bag, caboose or even handy linen closet. But the sight of that canvas-roofed automobile was naturally and immensely more than a womb image. I hate to say this. I was making, God help us all, aesthetic judgments. I was recognizing pleasing design.

As the Ford Phaeton passed me, I stood up, and I could see that it had leather upholstery. Now I had read about leather upholstery and knew vaguely what it meant. It meant that the seats were leather, that's all but the word "upholstery" beguiled me. Leather upholstery. The phrase had the power of an incantation, and I succumbed to it in the experience of a kind of pleasure that is unqualified and utterly unlike any other, and particularly unlike that of sex. The charm, the fitness, the appropriateness, the cleanliness of good design . . . the way it makes your body feel well-knit without causing erection—a state which I could not in any case have experienced at that time.

Later that year, and for years thereafter, I walked along our street looking carefully at the shapes of things. Design abounded. Toronto was full of one-family brick houses with front porches that had classical columns supporting their roofs, gables, complex patterns of red and yellow brick, found also throughout rural Ontario. Sometimes these small houses had been built, as they are still, in repeated variations of a single basic design; but just as often you would find no more than two or three houses along a terrace in the same pattern. Sometimes, as was the case with Mr. Faucett's design for our house, a single dwelling had been taken from the pattern. If I were to sum up Toronto living in the early thirties, I'd have to think through the phenomenon of the small one-family home of six or seven or eight rooms, often with an attic, rarely with a recreation room. If there were four or five bedrooms, a pair of grandparents and a maid might live in the house; if only three, a sunporch might serve as guest bedroom in warm weather. I understand how the native domestic architecture shaped our choice of ways to live, and was in turn shaped by them, until a consensus was reached.

I'm not talking about the kind of house that exemplified south Rosedale at the beginning of the century, enormous places some of these were, built to individual plans by architects with professional Beaux Arts tradition, training, *formation*, behind them, sometimes with ornamental carving in red sandstone, of great intricacy. In Toronto from the nineties onward, the dominant class was composed centrally of rich wholesalers—the essential middlemen—who controlled by their purchasing power and their pricing to the individual storekeeper the modes of production of consumer goods: clothing, kitchenware, furniture. The story of Toronto is inseparable from the growing up of the great mercantile houses, the department stores and those epic-scale jobbers like Cassidys, or Higgins and Burke, or Hayhoes Limited, whose weathered warehouses along Wellington Street or Front Street I used to admire for their solidity and architectural self-assertiveness in heavy rusticated smoky building blocks, when I roamed around downtown as a liberated adolescent.

When the chairman of the board of one of the leading department stores had his life-story ghost-written for him—a tale of growing up in Toronto in the eighteen-eighties and -nineties, an era when my grandparents were likewise coming to maturity—he dwelt at length on the dominance, in character and by financial acuteness, of these jobbers. Toronto is not primarily an industrial city; it's a centre of trade and shopkeeping and shipping, and the department store is the natural architectural *chef d'oeuvre* of the city, as it is of Chicago.

It isn't a surprise that the Santa Claus Parade and the enormous show windows on the corners of Queen and

Yonge, Richmond and Yonge, and along Yonge Street where certain lesser emporia were situated, directed and stimulated, almost absorbed, the emotional life of the citizens. These windows, high in emotional key and pitch, often intensely Christian in their streamed-out messages of holiday goodwill, were the possession, public relations outlet, epiphany, of enormous mercantile forces.

In south Rosedale a wholesaler's mansion might run to four storeys, here and there to 50 rooms. I have been in houses, though never as an invited guest and always by the side or back door, where the attic was the fifth floor, in whose recesses and at the top of whose depressing back stairs were long galleries of maids' rooms, walls the colour of an inferior Ontario cheddar, a pale soapy yellow devoid of decorative impulse or effect, where now and then a cutout from a rotogravure, most often the *Star Weekly*, might droop from the slanting wall. These rooms were irregular in shape, tucked up under hipped or gabled roofing. One bathroom on the top floor. Short little bathtub. A good deal of danger from fire; these would have been difficult attics to escape from. Mercifully such calamities were infrequent. East of Glen Road and south of the Glen Road ravine. Maple. Elm. Castle Frank. South Drive. Around Craigleigh Gardens. Unmitigated south Rosedale, redolent of fiscal power, charmless. Not intended to charm. Seeing them now at 40 years' remove I guess these houses were meant to cow the paid police force, impress the casual passerby with opulence, house multitudes and encourage large families, shelter at long term from testing weather, finally to provide employment to the building trade and to the itinerant architect whose name seems rarely to have been preserved.

I never understood those houses and how they shamed me and made me feel poor, but I took in all of Summerhill Avenue perfectly. I had seen Mr. Faucett and knew that he was short, rotund, redfaced. He sweated a lot. He wore braces and a vest. Was not rich but owned our house and two others, one in Long Branch, one in Mimico. Mr. Faucett knew all the history of north Rosedale; it was he who first suggested to me that the McNallys' house had at one time been alone in the country.

"See, sonny, see how it's off to the one side of its lot? I'd never have planted it there; it doesn't use the space. It was there before the lots were surveyed, but it don't look like any farmhouse to me, not to me it don't."

He had this trick of repeating his phrases with slight changes of wording.

"Built about 1870, that house was."

I said, "That's my grandfather's birthday, 1870. January 1870. My grandfather Goderich, that is."

"Is that so? Well, you see, the country was just growing up then; it seems longer than it is, to you. I can almost remember that far back. I was born in 1888. I'm older than your Dad, you see. "

"I could tell. My Dad is the same age as the century."

He showed discoloured teeth, perhaps ill-fitting dentures, in a friendly grin. "How can you tell?"

"Lots of ways."

He didn't follow this up. "They'll be pulling that place down one of these days, taking it down, yes. I'll tell you what it must have been. The house for some blacksmith or carpenter who worked down in the city in the old days, and helped to build up this neighbourhood."

"How can you tell?" I asked in my turn.

"There's a lot of hand craft gone into that house, my laddie. Look at that weathervane; that's handwrought ironwork, that is. A master blacksmith made that, *and* the lightning rod, *and* the eavestroughing. I'll bet the floors are doweled."

"The floors are covered with lino, Mr. Faucett."

"I'd like to look at them," he said, musing. My father sauntered along the sidewalk and handed him some money. "Thank you, Mr. Goderich."

"Thank *you*, Mr. Faucett. Are you teaching Matt the history of Summerhill Avenue? A useful thing to know." He smiled and turned away.

"Your father is a great believer in education," said Mr. Faucett.

"Oh yes, he is, all the Goderich family are, all of us."

Mr. Faucett watched my father climb the stairs to our verandah, his face a little puzzled, which didn't surprise me. I'd noticed early that people often looked slightly perplexed after an encounter with Dad. I did myself.

"He's still at the university then?" said Mr. Faucett.

"Not today. He's here. You just saw him."

"I meant as a regular thing."

"Only in the school time."

"Well, but then."

"Oh, yes."

"You'll be going to school yourself one of these days, I suppose."

"My father doesn't want me to go this year. He's afraid I'm too little for the other kids my age."

Naturally I didn't have the least notion what my father was getting at, when he chose to start me in school a half-year later than other kids, instead of a half-year early as he could have done because of my April birth date. He used to explain his thinking laboriously to my mother, on this as on all subjects, where he felt conscientiously constrained to establish perfect clarity. My mother, a convinced and early feminist, though never doctrinaire, an earnest voter and observer of political candidates, a university woman—the first in her family—and something of a rebel against the social ideas of the group into which she'd been born, French-speaking Torontonians of Québec origin, was regularly obliged to protest that my father made his thinking clearer to her than was necessary.

"Of course I want to be your mental companion," she would profess, "but not at this length."

A look of perplexity would invade my father's face, and

he'd start to rephrase his thought. "Perhaps I haven't made myself clear," he would say; it was almost his favourite phrase, one of the incantatory recurrent bits of dialogue we used to tease him about. "Perhaps I haven't made myself clear." He hated wilful obscurity. He wanted contracts and social relations to be as unambiguous as possible, whether because he felt drawn toward ambiguity in his heart I do not know. By this time he had written his first two books, one on ethical theory whose title charmed me at the age of six—it made so little sense to me. *The Place of Conceptual Thought in Ethical Judgments*. And a second on social ethics and politics called, for some reason, *Property and Value*. I have looked into both since I grew up. While they tell me very little about their ostensible subjects, they tell me an enormous amount about my father, and his father, and far far too much about myself.

People would come to the house in the evening to listen to my father explaining himself; it seemed to me an embarrassing neighbourhood show, or exhibition. He was so circumlocutory that his speech reminded you of a trout fisherman with a nibble. Far down the line of his reflections he might feel a faint movement, the twitch of a notion, as though idea were finned and gilled. And he would play it, how he would play it. I never could tell all by myself when he'd landed a catch, but older folks could. Once or twice, I remember, a half-dozen grownups broke into spontaneous applause when he finished a sentence with these or similar words, overheard by me on my way through to bed: ". . . thereby grounding axiological fiat in absolutist ontology."

When I heard from my father that there was a body of knowledge, or at least of propositions, called axiology, I asked him if it had anything to do with cars. "Indirectly," he said, and now I see how truthful his reply was. He couldn't easily form such truthful sentences to adults, especially to my mother. "I believe you, Andrew," she would say, rolling an eye.

"He's smaller than other boys in his age-group."

"Quite right."

"He'd be at a continuous minor disadvantage, being in the same school year with them."

"Yes, yes."

"We should leave him back a year. It won't hurt him. He could skip a grade later on if necessary."

"You have confidence in Matt."

"Of course I have. He may take a growth-spurt in a year or two, then he can skip if he wants. But it's better to be bigger and a bit older, than a bit smaller and younger. We'll hold him back, and if the school wonders where he is, I'll go and explain."

"What should they know?" said my mother, laughing uneasily.

"They must know through Amanda Louise that she has a brother of school age."

"Andrew, I assure you, Sister Matilda will not pursue you."

"Then you agree?"

"Perfectly," she would say; she was willing to soften the condition of total clarity in order to abridge the discussion, but she was not a dishonest woman, simply a woman who did not want to generate more sentences than the given occasion required. I didn't get to school till I was six and a half. I didn't miss it.

I had a whole extra year to wander as far as I could without crossing dangerous streets; this permitted me to cross Jean Street, and Summerhill, but not Glen Road nor MacLennan. Within this range there was plenty of ground to cover. I could get to the north side of St. Andrew's Gardens and wander along its length between Glen Road and MacLennan. I could worm through backyards on Jean Street onto Edgewood Crescent, and on a very loose interpretation of the rules about crossing streets, I could get up to the end of Edgewood and around onto its east side—it was a dead end—without having my feet touch the forbidden pavement, and this would allow me to roam even further toward the mysterious east.

I didn't usually do this because I understood clearly that my father didn't want me to go that far. I was able to get half a mile away from home without breaking the spirit of the law, or even the letter, and temptation to stray was not severe. There were many other kids living in the space enclosed by Dad's rules, and since many of them went to school the year before I did, I got to be something of a pet for the young mothers of the neighbourhood. I had my little rounds. I might drop in on Mrs. Bannon to say good morning, on my way along Summerhill. George and Molly were both considerably older than me. Molly, a very vivacious girl with long, flowing, deep-brown hair, must have been the same age as Mostyn McNally, perhaps eleven, and George, already and always known as Georgie-Balls for whatever reason, was eight or nine, the best young hockey player in north Rosedale, notorious or renowned, depending on your viewpoint, around Rosedale Lacrosse Grounds, for his reluctance to give up the puck in a game of shinny. Georgie wouldn't relinquish the puck, but nobody could get it off him either. He was a natural, that's all. He made me wonder about his father, whom I learned, years later, had died absurdly young and been buried by mistake in a rented tuxedo. Never a steady life, Mr. Bannon's, but Georgie-Balls must have inherited his athletic gifts from him because Mrs. Bannon certainly had none; she was a fragile lady with the deportment of a Tennessee Williams heroine *avant de la lettre*, a little distracted, a waver of both arms, Esther Bannon. With masses of dark-red hair and, peculiarly, pince-nez reading glasses. Paying morning calls on this lady at the age of six, in the expectation of something to drink and perhaps 2¢ for candy—as I say, the young ladies of the district petted me extravagantly, giving me a strong liking for woman's society, which I've never lost, thank God—I gained a mixed, misty impression of her appearance. She wore blue a lot, and it went well with the floating dark-red tresses. She was the same age as my mother, perhaps even a year younger, though Molly Bannon was a good bit older than Amanda Louise. One summer we shared a cottage at Rouge Hills with the Bannons; the relationship, usually friendly, was tense from time to time, since there was no Mr. Bannon to counterbalance my father's oddities. The two young mothers used sometimes to pick at each other out of idleness.

I think now that Esther Bannon was the first woman who ever made me feel the oppositeness of womankind, the closed unapproachable untranslateable structure of female experience, which no amount of feminist rhetoric, designed to obscure the difference, can in fact deny. The difference is there. I can't be a woman or think like one. No matter how close I get. My dear sister Amanda Louise seemed like a *person* to me, somebody just like myself, to wrestle with. She had fought Jakie Forbes, in one of the epic encounters of the neighbourhood, and been one-sidedly defeated, a defeat that I was expected to avenge and never did. My mother was too close to me to be seen in any way distanced, removed from my own nature. Mme. Archambault was the incarnation of law—God the Grandmother—in its unbending and arbitrary character, primitive and inexplicable.

Esther Bannon, on the other hand, had a sexual nature, and the Bannon household seemed secretly soaked in sex. It was Georgie-Balls who told me the first sex joke that I remember.

"A lady goes into a record store and asks the saleman if he has the record 'Hot Lips and Seven Kisses.' "

"Yeah, yeah, what then?"

"The salesman says, 'No, lady, but I've got hot balls and seven itches.' And she says . . .'' (Georgie begins to guffaw) ''. . . she says, 'Is that a record?' And he says . . .'' (laughing loudly) ''. . . he says, 'No, but it's a darn good average.' ''

I couldn't make head or tail of this. I knew that there was something about the tale, involved with the way Georgie laughed, which precluded its analysis at the family dinner table. Here was a kind or quality of experience that was foreign. I would have to make my way into it slowly, making educated guesses as I proceeded. "Hot balls and seven itches." That seemed very feeble to me.

But the Bannons were mildly sexy, Mrs. Bannon more than the children. I see now that the years have blended her image with that of numberless vaguely-located ladies in movies, parts played by actresses like Claire Trevor and, in different emotional tone, Joan Blondell or Glenda Farrell. It was the red hair.

Later in the morning I would leave the Bannon backyard and wander along the street to the bus stop at the top of Glen Road, where the bus turned onto Summerhill. This was where Letty Millen lived and she, questions of sexuality wholly apart, she now was a lovely girl. She was eleven. And if Esther Bannon was a decayed southern gentlewoman of the T. Williams persuasion, Letty Millen was a brisk Canadian girl, nothing languorous about her, a Bonita Granville, possibly even a Deanna Durbin, though Letty Millen was fair-haired. Her attraction for me was a confusing, rich twining of conflicting motives and identifications. Taking young Miss Millen's point of view, I suppose that she never identified my feelings. What she would have seen, coming out of her house to catch the bus to school, or alighting from it at three in the afternoon, was a rather sticky, rather dirty, short person about the height of a fire hydrant but not as bulky, six years old and of no interest to her whatsoever, barely identifiable as some fairly distant neighbour's child.

Once or twice I caught the trace of a faint gleam in the eye of Mr. Busdriver Smith as the fair Letty got down from his conveyance, which filled me with rage and impotent jealousy. Fantastic, one thinks, crazy, a six-year-old boy jealous of a middle-aged man over a girl on the brink of adolescence totally unaware of either of them. A weird love triangle. Yes. I see that it is weird, but only because not much discussed or written about; there are no long romantic epics about the loves of six-year-olds. This is only because there are no six-year-old epic poets, though the idea of such a poet is not at all logically self-contradictory. I had intensely lived fantasies about Letty Millen, mostly involving being taken by the hand and accompanied to the grocery store for candy. Sometimes I imagined myself held snugly in her arms on her knee, an image that shook my child's soul with delight, quite literally. I can clearly remember seeing Letty Millen stand on her verandah and give me a melting look, I think now totally unaware of my presence, but melting, dissolving me to impersonality.

A six-year-old boy's sexual feelings are, one supposes, indistinct, imperfectly focused. I was not aware of being sexually male as that girl looked me over, or overlooked me, more likely. I did not want to fold her in my arms and shower burning kisses on her upturned face. Quite the contrary. I wanted her—to be as unambiguous about it as possible—to cuddle me. But this wish was not exactly a wish to be mothered. What my mother did to and for me was untender. It was firm and clear. My mother used to talk to me almost, not exactly but almost, as if we were the same age, about 31. I was never babied after I learned to read and to express myself in complex syntax, which I did far too soon, perhaps, for emotional ease.

I may have wanted from the girl at the end of the street what my mother did not supply, an emotional bath of warm and indistinct abdication (a word very big at that epoch) of selected motive, an acceptance of mixed motive proffered by obscure need. Anyway whatever it was I wanted from this big girl I didn't get. It was two years before Letty Millen learned my name; by this time she was going to Jarvis Collegiate. She was, I believe, a precocious student, and high school drew her into distant orbitings. I didn't see her again for years.

But there were other girls; there was Alysoun Selkirk who lived in a house a few doors west of Letty Millen's, across Jean Street on my way home. Alysoun—her name was always spelled in this idiosyncratic way but pronounced ordinarily—was apple-faced, there is no other way to express it. She had a geometrically round pink face and tiny Chinese eyes, with toffee-coloured hair hanging in perfectly straight bangs on her forehead. She wore short dresses with a lot of smocking on them, and had a big sister called Alexandra who played the piano, not well but with assiduity. The Selkirks' house always seemed shady and withdrawn because of the large horse-chestnut tree standing on the front lawn, source for the boys along the street of strange, green, spiny balls that yielded pale lumps when split open, yellow-white nuts which darkened upon exposure to air, forming the fibrous casing we used to test in formal battles. We would attach these chestnuts to strong cords, then play a game whose Canadian name I've forgotten. In England they call it "conkers," a word that probably means just what it sounds like. The object of the game was to conquer your opponent's chestnut by splitting it with a blow from your own, swung sharply overhand with a snap of the wrist. We baked these nuts in the oven to harden them, put them in the refrigerator, soaked them overnight in water. Jakie Forbes found chestnuts every year that overcame opponent after opponent, splitting, cracking, wounding. However he was not good at games with marbles.

Alysoun and I were almost the same age. Her mother's tales of her pregnancy—not qualified to us as such—echoed through my early childhood. Often she would associate us as dwellers simultaneously in neighbouring wombs, asserting what I felt to be a spurious intimacy with my mother. As a matter of fact, Mrs. Selkirk had known my mother before I was born, even before Amanda Louise had been born. Her maiden name was an unusual one which I have only seen once or twice since, Brandreth. Emma Brandreth. Like Letty Millen's mother, Emma Brandreth had been known for her good looks when she was in college. She and my mother had been at UC together at the beginning of the nineteen-twenties; the college community was far smaller then and she and my mother, and Letty Millen's mother too, had known each other, might even have been considered as in some sort rivals, though my mother would never have put herself forward, or been proposed by others, as an obvious "beauty."

Emma Brandreth and Enid Ivings (afterward Enid

Millen) were well enough publicized as beauties for their
renown to have persisted for a decade or more. I can
remember the look my mother usually assumed when speaking of either, at once comical and satiric, if the distinction is
clear. She didn't mind not looking like those girls but she
did. They had—the trio—some sort of subterranean relationship which made it the more surprising that the passage
of a decade had brought all three to the same backwater,
Summerhill Avenue in north Rosedale. At University College in 1921 my mother had figured as a curiosity. Isabelle
Archambault, French Canadian and Catholic, who for
obscure and maybe threatening reasons had decided not to
attend St. Michael's College, which was the customary place
for Catholic girls from Toronto to locate themselves.

"Tried it for a day and hated it," said my mother when
asked about this, and I have found that she spoke literal
truth. Registered for one and only one day at the Basilian institution, she had there seen so many people she'd been to
high school with, or to weekly Mass with for fifteen years,
and hadn't much liked, that she'd trotted across Queen's
Park and slyly insinuated herself onto the rolls of a wholly
secular college, without her parents having been in any way
aware of the magnitude of the decision. This was a fateful
choice; she met my father there when she was a sophomore
and he was a beginning lecturer in philosophy.

Once these social/historical circles and vortices establish
themselves, they don't stop. Filaments of connections bound
me to Mrs. Selkirk and Mrs. Millen in a more than faintly
incestuous way, long before I was born. Arrived at adult-
hood I figured out that both these ladies had had their eyes
fondly upon Andrew Goderich the moment he appeared on
the scene, the brine of Nova Scotian coasts white on his
shoulders, just drying. But it was the little French-Canadian
girl, sly early ecumenical, who got him. Naturally my father
was a Catholic, but his religious education hadn't at all been
what it would have been in Québec or Ontario. He'd been
sent to Dalhousie quite deliberately by his family to ensure

his place in the upper middle-class community, Catholic or not.

Neither of my parents at all fitted the mould of the English-speaking Catholic of Toronto in the twenties, which made them an irritating puzzle to their co-parishioners, as well as to people like the former Emma Brandreth, English, Protestant, married to a near-Scotchman, not at all badly off with a number of rich relatives. She would look at me, so clearly wondering whether I ought to be allowed to play with Alysoun that it was clear even to me. Jakie Forbes, for example, was *not* allowed anywhere near Alysoun and Alexandra, with alarming consquences later in life, for reasons obviously snobbish and ill-founded. Jakie didn't mind it a bit because he was kinging it over the rest of the kids in the neighbourhood with his fists and his inextinguishable grin. He lived around the corner from the Selkirks, up at the end of Jean Street almost at the tracks, his house separated from the wire fence and the right of way by a large vacant lot. Memory suggests that it was a lot big enough to take two houses, and I remember that later on a single house was built there, leaving a good-sized field still unimproved.

This vacant lot was an epic battleground. I didn't go down there too much before I went to school, unless Jakie wasn't around. I could see with horrid certitude that when we began to see a lot of each other we would have a lot of fights, and I would get licked more often than not. Jakie was plenty tough. He had punched Amanda Louise in the face bang bang bang, made her weep bitterly and sent her home. He had pale squinty narrow blue eyes and very fair hair which stuck up in tufts as though it had been inexpertly barbered. When he boxed, he kept looking at you. When I boxed, I couldn't resist the impulse to avert my head, so as not to get hit directly in the mush. "Sock him in the mush," people would holler. "Clean up on him, Jakie," and he would wham me in the face. I got used to this later on, and I didn't lose every fight I had with him. Sometimes I would jump on him angrily and get him down, then punch him a few in the face while I was on top. But when we stayed on our feet and boxed I got beaten consistently, and without too many hard feelings. I would watch with enjoyment and holler as loud as anybody in support of my pal Jakie when he was cleaning up on a stranger.

There were tough kids, like Jakie, and there were poor tough kids. Maurice and Eddie Reilly were poor tough kids. Jakie Forbes was almost but not quite as tough as Eddie Reilly, but no poorer than any of the rest of us. Mr. Forbes sold coal and fuel-oil, the latter commodity just coming into popularity. Our house, for example, was heated by a coal furnace, and very inconvenient it was too, coal-delivery by men with burnished, sweating black faces and contrasting white teeth, sweatcloths around their necks, grimed seamy lines on faces and under their chins, grunting as they swung hundred-pound sacks of anthracite onto their backs, carried them up the driveway, then dumped them into our coal chute, where a black miasma of dust mounted, slowly dissipating some time after they had gone. My father swore by Welsh anthracite. I can remember him wandering around the house mumbling about Welsh blower coal, nut, pea, coke, and about the inferior combustion of bituminous coal. "Burns Coal Burns Best," he would sing, going on to warn the air at large of the gassy, smelly, dangerous fumes from bituminous coal.

Harold Forbes was employed by one of Burns Coal's principal competitors, Lake Simcoe Ice and Fuel, whose ice-house on Dupont Street was one of the enchanted palaces of midtown Toronto, soundproofed by coarse reddish-brown sawdust on the floor. I suppose they shipped ice from Lake Simcoe originally, storing it in the city ice-house all year round. I used to imagine palaces of clear transparent blocks of Lake Simcoe Ice, castles with blurry walls, winding passages and turrets of ice, protected inside the ice-house all summer long from sun and heat, sprinkled with clotted thick mealy sawdust. Then there was Belle Ewart Ice and Fuel, specializing more in ice than in combustibles. Belle Ewart, who was she? I associate Belle Ewart with Scotch romance and with Sir Walter Scott, but in Toronto in 1935 she was the name of an ice company whose horse-drawn wagons circulated throughout Rosedale summers, to the intense relief of all children. Jakie Forbes and I used to conciliate one another by running behind the slowly moving wagon and sitting on the back step. When the wagon stopped and the iceman came around back to select a 25- or 50-pound lump for delivery, we would make ourselves inconspicuous, then rush forward and steal pieces of ice when he had gone up to the house, the heavy block of ice suspended from tongs a couple of feet long, with curious ovoid handles. There were signs in the windows of houses, with large numbers, "25" on one side, "50" on the other, and an advertising message from Belle Ewart or the competitors, Lake Simcoe.

Burns Coal were not in the ice business; they stuck to coal and later on, I believe, to fuel-oil, having spotted early the start of the decline in the ice trade, electric refrigerators already widely supplanting iceboxes. Mr. Forbes used to tell us that Lake Simcoe would have to get right out of ice.

"We'll only sell ice a while longer, to folks that are getting along, and don't want a Frigidaire in the house because they're frightened of them."

Jakie and I would laugh when he said this.

"No," Mr. Forbes would continue, "you'd be surprised how many of my customers are afraid of electricity in the house. An electric refrigerator makes a lot of noise at night, whirring and bumping on and off, and people get scared. All the same, that's the cooler with the future. I'm concentrating on fuel-oil."

He must have concentrated to good effect because he ended as a company vice-president who left a large block of stock to Jerry and Jakie. I liked Mr. Forbes, who was a rawboned, not-very-well-co-ordinated man who had never got his Senior Matric. He had had to go out to work in his midteens. Perhaps this was what made him much easier to get along with than his son Jakie. Once, I have good reason to suppose, he saved my life. There were several deep holes or pits in the vacant lot beside the Forbes house, some of them the size of a shell hole; we used to play Great War in them, filling out our uneasy, rather fearful though imperfect knowledge of the War with details learned from *Chums*, the *Boy's Own Annual*, or the weekly numbers of *Triumph*, *Hotspur* or *Champion*. Our reading did not become wholly dependent on US sources until after the coming of the comic book, with the publication around 1935 of the first issues of *Famous Funnies* and then *Popular Comics*.

One very rainy spring—it must have been my last spring as a carefree pre-schooler—this vacant lot was thoroughly flooded, oozing like a marsh with soaked-up water, and the pits or shell-holes, and our excavations in them, were full. Jerry and Jakie and I, and some of the bigger boys from the neighbourhood, dug around and made earthworks and tunnels and all sorts of dangerous underminings in the rich yellow mud.

One wet day my mother called me into the living-room after the horse-drawn Eaton's delivery wagon had called at the house, to show me a new pair of high-cut boots she had bought me. I was delighted beyond words, had been wheedling for them for weeks. They had a little pocket in the side of the right boot, with a snap fastener, and in this pocket was a small hunting knife. It wasn't even my birthday. As things turned out, it was almost the reverse.

"You work them up with Dubbin," said my mother, "and it waterproofs them. I'll show you." She produced a flat tin can of the preparation from among sheets of tissue paper and began to smear goo on my boots, using her bare hands, clearly enjoying herself. I must admit it looked like fun.

"Oo-goo," she said absently, "oo-goo."

"Let me!"

"Next time."

"Oh all right." I was getting the boots so I supposed that she was entitled to some fun. When they were thoroughly waterproofed, I laced them on and clumped away along Summerhill toward Jean Street, hoping to irritate Jakie as intensely as possible with the sight of these remarkable boots. The sidewalk was shiny dark-brown-cement wet, and leaves left over from last fall were plastered on the roadway and in gutters. I came up Jean Street at a trot and when I came in sight of the vacant lot I saw that the Forbes kids and the O'Briens and Georgie-Balls had built a raft with a clubhouse on it right in the middle of one of our shell-holes. What an idea! It looked—I said to myself—like Huckleberry Finn, a book I had just tackled with partial success.

They all shouted together, "Hey, look at our raft."

"Hey, look at my boots," I said simultaneously, but they paid no attention, much excited with their construction.

"They're completely waterproof," I said. "Look!" I thought that the raft was floating in maybe a foot of water, yellowish-brown and greasy, slopping up around the edges of the planking; you had to jump from the collapsing banks of the hole onto the raft. There was a bit of open water all around it.

"Watch this," I said, meaning to demonstrate the water-repellent qualities of my high-cut boots. Just as they shouted with a single voice, "Look out, Matt, look out," I stepped into the water and sank straight down into depths over my head. My boots hit bottom and I kicked involuntarily. The water was opaque, paralyzingly cold, I couldn't see a thing. I shot upward and bumped my head hard on the underside of the raft, which had slid in against the side of the hole directly above me.

I couldn't swim or breathe in or out, naturally, and as the water was so muddy I couldn't force myself to open my eyes. But I wasn't frightened. The whole incident happened so damned fast. I was just frozen and furious because they hadn't told me the water was so deep. Mind you, they hadn't had the time.

I bounced off the slimy bottom of the hole a second time, giving my skull another resounding thump. It was probably this second bump that saved me because the people up on top didn't know which way to move the raft so as to be able to reach me. It was far, far too heavy, partially waterlogged, weighted down with the shack standing on it, to be lifted out of the hole before I drowned.

Mr. Forbes came on the dead run when he heard the amazed shouts. He noticed the bumping from beneath. He got the kids to ram the raft hard up against the opposite bank. Then he leaned way over, and reaching into the depths with both arms, down into the freezing water, he felt around and grabbed until he caught hold of me like some crazy flopping fish or baby seal. They tell me I was moving around pretty good in there. He got me by the armpits and shouted. The boys held onto his legs and he heaved me out of there. Didn't give me one second to gasp for air, wrapped the coat of his suit around me and galloped down Jean and along Summerhill.

By now the word had gone around north Rosedale—in 30 seconds so it would seem—that Matt Goderich was trying to drown himself in the vacant lot. All the little girls on the block were out there gaping as I was hustled past: Alysoun and Alexandra and Amanda Louise. Why, I wondered, did their names all begin with the letter A? Halfway along the block, just in front of the stoneyard, we met my mother nipping along at a good pace with a look of resolution on her face, my little brother scampering up behind with the smug look of guiltlessness written large upon his features, bless him. They had heard, and I guessed I was in for it. But strangely my mother made no fuss. She just turned beside Harold Forbes and walked along with him to our house, not offering to take me from him, making good speed. They brought me inside, and my grandmother appeared with a tiny silver drinking cup in her hand.

"Drink this," she commanded in a voice that allowed no dissent. She put the shining cup to my lips and I swallowed fast, twice, and nearly choked on my third great surprise of the day. It was brandy, so fiery and heady that it seemed to me as astounding as the dirty water, in just the opposite way. I coughed bewilderedly. From first to last I had not felt fear, but now as they yanked off my beautiful new boots, having much trouble with the cramped, sticking thongs, then pulled down my pants and peeled off my soaking sweater, rolled me in a comforter and practically sat on me, I started to think about what might have happened. I didn't cry, but I sure felt like it.

"I didn't mean to do that," I said.

"I know," said my mother. Mme. Archambault smiled sympathetically.

"I didn't know it would come over my boots," I said with a rising inflection.

My mother said, "That's all right. We'll dry them by the register. They'll be as good as new." She was wrong; they dried very stiff, with some kind of whitish deposit on them which never wore off, reminding me of this disagreeable accidental immersion long after.

"You were trying the boots, weren't you?"

"Yes." I began to drowse.

My brother Tony was the only one present who seemed annoyed or disappointed. I think he'd been expecting to see me severely punished; each of us looked forward to the other's misdeeds and expiations in the usual fraternal way, not exactly promoting awareness of the other's guilt, yet not concealing or minimizing it. We were never punished physically by either of my parents. Of our four grandparents, only Mme. Archambault would hazard as much as a wounding word, usually invoking the close surveillance of the Deity. Punishment to us was mainly a matter of one or other parent looking at us sorrowfully and saying something like, "That was very silly."

But even gentle correction can have its scale of more or less severe. I sometimes think nowadays that I'd have been better off with an occasional whack on the bum than with these mild phrases, which acquired sting from their restraint, in a curious way. My father and mother were in no sense hostile or aggressive toward their children, erring, if it is possible, in their radical mildness. But when my mother looked at you straight, saying, "Very idle and silly," you felt it.

Adults felt it, I noticed, and felt the intensity of her terseness in other ways. She didn't fall all over Harold Forbes for saving my life. She was obviously certain, in cold fact, that he had saved my life. I'd never have gotten out of that bloody muddy hole by myself. I'd be there still if it had been left to me. My mother gave Mr. Forbes a stealthy grin, with a peculiarly conspiratorial air.

"Still selling the oil, are you, Harold?"

"That's it, Ishy," said Mr. Forbes. Even through the shakings and shiverings that were punctuating my drowsiness, I noted this novel form of address, wondering when Mr. Forbes had known my mother well enough to be on that footing with her. Only three other people called her that, her parents and my father. "Ishy," for goodness sake!

"We burn coal," said my mother, laughing, "and as you know, Burns Coal Burns Best."

Mr. Forbes began to laugh too. "Did Andy tell you that?"

"No, I read it in the paper."

"At Lake Simcoe we can give you a better arrangement at lower cost. Had you thought at all about changing to oil?"

"We'd have to discuss it with Mr. Faucett, Hal. We only rent this house, you know."

"No, I didn't know that, I didn't realize . . . anyway if Faucett ever decides to convert, let me know."

"I certainly will," said my mother, smiling at him as he left the house. She never even said "thank you," which annoyed me slightly.

"You're all right now," she said to me, "but I want you to go to bed and stay there, in case of a chill. Are you still shivering?"

"No." I saw that I wasn't going to be punished, and felt a strong confirmation of my notion of justice. It would have been wrong, I felt, to punish me since I had meant no harm, had simply been undone by accidental events. Clearly no sensible person, young or old, would take that sort of misstep intentionally. My parents were quite able to see this.

I remember that day for another reason. I spent the remainder of it warmly blanketed in the front bedroom, which I now shared with Tony and Amanda Louise, but I wasn't supposed to be asleep. The lights were on in the hall. I heard various comings and goings in the evening, guests in the house of the kind that used to populate our living- and dining-rooms maybe twice a month, or oftener through the winter. These were friends and admirers of my father, university people more often than not, members of this or that tiny political structure, minatory in conception and behaviour, of a type that proliferated in the mid-thirties in Canadian university cities. Most of the people who came to the house for these informal socialist gatherings turned up years—or decades—later as declared candidates for the CCF, and later still for the NDP (or NPD if one resided in Québec). Several of them held office in the nascent party organization; now and then my father was sounded about the likelihood of his contesting some sort of election—never in a safe seat because there were no safe seats for Socialists.

I drowsed comfortably, the icy chill which had entered the very marrow of my childish frame now dissipated by brandy, hot food and several pounds of blankets and comforter. It must have been about a quarter to nine, well on toward my customary bedtime, when my father stole into the room with another man behind him who said quietly, *"Il dort, le pauvre petit."* I could understand this, and identify the speaker as someone who spoke with a different accent than, say, Mme. Archambault.

"Je crois que non," said my father. "Are you asleep, Matt? I've brought a friend to say hello to you."

I did not know that it was a meeting I'd want to recall later, and I barely opened my lids, squinting through my lashes at a thin man with a long narrow head, silver hair, a curiously Oriental expression and a peculiar air of benevolence and beneficence. I didn't pay him more than minimally polite attention. Then I really did fall suddenly asleep, and I suppose my father and the stranger left the room.

The next day my grandmother repeated rebelliously to my mother, *"Il me paraît un curé déguisé."* My evening visitor with pale hair and slanting eyes had been Jacques Maritain, then spending part of each year in Toronto at the Pontifical Institute of Mediaeval Studies, whose foundation he had supported and encouraged. Hardly anybody in Toronto in those days had the least idea who Maritain was or what he did for a living (nor did they when he died, on my birthday as it happened, in 1973) any more than they had any idea who Hemingway was a decade earlier, when he passed the winter at 1595 Bathurst Street. If anybody had suggested to Torontonians of that epoch that their city might one day be famous chiefly because these men had passed through it in the twenties and thirties, the citizenry would have hooted at the suggestion. But there is something to it.

Maritain spent most of his energies in the nineteen-thirties, for obvious reasons, on social thought; the previous decade had seen the gestation of his most important writing on epistemological and psychological matters. He gave much of his energy to various causes and groups of an insurgent character and was, like my father, a Catholic leftist, in the thirties a very rare bird indeed. In 1936 and 1937 he spoke out against Franco and the Falange in a way that gave great offence to Toronto opinion, and indeed Roman opinion. His big book on property and society, *L'Humanisme intégrale,* came out in English in North America in 1939 as *True Humanism.* When France fell in the following year, Maritain came to North America and was for many years in residence alternately in Princeton and Toronto. When my father was paying the social penalties that his increasingly radical views exacted, when we were sometimes without much money and an assured dwelling, it was pleasant and heartening to receive the philosopher's visits.

All I knew about Spain, on the day that I fell in the hole, nearly drowned, met Maritain, was that something had been going on around the Alcazar. I knew this because the euphony of the word had registered in my imagination, though I had no idea what the Alcazar was or who were doing what in its vicinity. I could read perfectly well by then, and I used to see pictures of shattered wall, and piles of broken building stone, and large headlines in the *Star* about the Alcazar, then about Madrid and Barcelona. There was no way I could link these newspaper events, or those taking place in a land called the Ruhr, with what my father was up to with his books. *Property and Value* in particular had managed to offend just about everyone whom my father might reasonably have wished to conciliate. It was a book of the far left, which would have offended almost every Catholic in Canada, had they suspected its existence. Certainly all the Catholics who read it—perhaps a dozen—were certain that Moscow was the next stop on my father's itinerary. It offended his family; his father found difficulty in understanding it, but was sure that it would undermine all prospect of academic advancement. He was right, of course. He knew much about the advancement and retardation of career ambitions, how these are managed.

The Board of Governors of the University, august body, were not certain what the book meant, but they sensed that it was not favourable to them. Maritain too, despite the intense respectability of his, as it were, covering connections, was by no means immune from jaundiced suspicion. He spoke too freely, did M. Maritain; he had no sense of good public relations.

Events now began to succeed one another with bewildering speed: the death of old King George, the accession of Edward VIII and his almost instantaneous abdication, various German adventures along their frontiers, of a piratical and gangsterish kind. About all these things I was as ignorant as the Board of Governors of the University of Toronto, though not at six years more ignorant than they. I wondered about

these people who came to the house. I never got quite
straight in my mind who lived with us and who was merely
passing through. M. Maritain, evidently, was a casual
though frequent visitor. Another ageing gentleman of equally
saintly mien, but with less command of the French language
(in fact none that I recall) though he had a beard in the European style, came to the house from time to time, a Mr.
Woodsworth. And there was a very young, immensely
energetic and attractive woman with a big square jaw, said to
be a poet, who came to talk politics. And many people from
the philosophy department. Priests too, but priests of a stripe
of which Mme. Archambault found it impossible to approve.
She complained that they paid insufficient attention to their
pastoral cares and too much to world affairs. University
priests, not honest industrious parish priests like Father
Lamarche from Saint-Lin.

There were maids in the house, one at a time, who used to
sit in the kitchen with my mother and listen, hour after hour
on idle weekday afternoons, to a succession of fifteen-minute
radio programs accompanied and punctuated by stinging
organ music, which I heard as I sat on the dining-room floor
playing with Tootsietoys. First came the Happy Gang at one
o'clock: Bert Pearl, Blain Mathé, Bob Farnon, with
Kathleen Stokes at the organ . . . and at 1:30 the long parade
of quarter-hour dramatic segments began, ending at 4:30
when Vic and Sade went off the air to be followed by Speed
Gibson, Dick Tracy and Orphan Annie in the time remaining before Amanda and I were directed to wash our hands
for supper. I remember two of our maids especially well.
There was Rita Deschamps, a slim redheaded girl from
Sturgeon Falls, whom my grandparents had brought down
with them one year when they came for a visit. When they
went back up north, Rita insisted on staying, having by then
made friends around the French church, Sacré-Coeur on
King Street, and grown addicted to city life. I don't recall exactly what her duties were: she may have done some looking
after children. Baby-sitting hadn't yet been invented. She

certainly did no cooking, neither did our earlier maid,
Helma, a Finnish woman who came from heaven only
knows what northern fastness of brooding lakes and tundra.
She trailed a heavy pall of gloom along with her, an impression of the twilight sub-arctic. This may have been because
she spoke virtually no English. I wondered if Finnish were
just a kind of horribly mangled English, because Helma used
to use a word that sounded like "keerko" when she meant
"church." When the family crowded into the Durant and
headed for Our Lady of Perpetual Help Church on a Sunday
morning, I might be left behind because four adults and
Amanda Louise had already squeezed into that fatigued
sedan. At these times Helma would clutch me around my
middle agitatedly, muttering "keerko, keerko."

Where can she have come from, how did she find her way
to Toronto? I associate her with the west, with harvesters
and railway trains full of young people who went west to get
in the crops, on obscure farmsteads west of the Lakehead,
and imaginatively with the novels of Frederick Philip Grove;
she had their intensity and their awkwardness of articulation.

M. and Mme. Archambault were the other principal
tenants of our straitened upstairs living quarters. Typically,
the maid slept downstairs in the sunporch. All three of us
kids slept in the large front bedroom next to the bathroom;
my mother and father had the small rear bedroom at the
head of the stairs. The big back bedroom was the Toronto
pied à terre of my grandparents. My father never complained
of this preponderance in living space allowed his in-laws. If
anything, it was my mother who most often showed her
sense of being inconvenienced. Of course relations between
grown married women with children and their mothers are
often strained.

My mother had squadrons, fleets, of cousins, the children
of Mme. Archambault's five brothers and four sisters, *les
Michaud*. I can remember playing with Lois Michaud in
some green and sequestered park in old downtown Toronto
at the age of five, having been taken for the day by my

grandmother to visit some of her Toronto relatives. Lois
Michaud, who was she? Most likely the grandchild of one of
my great-uncles, therefore my. . . what. . . second cousin?
God knows! Cousinship is a relationship no longer much
cherished. My mother would have been a first cousin of Léon
Michaud, Lois' father, so she and I were second cousins, if
anybody cares to know. Where is she now? And where are
the 50 other kids my own age I used to meet on similar rang-
ings around Sackville, Winchester and Amelia Streets, in the
wake of my energetic and commanding grandmother?

That big back bedroom where Papa Archambault and his
lady dwelt in season was a good-sized room with an ap-
preciable ell to it, and a walk-in closet. It had almost the proportions of a small flat or apartment, when a curtain had
been drawn across the ell where my grandfather kept his
small workbench. He was in all ways a remarkable man,
noteworthy for the extreme contrast of his character with
that of his spouse. He was quiet, reticent to the point of being withdrawn. He once shot seventeen cats overnight with a
light sporting rifle, longtime prowlers along a back fence in
Sturgeon Falls. But he was not at all a mountain of repres-
sion, as might be suggested by the incident of the cats in the
night. On the contrary, he was pleased with life and with
himself. He could do most things with his hands, was a
painter and draughtsman who produced many pictures best
described as highly accomplished primitives. One of them, a
crayon seascape called "When Steam was Young and Sail
Supreme," hung in our bedroom for years and gave me intense pleasure in its contemplation.

He worked in brass and other metals, and in wood, with a
high degree of finish. He made each of us children a sizeable
personal bank or strongbox, in descending order of size to
match our ages. My brother Tony's was made of a large
Ovaltine can, scraped and repainted and faced with wooden
ends. Each of these safes had a secret locking device, all of
them of considerable ingenuity.

He died early on, when I was five years old. He had contracted a great fondness for my young brother Tony, then barely two, and his last words were, "How's little Tony?" I mention this because they are the only authentic set of last words recorded in the family. A complex personality, Papa Archambault's. He was no businessman. He opened a shoe-store in Sturgeon Falls in the absolute and total depths of the great depression, and in a very short time everybody in town was wearing a pair of his shoes, and he had a cash drawer full of relief vouchers of the municipality of Sturgeon Falls. In due course, the town went bust, its obligations were repudiated, and M. Archambault reappeared on Summerhill Avenue, no longer in business for himself.

A lesser man than my father might have been fatally impressed by Papa Archambault's ill-fortune (and bad management too, most likely) and when the time came to try business for himself might have been somewhat daunted. Not my dad! He was ready to risk all when the opportunity was presented, in no way deterred by his father-in-law's heavy losses. There was a strong sympathy between the two men; it was Dad who heard and repeated the dying man's words, "How's little Tony?"

Tony isn't little any more. In those days I might have been excused for wishing him not simply little, but so small as not to exist at all. I wasn't precisely jealous of his special relationship with Papa Archambault, not at that time anyway, but I was pretty dashed when he came upon the scene, managing to leave myself with a permanent record of my annoyance, in a clear-cut instance of the willed accident.

Most of the family had gone up to OLPH church, for Tony's official christening, that afternoon: my mother and father, Amanda Louise, two grandfathers, Uncle Philip. I was left alone in my bedroom, three years old, supposed to be taking my nap. I hated this notion of a nap, and was not best pleased to have been left in my grandmother's care. And she, I suppose, would have preferred to attend the baptismal rite. She persuaded me to lie on my bed and doze, or otherwise simulate slumber, while she did something or other downstairs. Perhaps I did in fact go off for a moment or two; my room had been darkened and the house was deathly still. I woke with a sharp start sometime later, for some reason feeling frightened. I got hastily to my feet, took a step in the dark and another, and suddenly slipped by placing my foot unexpectedly on a roller-skate. I fell backward quite hard, and stabbed myself in the back as I fell with great force onto the upper edge of a woven wastepaper basket made of wooden slatting or stripping, whose upper edge had been cut out in a series of Gothic points. Nobody in the family had ever had any reason to suspect the stabbing power of these small sharp projections. One of them slid into the skin on my back, near the spinal column, like an assassin's blade, inflicting a wound whose scar I still carry. I was dazed by the wound, picked myself up, saw blood dripping onto the floor behind me, and let out a mournful wail that brought my grandmother on the run. Never slow to react, she saw the trouble at once. I was apparently bleeding copiously, and a flap of sliced-open skin was curled back from an alarming gap in the flesh. Whether she had had any experience of first aid, I never knew, but she got me into the bathroom immediately and bent me over forward, twisted across her knee in such a way as to cause the sides of the wound to press shut against each other and bleed less. She sponged it carefully with warm and sudsy water, which hurt, but not unbearably, then patted it dry with a freshly laundered towel, and without giving any forewarning splashed the still open and slowly bleeding cut with iodine.

This caused me to let out a dolorous howl of shocked surprise just as the family arrived back from the church with the newly baptized Tony at their centre, clad in the traditional long christening garment. People began to take snapshots of family groups. My grandmother was called for. Seeing that she had stopped my bleeding, she applied a dressing of gauze and adhesive tape to my back and carried me back to bed, where I was to lie quietly flat on my stomach, till a reassessment of the injury could be made later on when the house was quieter.

My back hurt a lot. The wooden point must have penetrated near the large cluster of ganglia up there between the shoulder blades. It seemed to me that the dressing was wet—there might be fresh bleeding but I was very fearful of turning around to see, thinking that I might pop the sliced skin open anew. The room was dark. I was emotionally overwrought, the rites of baptism, the claims of sibling rivalry and this stab in the back all mixed together. I felt guilty. I felt as if this wound were deliberately self-inflicted, and yet I was certain that the roller-skate on which I'd slipped was not mine, but Amanda's.

Too young at three years to have any idea of the desperate human need to call attention to oneself, having the need but not, as it were, the concept of the need, I now lay still, deciding from motives of policy not to interrupt the celebrations below. Sometimes I overheard a tired wail from Tony, who must have minded the swaddling christening dress intensely, though he has always resolutely denied any vestigial memory of the occasion. Eventually he was brought into our room and placed in his bed, where he burped and gurgled for some time before falling asleep. By then I was sound asleep myself, dreaming of circuses. My back hurt.

That evening, Dr. Bloy, a friend of the family, but not our family physician on account of his supposed incompetence, happened to be in the house, and my father asked him to look at the cut on my back, being perhaps not quite certain of the efficacy of my grandmother's treatment. I lay there on my stomach, very tired and cranky, having had a late supper after an overlong nap. The doctor relentlessly peeled away the adhesive tape which my grandmother had applied rather too liberally, then carefully scissored away some gauze which had stuck to the cut. He cleaned off some shreds of dressing with alcohol, taking care not to reopen the slit. When he had it all cleaned off he gave a reflective whistle. "If I'd been here, I'd have stitched it up," he said and I felt frightened. In those days stitches had a very poor reputation among us three-year-olds.

"Could you do it now?"

"No, the healing's started. He'll have a scar, for sure."

Dr. Bloy was quite right. I had a scar for many years (still faintly visible) to remind me of my brother's arriving in this world to claim a share of the family fortunes and name. And long after the scar tissue disappeared and the seven-year cycle of replacement of body tissue had been undergone twice, thrice, more, I still had a deep, depressed triangular red mark below my shoulder blades, to the right of the spinal column. My mother sometimes used to refer to this memento, not wholly jokingly, as the brand of Cain, this perhaps after I'd beaten up on Tony or broken something that belonged to him. And the Biblical reference, once I understood it, infuriated me. Tony was no Abel, I knew, and I was no Cain.

Life in those days did however sometimes wear the aspect of an imposed exile from a very good place, if not quite a great good one. As soon as Tony could talk a bit, the front bedroom shared by the three of us assumed the character of a forum, sometimes a cockpit, in which three increasingly loquacious individuals carried on late evening debates.

"Shut up, you kids, I'm tired, I want to sleep," Amanda Louise would insist from her big bed next the window, while we went on giggling or wrestling in our bed. If we struck an interesting subject, she would gradually get drawn into the talk. Finally my mother—never my father—would burst into the room and command us to be silent, and go to sleep like good children; more often than not we obeyed her, because she never appeared till very late. When I went off to school when I was going on seven, I began to sympathize with my sister's wish to get to sleep in good time, and the long, laughing conferences with Tony under the bedclothes were curtailed. I had to get up in the morning.

That fall I was escorted to OLPH school by Georgie-Balls Bannon, more as a gesture of parental supervision than anything else. I found my way along the five-block walk to Our Lady of Perpetual Help very easily, and discovered labyrinthine shortcuts—really longcuts—in the company of Jerry and Jakie Forbes along Sighthill, Rosedale Heights, and down the bridle path on the side of the hill above the tracks, criss-crossed by paths through tall grass cut by the comings and goings of the kids from Perpetual Help, and the bums from Whitney School with whom we carried on nomadic perpetual war. Going up and down the hill we fired snowballs in season, and balls of horse manure in season, at the Whitney bums on their way to school, up the other side of MacLennan.

Returning from some sortie into Whitney territory eastward above the tracks, I could see our backyard and the swing beside the garage, and sometimes I would see Tony pumping it back and forth, not getting anywhere special. Remorse might strike me, a big kid observing my lonely little brother. When I got home, I might very occasionally go around back to play in the swing with Tony.

The last time I remember—it must have been the year we moved to Moore Park—I tried to squeeze down beside my brother in the space under one of the bench seats. It seemed as if the space were smaller and more cramped; there was no room for my knees. After that I stopped playing in the swing in the garden, and didn't see another one like it for 30 years.

2

On sunny spring forenoons, usually on Thursdays, the men
from the Beverly would assemble on the corner of Garfield
and Clifton Road, outside the schoolyard, from which their
presence was solemnly interdicted. Sometimes we would be
lined up in rows on the playground doing PT under the direction of leathery Sergeant Hornback, doing our level best to
land a blow with an Indian club on calisthenic neighbour or
partner, in simulated accident. A blow on the funnybone
from one of these hardwood clubs would induce spasms of
alternate tears and laughter that were genuinely crippling.
There we would be, swinging arms and legs to the loud
count, and outside the fence a respectably dressed quartet of
representatives of Hollywood would materialize afoot, the
least of their number bearing a folded card table, others
holding bulky brown cardboard boxes. They must have
hiked over from St. Clair and Yonge, a considerable distance
to carry that much weight.

The nuns, and Miss McHale and Miss Conroy, would eye
the interlopers—as they considered them—from behind tall
classroom windows, on each of whose many panes a
chocolate-coloured Easter egg or yellow chick, or purple
bouquet of unidentifiable flowers, might be blazoned, for
this was mid-April. Sisman's Scampers lightfoot weather,
when the speedways for Dinky Toys were solid-packed
yellow clay down the hill into the ravine behind the school,
when Monty McNally and I would unwillingly turn our

steps away from our raceways to investigate the enticements of filmland.

Sister Matilda, Sister St. Jane and Sister Claude were sworn enemies of the movies, regarding them as vulgar and worse, sinful. A decade earlier, the film capital had been rent by intimations of scandal, then by accidental revelations of this or that sexual intrigue, finally by an unhappy girl's death during a party of the kind then conventionally considered wild. Whether this party took place at a roadhouse or not cannot now be ascertained; but wild parties at roadhouses, where gin and jazz figured largely as staples of the ambiance, as well as rollers of paper streamers, formed a principal commodity among the wares of those who then, as now, dealt in the reforming activity which was to create a series of stenches (as the phrase went) in the nostrils of the decent.

I was always fascinated by that expression; it seemed extreme. I never actually saw Fatty Arbuckle in a film, but pictures of this luckless mummer were still discoverable as late as the mid-thirties in discarded fan magazines lost in closets: *Silver Screen, Photoplay, Screen Mirror, Modern Screen, Screen Romances.* From the agreeable aspect of the comedian in these shots it was hard to determine why he should be such a stench. But there it was; public morality had surely been transgressed and a scapegoat had to be found. An office of film censorship was established with a former Postmaster-General of the US, a Mr. Hays, at its head. The rulings of the Hays Office were to become legendary as years went by, because of their exotic mixture of nasty-mindedness and innocence. At this time too the Legion of Decency asserted its sway over Catholic filmgoers, who were required in parish or school to subscribe without qualification to the Legion's pledge.

But even these bulwarks of public morals could not erase from the imaginations of Sister Matilda, Sister St. Jane, Sister Claude, Miss McHale, Miss Conroy and the redoubtable Father Regan, their growing suspicion that the

cinema—always simply called "the movies"—threatened
their ascendancy over pupils, parents, parishioners, and
would in the end undermine it completely. The movie-going
habit might be described as noxious in Junior First or Senior
Second, might be likened to certain unnameable solitary
vices, which I never persuaded anybody to identify for me or
even describe, by assiduous pastor or anxious curate: Father
Regan, Father O'Reilly, Father Fullerton, Father McCoy.
But it could not be banished; it flourished.

At ten to twelve we came out the side door, at the north
end of the school, the boys did. The girls came out the south
door, I believe. They must have done, because they certainly
didn't line up with us, and the south entrance had GIRLS
carved over the lintel. Strict segregation obtained whilst we
were in movement to and from the classroom, but grew less
strict when we were actually seated and engaged in learning.
Here desegregation came into play, often as a disciplinary
measure. I was always being ordered to "go and sit with the
girls, Matt Goderich." This was ineffective discipline
because I didn't mind sitting with the girls. I liked it. I had a
chance to examine a lot of girls from close up: Frankie
Walsh, Alanna Begin, Paddy Ann McCarthy, to instance
three eight-year-old lovelies at whom I threw inkballs. I enjoyed their society greatly, and this enjoyment proved to be
in no way simple or indiscriminate, but complex and most
variously pleasant. None of these girls had her hair cut in the
severe Buster Brown style favoured by Alysoun Selkirk.
They had long silky hair, good for dipping in the inkwell at
the upper right corner of one's desk. Sometimes when one's
inkwell had been well stuffed with balls of drawing paper,
then partially filled with ink from the tall Waterman's bottle
with the globe on it in glassy relief, a tarry blue-black decoc-
tion would precipitate itself, glinting with almost coppery
tones, into which Alanna Begin's hair, a lustrous taffy colour, might be intruded with alarming results. One noonday
on Holy Thursday in the mid-thirties I got the unfortunate
girls' hair so clotted and entangled in my inkwell that the

tiny glass liner pulled right out of its hole attached to her left braid, a darkly purple stain spreading below it over her dress. The colour was appropriately penitential in tone, about the same shade of purple as shrouded the statues up at the church during that liturgical season. Nobody had the heart to tattle on me, I'm glad to say, not even the class tattletale, Paul Wickett.

So Alanna and the other girls filed away just about noon, out the south door and around the front of the building, meeting us boys just at the border of the schoolyard. We could sense the teachers staring at our shoulderblades as we moved off the property. All at once I heard Miss McHale shout, "Alanna Begin, what *have* you done to your dress?" I kept right on moving. School was temporarily out. On the sidewalk the men from the Beverly had set up their display, a cheerful sight perhaps unsuited to the temper of the season, for tomorrow would be Good Friday.

They always came to us at noon, moving on a further half-mile in the afternoon to stand outside Whitney School at three o'clock. Years later I learned from a contemporary who had gone to school with the other dirty Protestants at Whitney that Christian morality was not there felt to be so vulnerable, so under attack, as at OLPH. Sometimes these men from Hollywood came right onto the Whitney schoolgrounds, giving of their plenty to the very teachers. Hints of an easy alliance between Protestantism and the cinema used to fascinate me, and once or twice I mooted the question to my parents over supper.

"There's nothing specifically Lutheran or Calvinist about the movies," said my mother. She seemed to find the question of theoretical interest. "I can't see any connection."

"They're both godless and secular," said my grandmother with much complacence.

"Are we to consider the matter sociologically?" asked my father, spooning up mouthfuls of maple-walnut ice cream, a dessert of which he was surpassingly fond. He looked around the shaded, cosy table at all of us, grinned and wiped his chin, where a small lump of ice cream had lodged. "The question of the ownership of these theatre chains, and of the film-producing corporations, is very involved, very complex. A ramified example of the industrialization of the simple human need to be entertained."

"Andrew, Andrew."

"All right, darling." He turned to me. "So far as I can see, there is no hidden connection between Protestantism and the films. Some arts really are connected to particular people, particular places. You might argue that of symphonic music, best written by Germans, for some infinitely obscure reason. Perhaps I should say, by Germans and Austrians. The English have a rich and various poetry of a kind found nowhere else; they excel in no other form of art, except possibly ecclesiastical architecture. Perhaps *aquarelle*. I can't detect a cultural identity in the movies. Mind you, their industrial aspect suggests North American patterns of production. We might find the routine movie, the average, competently produced, program picture, more expertly produced here than elsewhere, because not considered an object of hand craftsmanship. . . . I'm going to stop talking."

"Thank goodness," said my mother, looking to Mme. Archambault for her usual ready concurrence.

My grandmother surprised us all. "Andrew is right," she said, "the best films must be made slowly, by hand, like everything else." She then lapsed into an unusual taciturnity, clearly thinking of Papa Archambault, now two years dead, and a great exponent of the hand crafts.

This conversation did not tell me why the men from the neighbourhood theatre could get into the Whitney schoolyard, but not ours. Long after, an obvious reason occurred to me. There was only one man, an elderly and extremely grumpy janitor, Mr. Finn, on the staff at OLPH. I think now that the sisters and the lay lady teachers felt threatened by this gang of more or less strange men, not identifiable as Catholics or fellow parishioners. They welcomed visits from a wide variety of priests, of course: Oblates, Passionists,

Redemptorists, Paulists, Franciscans, an occasional Jesuit. No Benedictines. Presentation and Alexian brothers. Recruiters from the two Catholic high schools for boys. Christian Brothers from Oaklands and Basilian Fathers from St. Mike's. And always squadrons of nuns in habits of grey or black, coiffed and wimpled in the height of fifteenth-century chic.

Nobody thought then, as I do now, that the movies and the Christian Church are near cousins, celebratory, deliverers of the good news in joint, or at least analogous, propagandizings. Pro-paganda. For the pagans. Is that what the word really means?

"What *have* you done to your dress?" I saw Alanna stiffen in amazement as Miss McHale bellowed at her from above and behind. I went ahead and tried to lose myself in the crowd around the men from the theatre. Their card table was loaded with free gifts for the OLPH audience. They gave away candy. Hard round short sticks of barley sugar of a kind I never saw anywhere else. Like truncated pieces of Brighton rock, suckable for hours. I used to get into trouble for being unable to recite when called upon, because of chunks of this hard candy. Once I nearly strangled on the juice of a piece, too hastily swallowed in an effort at concealment.

"Matt Goderich! Stand and say 'Come little leaves, said the wind one day.' "

I got to my feet choking slightly, and gurgled, "Come glug glug glug. . . .

". . . glug, cough, 'over the fields with me cough to play. . . .' "

She had selected a poem somewhat advanced for Senior First, perhaps to confer an obscure self-justification. She had me reading from Book Four of the Canadian Catholic Corona Readers, whereas Senior First was only what would now be called Grade Two. The names of the primary grades, and their number, kept shifting around all through the second half of the thirties. When I went to *real* school (not kindergarten) with books and desks and globes and chalk and cutouts in the windows, the first year was called Junior First. There were supposed to be junior and senior grades through four levels, thus: Junior First, Senior First, Junior Second, Senior Second, Junior Third, Senior Third, Junior Fourth, Senior Fourth, which reminds me powerfully of the lower and upper grades of an English public school, as described in boys' books and magazines. Anybody born in Ontario before 1932 or 1933 will remember this system. Eight grades of primary school leading to high-school entrance. The final grade, Senior Fourth, was also known as Entrance. No-one has forgotten that.

"He went down to Whitby Collegiate to write his Entrance."

"Got my Entrance." And so forth.

This meant that the aspirant had completed a really quite exacting primary education and could now proceed to a high school, a "continuation" school (usually a country primary school with the first and perhaps the second year of high school available for local students), or what were still called in Toronto Collegiate Institutes, at one time private, fee-supported institutions, later incorporated into the public system.

Up till the mid-thirties, it was conventionally accepted that eight grades of primary schooling were normal, doubtless because a large proportion of scholars completed their schooling with the Entrance year. In eight primary years, a pretty complete basic education could be acquired. Many distinguished persons rose high in Canadian life after completing the Entrance year, Senior Fourth, and ending their formal education at that point.

But by about 1935 in Canada as well as in the US, far larger numbers began to go to high school, and a movement to shorten the primary course by one year became widespread. I used to be mighty perplexed when I was going to OLPH, about what had happened to Junior Second. There didn't seem to be any such year. I only ever attended *seven* grades of primary school. The year I reached it, Senior Fourth, that hallowed Entrance year, had its name changed, arbitrarily as we all considered it, to Grade Eight! We never got to write our Entrance exam, thereby missing out on a sacrification rite of early adolescence which had given nightmares to three generations of Ontario schoolchildren since about the time of Confederation.

After that seven primary grades were usually considered normal, and one began to hear disquieting rumours of a thing called in the States "Junior High," in which the seventh and eighth grades were treated as a separate entity preparatory to the last four years of high school. The cult of the teenager, the sub-deb, high school, Andy Hardy, now began to blossom as, all unawares, those of us who missed out Junior Second participated in a great social revolution that eventually re-made Canadian life. The expectation that one's formal schooling would end with the Entrance year, or at the latest after two years of "continuation" school, had for long reflected the predominantly rural and small-town character of Canadian life.

In the mid-thirties, unemployment and the growing urbanization of our lives, and changes in the distribution of wealth, and in the role of various governments in peoples' personal affairs, meant that very much larger numbers of us kids went on to high school, as far at least as the twelfth year, called in Ontario Junior Matriculation. By 1940, a pattern of seven or eight years of primary education *plus* four years of secondary—essentially the pattern found today all over North America—was becoming standard in Ontario. You could get into most of the provincial universities if you had the Junior Matriculation certificate. I think only the obdurate and august University of Toronto exacted the fifth high-school year, the notoriously difficult Senior Matric, or Grade Thirteen (fateful number) for university entrance.

In the mid-to-late thirties there were viciously anti-democratic educators lodged in place in most of our school boards who deplored the influence of American models upon

Ontario education, who thought that on the whole it was not a good thing for most students to proceed as far as family finances would allow in high school. But these persons and their views were, happily, borne down by the new trends. By the time my sister Amanda Louise went to high school, all her friends from OLPH did so as well, almost without exception. Some went to Catholic private high schools, Loretto or St. Joseph, most to public Collegiate Institutes at public expense.

I think it was this change of expectations more than almost anything else I remember that altered my life, and the lives of my pals, born around 1930. All of us took it for granted that we would go through high school, or at least as far through as our wits would carry us: we all entertained grave misgivings about Senior Matric. All my life I've been on close terms with guys my own age who were the first members of their family to get through high school. And it was a very long time, I tell you, buddy-boy, before university *attendance*, never mind graduation, was widespread. In the late thirties, one student would complete a BA degree out of every *hundred* who started high school. To have two parents—as I did—who had graduated from university in the generation before mine, in the second and third decades of the century, was extremely rare among rich people, and simply never at all the case of the less than rich. My parents were a rare pair, for God knows we weren't rich, and in a year or two we became very poor!

My father was a professor. How long this happy state would continue grew more and more doubtful as the thirties drew on. Those poor men from the Beverly theatre who gave away candy, the hoboes along the railway tracks behind our garden, news from the Alcazar, the game called "sit-down strike" that I played with Jakie and his brother, the shifts in educational policy, the replacement of the traditional readers in school by the new "Life and Literature" series (not a bad title, that), the replacement of History, as a school subject, by Social Studies, all these complexities of living, when I was aged seven, eight, nine, were the growing signs of social upheavals whose meaning was as yet closed to me, and to my elders.

I saw my father each night more unsettled, less spontaneous in his natural and endearing gaiety, my mother more openly sympathetic with him and oddly more and more fearful. In the background Mme. Archambault loomed as a threatening attendant chorus. My uncle Philip lost one job after another, finally growing virtually incapable of finding work. One of the men from the Beverly was about Uncle Philip's age, the early twenties. They resembled one another; every now and then I thought of asking my uncle why he didn't get a job as an usher at the Beverly.

The four men who came over to the school from the theatre, every Thursday afternoon during the fine weather before the summer vacation, comprised the entire staff of a small neighbourhood movie theatre excepting the girl cashier and the projectionist. The manager, two ushers, and the ticket-taker and guardian of the door and lobby. The manager, a harassed balding man, was the only one of them past 30. He had a wife and a number of childen whom I used to see clustered around him on Saturday afternoons. I knew they belonged to him because of the affectionate way they clutched his hand or his cuff, or the trouser-leg of his neat, dark, almost threadbare suit. At this time, this man earned $24 a week, and he continued in this job from the time I went to school and began to go to the movies regularly in 1936, until the mid-fifties, when his weekly earnings had probably tripled.

The ushers and the ticket-taker usually didn't last more than a year or two. This turnover made me wonder whether my uncle might not carve out a career in film-exhibition. Plenty of men in those days, and later on too, were taking on jobs for which they had not been trained, after finding themselves unable to get work in their areas of special knowledge. I can remember graduate engineers complaining to my dad that there was no work for them. I don't suppose that any medical doctor ever went long without employment, but I know of graduate dentists who treated no patients whatsoever in small Ontario towns in the mid-thirties, when they had office rent to pay, and the salary of part-time office help, and instalments on their purchases of operating equipment. Times continued tough, very tough.

On this Thursday of Holy Week at noon, the manager and his ticket-taker and ushers had spread before them the customary range of gifts they used to persuade their clientele to attend the forthcoming Saturday matinée. The Beverly was a smallish neighbourhood house on the west side of Yonge Street, half a block north of St. Clair in a building long since disappeared. It faced drastic competition from the much larger and grander Hollywood Theatre across the street, a little farther north. Later on in the late forties the Hollywood was twinned, a second auditorium being built alongside the first such that both halves of a double-feature could be run simultaneously—you could choose which of the features you wanted to see first, or you could watch one through on one side of the building, then proceed to the adjoining auditorium and sit through it a second time, if you felt like it. A surprising number of people used to do this. I believe that certain fans of Bette Davis and Joan Crawford, especially, most of them ladies, used to oscillate back and forth in the double auditorium, watching the film of their preference three or four times in a row.

Around 1947 a third theatre was built to serve the St. Clair-Yonge district, an Odeon House, the Hyland. By this time, the décor and the exhibiting policy of the old Beverly were long superseded; it name had been changed from Beverly to Kent (not its first name-change either) and little by little people stopped coming.

But in 1936 and 1937 moviegoing was still our central form of entertainment. The only reason the manager of the Beverly had to make his regular promotional sweeps was that most of us had almost nothing to spend on entertainment. This was the golden age of one-cent candy, merchandised precisely because one cent was a meaningful selling price. It cost a dime to get into the Saturday matinée at the Beverly; that was a standard kids' admission price all over town, though there persisted throughout my childhood a rumour that there was a theatre somewhere out along the Danforth, where you could get in for a nickel. I think that this rumour, whose foundations I could never uncover, was probably false, but an interesting survival from much earlier in the century, around 1920, when admission for a kid was in fact five cents.

There were many Saturdays when all I had was a nickel; once or twice I hiked through the Don Valley to Broadview Avenue and out the Danforth, a distance of several miles, in search of the mythical five-cent admission, but I never actually found it, though I passed plenty of neighbourhood houses like the Pape and the Broadview.

They gave us those granitic chunks of hard candy. They gave us pencils, pens with pen-nibs that didn't write well, splayed and scratchy. Pencil boxes. Scribblers. I especially remember the blotters; we were always much in want of blotters, particularly those of us who were just beginning to be allowed to use ink, for writing or for dyeing girls' braids. These blotters had the name of the theatre on them, its address and phone number, and the forthcoming bills for Saturday, Monday and Tuesday, and for Wednesday, Thursday and Friday. The bill changed twice weekly, and there was only one matinée a week, on Saturday afternoon when a *third* feature, a 60-minute cowboy picture from Republic, was added to the program. For 10¢ you got to see two features of normal length, the cowboy movie, and a newsreel, as well as two or three animated cartoons and of course the trailers for coming attractions. Figuring 80 minutes apiece for the normal features, 60 for the cowboy film—that gives you three hours and 40 minutes, ten for the newsreel, fifteen for the cartoons, then the trailers—this gives you a program four and half hours long, and that doesn't count short periods when the screen was blank and curtained over. I see that my recollection of long Saturday afternoons passed in darkness is perfectly accurate. We used to arrive around one o'clock and leave the theatre well after five, eyes aching, heads whirling with incident.

At the Hollywood, where the ambiance was grander, but the admission the same, they used to have serials, and very enthralling they were too. Flash Gordon and the clay men who came out of the walls; Dick Tracy and a criminal aircraft that was one enormous wing, very scary. Warren Hull as the Spider. Comings and goings in black 1937 Buick Limiteds.

Paradise.

I remember all too clearly this triple bill: Sir Guy Standing and Richard Cromwell in *Annapolis Farewell*, Ralph Bellamy as Ellery Queen in the *Spanish Cape Mystery*, and Smith Ballew in *Yuma Stage*.

"Don't you hang around afterward and be late for supper, and be sure you get to Confession on the way home." My mother would hurl this injunction at us as we left the house on Saturday about noon, for the longish walk up MacLennan Hill, past OLPH school up Clifton Road to St. Clair, left turn at OLPH Church and westward toward Yonge. We always meant to pop into Perpetual Help Church on our way home so that Amanda Louise could go to Confession. I used to wonder what her sins were; she was an even-tempered girl, able to exert considerable physical force, not cowardly. She had been a useful protector for me on occasions when our combined force had rebuffed a cruel onslaught from, say, Maurice Reilly.

Monty McNally was in love with Amanda Louise, according to a bunch of silly girls in my class. Those times when we left the Beverly early enough for Amanda to get to Confession before Father Fullerton left the box, we were always accompanied by Monty; this seems precocious. He and Amanda were about ten years old; they were undeniably fast friends. I don't know what other flavour their friendship can have had, in the two years when it was at its most intense;

certainly Monty did me a good many favours for a long time.

It took us close to three quarters of an hour to get from Summerhill to the Beverly. Before we bought our tickets, if we had any extra money, even a nickel, we would go to Woolworth's next door and buy candy at the long cheerful counter next to the entry. If we had, say, ten cents extra between us, we would buy a nickel's worth of sponge taffy and the same in jelly beans. The jelly beans were for eating—sometimes we bought mixed nuts instead. The sponge taffy was for ammunition. Oh, now and then we ate bits of it, but it functioned, when broken into chunks the size of a small piece of cake, as a weapon of offence and defence.

At five minutes before one the afternoon crowd of kids would be fully assembled in the theatre auditorium and the din would be excruciating; you could hear it out on Yonge Street even with the inner doors sealed shut, and when they were opened to allow the ushers to throw some kid out, waves of sound would roll forth, to the extreme consternation of passersby. It sounded like Gehenna or Armageddon, or the awakening of the Divine Beast in the Revelation to St. John on Patmos. We would whiz up and down the aisles, allowing the less nimble ushers almost to catch us, then turning on the afterburners, spurting away and evading them by slipping along a row of our buddies from school, whose legs and elbows would impede the usher as he snatched at our windbreakers.

When the sponge taffy had lain some time in its bag, say the length of the first feature, its consistency would be softened and altered such that it would hurt on impact—a chunk of average size would have the weight and momentum of the rubber ball used in jacks—and it would also lodge, if accurately thrown, in the recipient's hair, there to entangle itself irremoveably. How I remember those joyful afternoons in the Beverly when girl-child after girl-child launched herself up the gangway in howling, tearful pursuit of her tormentors, lumps of sticky, brownish-yellow taffy dangling from her scalp like Christmas tree ornaments. Meanwhile the noise raged and the ushers tried in vain to calm us. Once in a while they would cause the show to be interrupted, but this was a wrong bit of strategy because then the sound of the throng grew positively menacing and the first members of a dreadful advance party would appear on the stage apron, a very bad sign. Then the projectionist would roll 'em in desperation and the stilled image on the screen would leap into life. There would be cheers, or a moment of stunned silence in which we would hear Adam Sinclair weeping, often, in fact almost always, from under a row of seats down front, where he was being held captive.

I often wondered why Adam kept on coming to the show. He was always treated roughly in his social role of notorious sissy. We would de-pant him to start; further indignities might follow. From time to time, when the afternoon's entertainment was over and the early evening show beginning—there was no interval, as there usually is now—I would pass around the theatre by Adam's side, actuated by obscure feelings of sympathy, principally the suspicion that if I were as unpopular as Adam I'd be treated just the same. We would be hunting for his pants. We would let his underpants go. I used to think that the fatherly manager must have a collection of Adam Sinclair's underpants in his lost-and-found drawer in the office. Maybe he did; maybe he took them home to his children. Adam would never follow my suggestion that he inquire about them. He couldn't bear to admit to the manager that he had been crawling around at the front of the auditorium with nothing on below the waist but a shirttail.

"How would you feel, Matthew?" he would sniffle, especially if the weather were cool. "Suppose it was you, how would you feel? Do you suppose I like it?" Adam was eighteen months to two years older than I, almost ten at the time I'm describing, but I always felt protective toward him, and ashamed of how I talked about him across our dinner-table, where he was invariably referred to as "yon wee Scotch farrrrtttt" or "Putty-Face" Sinclair.

"Putty-Face." He had a small round face like a hazel nut, with little wrinkles already appearing in the laugh lines on his cheeks, so that they seemed pinched and shrunken. My brother Tony invented this woundingly accurate nickname—his first verbal invention of record but by no means his last. We used to tease Tony, as soon as he was old enough to grasp that he was being teased, by calling him by his baby-name. Duddles. It made him wild. God knows how he managed to twist "Tony" around till it came out Duddles, but that was what he called himself till he could speak plainly. Afterward he called himself "Big T," a revenge that Amanda Louise and I felt very keenly. "Big T," for God's sake, where did he come up with "Big T"? He got it out of some first-reader, I believe, and it made me grind my teeth.

The first time my darling little brother cast his innocent, lustrous brown eyes on Adam Sinclair, he gave him the nickname "Putty-Face" and it proved ineradicable. People who didn't belong to our family started using the name. We must have employed it unconsciously in their presence, people who went to Whitney School with Adam, who may have relished its appositeness.

"Oh you're all so mean," he would whisper desparingly, and I would wander around the Beverly in the dark beside him, looking for his pants, which invariably came finally to light in one of the side rows ten to fifteen ranks back from the stage. As the search was carried forward while the possessor of the pants had only his shirttail to conceal his poor bare bum, it had to be prosecuted with circumspection. I would drift slowly along the side rows, apologizing to the few adults who had arrived toward 5:30 for the Saturday night show. Adam would have to crawl under the seats; this didn't seem to bother him as much as you would think. Habituated to infantile masochism, he now almost enjoyed attendance at the Saturday afternoon triple-bill in this ambiguous location. He could hear the soundtrack in return for his dime, even if immured pantless under the seats during the fourth reel of the first feature.

I always found his trousers. "Adam," I would whisper

sibilantly, "I've got them. Have you found your trainies?"

We always called those white cotton briefs "trainies." I guess this was an abbreviation of the term "training pants" but I didn't realize this at the time. I'd have scorned the phrase if I'd recognized its allusion to that period between babyhood and going to school, when wetting your pants was an accident still sometimes supervening in times of stress.

"I can't find them," he would whisper agonizedly.

"Forget about them. Come and put these on."

Once when it had taken us an unusually long time to locate his corduroy knickerbockers, just as I whispered the welcome news to him from a row of seats well over next a fire exit, a pair of young lovers not more than eighteen or nineteen suddenly seated themselves beside me and at once became locked—oblivious to the film—in an intimate embrace which, to say truth, rather shocked my nascent sexual feelings. They seemed so wholly preoccupied.

Scratchings from the floor. A ten-year-old arm appeared from under the seats in front of us, felt around in the darkness, then suddenly seized the shapely calf of the panting girl alongside me. She removed her mouth from her partner's just long enough to gasp, "Freddie, keep your hands to yourself." I gave a shout of laughter. The young couple straightened up and looked at me with suspicion, then with amazement as the semi-nude Sinclair rose up before them. He seized his clothing from me—we were all crowded together—and began to lift one leg at a time in a vain attempt to clothe himself. It was dark.

"The idea!" snorted the young woman, very offended.

"I'll call the manager," said her boy friend.

"We're just going," I said, making my voice as ingratiating as I could, "come on, Adam." I struggled past the little group, trying to restrain my giggles, not looking back.

"Oh why is everybody so awful to me?" I heard him wail. He got a sharp cuff on the side of the head from the young man, as he edged along the row. By then I was almost out of the building on my way to rejoin Amanda Louise and Monty, who had been loitering outside the theatre waiting for us. They could take Adam or leave him, and weren't eager to have him attach himself to us for the long walk home. Monty may well have suspected that the Sinclairs, the Cloughs, the Farquhars, looked down on him and his brother Mostyn, though how anybody could possibly feel superior to Mostyn, now fifteen and halfway through collegiate, escaped me totally, then and now. He had an enormous paper route which he delivered on an ancient CCM Cleveland that he'd acquired somewhere second-hand. One of the McNally boys would certainly rescue the family from poverty, when the general business slump had attenuated itself, by one means or another. The Sinclairs, on the other hand, seemed a family on a downward drift because of their inability to adjust to the Canadian social system.

Adam seemed then a prize example, somebody whose social role could only be that of ignominious scapegoat, born to be de-panted. I didn't fully understand how I felt about him. Whether I had grasped that our common element was purely and simply our humanness, our nature, I can't say. One judgment I was dead certain about, though, was that if there was torment or persecution going on in the neighbourhood it was infinitely preferable to be the tormentor, the persecutor, rather than the suffering victim, tormentee, persecutee. All my life, perhaps from as early on as those joyful afternoons in the Beverly, I have had a predilection for the winning side. I had not then heard the maxim, "If you don't want to be crucified, stay away from crosses." But I would have understood it, however obscurely, at once. I felt deeply moved by the axioms of the sports page. A good team makes its own breaks. Keep hustling. I knew that there was indeed such a thing as luck, good fortune, getting those big breaks, having chance on one's side. Adam Sinclair was my object lesson. And I knew that one could persuade luck to his side, make good fortune come when bidden. I was savagely superstitious, was and have remained an optimist.

I figured Adam could improve his lot, that he could

change the way things were going for him; on the long walks
home in the twilight on Saturday afternoons, I would urge
him to mend his ways and stop inviting disaster. "Asking for
it," was the phrase I used.

"It isn't that people don't like you, Adam," I would say,
feeling like biting my tongue because I knew quite well that
most people didn't like him, and it troubled me. "It isn't
that anybody wants to hurt you. It's just—oh I don't
know—it just seems like you were asking for it. You know?"

"No, I don't know. I don't want anybody to hurt me. I
only want to see the movies like the other kids. I want to be
left alone and have you for my friend, Matthew. Why can't
people let us alone?"

I felt somehow that this was quaky, boggy terrain, and
began to pick my way out of it. I was perplexed. I knew that
something about Adam's style of action begged for humiliation, and that he didn't intend to change. Yet he swore that
he wasn't "begging for it." This same terrible puzzle was
being woven and unravelled and woven again all over
Europe in those years, 1937, 1938, when a whole tragic people hated, feared, cursed and tried vainly to escape from the
dreadful criminal sacrifice being prepared, the holocaust in
which they figured as victim. No Jew wished this sacrificial
role for himself or his people. It is morally wrong to say,
"Well, why didn't they resist?" It is evil to make such a pro-
testation. They could not resist. Somehow it was not to be
found in history that they should resist. Why? I don't know
why. I don't know why. But I can tell you now that though I
felt sorry for Adam Sinclair, and though I was willing to be
his pal for short periods of time when nobody but my sister
and her trusted friend could see, I would not stand up for
Adam publicly. I would sooner persecute than be perse-
cuted; afterward I might gain in darkness the credit of helping him find his clothes.

We would walk along St. Clair Avenue toward Perpetual
Help in the end of the afternoon, hungry, with tired eyes,
feeling impatient at Amanda's expressed need to go into the
church to confession.

"Oh, come on, we'll be late for supper. Say you went, that's all. I mean, how can anybody find out? I mean, they won't phone up to ask Father Regan. Will they?"

"I feel like going. I want to go. I like going." This was something I didn't understand about Amanda Louise—this childlike need for attendance upon the penitential grace. I had not yet made my First Holy Communion, nor my first Confession, at that primaeval date. I would have maintained then, would now, that I knew nothing of sin. I was an ignorant young person. Where morals and conduct were concerned, my mind was shut. I knew about physical shape and form, whether this car was well-modelled where that one was ugly. I was beginning to have a sense of beauty in women and girls. Hair. I was beguiled by girls' hair, and knew which colours I preferred. Of the decencies and indecencies of action I knew nothing whatsoever, and I was not about to learn them from the Baltimore Catechism, that simple manual or guide to righteousness in universal use in the parish schools of the epoch.

"Who made the world?"

"God."

The opening words of the catechism. This referral to the beginning of things pleased me immensely when first I saw it. I saw that this book began in the right place. But I was always disappointed that that third line of the dialogue was not simply:

"Why?"

That question would have had to go unanswered, as I understand Christian doctrine, the inner movement of the Deity toward His Creation remaining a closed book to rational intelligence. Many years later I ran across the matter in a comic novel by a celebrated English satirist, which included in its cast of characters an Anglican clergyman who had been impelled to resign his vicariate precisely because he could not see why God had bothered to create. This poor man could understand the whole bag of tricks following upon the original act—Thirty-Nine Articles, advowson, presentation, the lot. He could not get over the first event in universal history. I'm glad now that I didn't get hooked on the question the first morning I picked up my Catechism to begin instruction prior to my first reception of the sacraments. I might never have gotten to Communion at all. Then this whole tale would have been greatly altered.

Adam and I would go on ahead, leaving Monty and Amanda to their penances, such that I would be home in time for supper, like a good boy, while my sister would be half an hour late and might even fall under some vague censure.

"Who brought you home?"

"I came with Adam."

"Adam Sinclair won't protect you from the pixies and the bogies and the other night creatures after it gets dark, and where's your sister?"

"She stayed for Confession. And there are no pixies and bogies."

"So you say. Well." My mother would purse her lips in serio-comic reflection. "Perhaps there aren't. But if there were, Adam would be small protection."

"Matt looks after Adam," said Tony precociously. He had grown tired of waiting for his dinner, as my father had. It was almost half past six when I got home, and Amanda missed supper altogether, a regular consequence of Saturday afternoon at the movies. We never really recovered, Amanda and I, and Monty, and even poor old Adam, from the idea that the movies were somehow our possession, our art, held by us determinedly against the encroachments of grown people; we were the first to take the movies seriously, so that when our parents complained aggrievedly that we came home too late for them to get their coats on and catch the evening show, we knew it didn't mean the same to them as it did to us. Parents needed *Photo Nite* or *Bank Nite* or gifts of *Dinnerware* to get them to go to the movies. All it took to induce us to go, the kids from OLPH, was the gift of a penny blotter, a chunk of unmeltable candy, pencil box, splayed pen-nib. Truth is, we went without being given any gift at all. The movies were all ours.

If the film and broadcast media are to be distributed among the generations in this century, radio must be allowed to our parents; they felt an allegiance to Amos and Andy, Lanny Ross, Kate Smith, Russ Colombo, Bing Crosby, Fred Allen, Jack Benny, the Yacht Club Boys, Donald Novis, Joe Penner, all those *Big Broadcast* movies, the Red Network, the Blue Network, the Mutual Network, the entire iconography of radio as mass communication, that we didn't share. What we had was dime admissions to triple bills and cartoons, and free blotters. At the movies.

Our children must be granted the delights of television. The generation born after 1950 never knew about radio the way my father did, never went to the movies the way I did. What the swinging children of the fifties got was Hanna-Barbera, Romper Room and Captain Kangaroo, and the Friendly Giant.

Reflections on the meaning of our age, this century *pas comme les autres*, lead us to judge it on the grounds of its enjoyment of, its special possession of these forms of communion, these new ecclesiologies. Old churches adapt or perish: there are first of all radio priests like Father Coughlin and Monsignor Fulton Sheen. There are movies full of priests like Bing Crosby in *Going My Way*. A cute priest. Bland. Unacquainted with evil worse than venial sexual transgression. In the late fifties, priests change their clothes and allow their hair to grow, emerging at the dawn of the sixties as the cult-leaders of the TV generation. Mick Jagger is born from the side of John Lennon. Timothy Leary preaches the Gospel and Jesus Christ makes it among the media as a superstar. In three generations, radio, movies, TV, my name ceases to mean what it used to mean. Matthew.

The nuns at OLPH were wise according to their generation to refuse access to their land to the men from the Beverly. On that Holy Thursday, wasting my lunch hour, going without food, I hung around their card table and collected whatever was going, fistfuls of free junk which I stuck in my schoolbag and hauled home with smarting hands at 3:15. I was soundly strapped that afternoon by high-tempered Miss McHale, who had managed to deduce my part in the staining of Alanna Begin's dress.

"Miss Conroy told me at lunch time, while you were wasting your time hanging around those nasty men. She saw you sitting behind Alanna. I've already had a telephone call from Mrs. Begin about that ink. The dress is ruined. What have you to say for yourself?"

A perverse imp put words in my mouth. "Could she dye the whole thing purple?"

It was for this smart remark that I got "the slugs." That's what we called the strap. I got six on each hand and the blows stung all right, but not unto death. I ought not to have been strapped by Miss McHale at all, according to strict rule, because she wasn't my teacher. Frail, dignified, Miss Conroy, already white-haired at 30 so that she seemed immensely old to us, should have administered my chastisement, but she was just not strong enough. She never got to give anybody the slugs; the culprit was sent along to the cloakroom of Senior Third, where the youthful and vigorous Miss McHale would appear, to a chorus of half-suppressed snickers from her students, very grown-up those Senior Third kids seemed, irritatingly smug as they whispered, "It's little Goderich this time."

Six on each palm made me a bit of a hero to the kids in Senior First, placated Alanna Begin's mother, made Jakie Forbes jealous and much amused my parents, who at no time made physical gestures toward their children that were not kisses and caresses, and later handshakes.

"Got the strap, eh?"

"Ya, ya, ya, ya, Matt's got sore paws." This was from Big T.

"Shut up, Tony."

"I wish you would not say 'shut up.' It betrays impoverishment of mind."

"Oh dad! What else should I say?"

"Nothing. Turn the other cheek. Pretend a mildness that you may not feel. Remind Tony about the phone books. In short, heap coals of fire on his head."

"Andrew, you shouldn't teach them such tactics."

"Maybe you're right."

"There, Tony, see? I helped you with the phone books and now you tease me, is that right?"

A bulbous tear appeared at the corner of my brother's left eye. He ground his teeth at me and my father and left the supper table in discomfiture. I had done him a real favour over those phone books, and his character was developing the defensive, protective carapace often characteristic of third children who are also younger brothers. Big T has never been in the least a competitive or malicious person; it might be contended that his genuine mildness has sometimes retarded the progress of an almost uniformly triumphant career. At the age of four, faced with my father's roundabout means of expression and my blithe glibness, he must often have found his vocabulary inadequate to his feelings. He had not said much at the conclusion of the phone-book episode, which had taken place the previous autumn, when he was three and a bit.

A new drugstore had materialized four doors up the street. To every neighbourhood home the proprietor despatched an advertising circular and an envelope containing some blue stickers bearing the name Merrill's Drugs and the phone numbers of the prescription department and the order department for toiletries, magazines and the general run of drugstore wares. There was also an announcement that any person bringing a telephone book to the drugstore on the grand opening day with one of these blue stickers attached to it would receive ABSOLUTELY FREE his choice of any five-cent candy bar in stock. Cunning promotion!

It was the phrase ABSOLUTELY FREE, Tony confessed later, that began as time went on to obsess him, the first time in his life that this unsupportable assertion of a state of affairs that exists nowhere in the physical world caused him to come to great grief. He knew that we had two phone books because we had two phones, a small handset which stood on a walnut bedside table in my parent's bedroom—the first of the "cradle" phones—and a clumsy wall set downstairs in the hall—the phones of the period. If he could get his hands on those phone books and lug them around to the drugstore he could get two free chocolate bars. He knew that Amanda Louise and Matt were off at school; he didn't know what that meant, exactly, or what we did there, but he was aware that we were gone for the day. On the morning of the grand opening he asserted a claim to the use of the phone books and to possession of the blue qualifying stickers, to which my mother gave an absent assent. She was going downtown to shop, and paid scant attention to what he was going on about.

Well and good. Noon came and went and my mother climbed aboard Mr. Busdriver Smith's red-and-yellow Twin Coach and disappeared downtown. The first thing Mme. Archambault did was to dismiss Tony from the house for the balance of the afternoon; she did not want, she said, to see him again till four o'clock. She pushed him onto the verandah and locked the front door. It is not known how she passed the afternoon.

Tony trotted up the street to Merrill's Drugs as fast as his short legs would carry him. Yes. They were open. All the lights in the windows and the showcases were full on. The windows had had their coating of Bon Ami rubbed off and the window displays, of Thermogene and Campana's Italian Balm, were stacked and pyramided in beguiling geometrical alignment.

He galloped home and pounded on the door. He called up to the second-floor windows, begging for the phone books. He went around to the back, whence his outcries might the more readily ascend. Nothing availed him. My father used to say that when Mme. Archambault had closed her mind to entreaty or complaint—those were precisely his words—the very powers of hell would not prevail against her. For she heard nothing, neither did she see. It was her ability to beat him pretty consistently in card games that incited this observation. Dad played auction, and later contract bridge with some skill, but according to Hoyle, as they say. Mme.

Archambault played a game all her own, either losing at every point or carrying all before her. She did not play "positional" bridge. In much the same way, when she played euchre or poker there was no way of guessing what was passing through her mind. Her poker was less uneven than her bridge, because of the difference in the nature of the games, I conjecture. She won consistently at poker.

I can hear my father say, "You should never have been in that contract, my dear Jeanne. Don't you ever allow for the distribution? Normally there will be three low hearts in east's hand."

"But there were none this time."

"Evidently not, but I'm speaking of the regular fall of the cards."

"I could feel they weren't there."

"No you couldn't. You could not! How could you?" My father resisted vigorously, in his professional capacity as a philosopher, and in his purely private life, any appeal to special intuition of a personal kind, inaccessible to rational canvass.

"I guessed . . . ," my grandmother would say, staring at my father without submission; she was a valiant woman. Most people refused to argue with my father because of his dialectic nimbleness, and in fact Mme. Archambault never argued with him—and he saw this—she simply outfaced him. His final recourse was invariably a mollified mirth; there was nothing to be gained by debate with Jeanne Archambault.

This capacity to march up to a position, envelop it, adopt it and refuse to budge from it, the salient modality of Mme. Archambault's character, transformed itself utterly in my mother into a willingness, more accurately a profound and desperate need, to approach any fixed stance in the most elastic way. I have known no woman more reasonable and less dogmatic than my mother. If it is possible to make a dogma of the open mind—ridiculous and finally vicious paradox—my mother has done just that. But there is no such thing as an insane sanity. You are sane or you aren't. My mother is the most sweetly reasonable person I have known, certainly among women, with a half-dozen close competitors to all of whom I have been devoted during my adult life. If there is a quality I admire unreservedly in women—in men too—it is open-minded fairness. Justice. Where can she have come at this mode of apperception? I suppose from the example of her parents. I sometimes feel the urge to dogmatize, to follow private witness, moving in myself like cancer, like an evil temptation, and then I think of Jeanne Archambault's bridge game.

Tony couldn't draw her attention, ranging madly round from backyard to verandah, by 2:30 blubbering, then crying outright with vile frustration. Always eager for the quick solution, Tony was, always hovering around trying to bring off a new resolution of the given situation. He couldn't bear to see action deferred. Men and women passing along the street tried to give comfort and succour. "What's wrong, little boy? Are you sick? Does it hurt somewhere?"

What was hurting Tony was a metaphysical wrinkle in being, which he now claims to have understood at the time. Social conditions, he saw with dreadful clarity, will not be modified by intense feeling. No matter how much he wanted his free candy bars, the oceanic pulsing desire, so real to him, altered in no way whatsoever the hard reality of his circumstances. It was not, he knew, the non-possession of chocolate that bothered him so badly. It was mainly that his wanting it so much made no difference to the world. This is a harsh lesson, one that it is well to get by heart at the age of three and a half. I sometimes tell Tony that he's a better man for having undergone this experience; he concurs.

I came home from school around 3:15 and found him sitting on the front steps weeping bitterly, his face streaked and his pants undeniably wet.

"Won't she let you in?"

"Mamma has gone to Eaton's."

"When's she coming home?"

"I don't know. I want the phone books, Matt."

I knew at once what he was talking about. "I can get in the cellar window, I know how," I said, and it is still one of my most pleasing memories, the image of my brother's face lighting up, as if the sun had appeared from long eclipse. I got into the house very easily through a window under the verandah. Tony couldn't have done it without falling—his legs weren't long enough, and anyway he didn't know the window could be waggled open. I went upstairs on tiptoe. I did not want to wake my grandmother if she were asleep, but I wanted that upstairs directory, so I risked it. She was asleep on her big double bed, door to her room wide open, the place she had shared for so long with Papa Archambault, her deep iron-grey hair straggling abundantly across the pillow. I paused by the doorway, looking at her. She seemed much smaller than when awake; perhaps I was growing a bit myself. I could hear a wheeze in her breathing. It struck me as I stood there that she was old enough to die. Her husband had died, I remembered, and they must have been almost the same age. Perhaps she would die; that would make three in the family, three grandparents out of four. Then there was Mr. Buttermere next door who had died two years ago. Dying seemed to be all around. I shrugged and went into my parents' bedroom, found the directory, then went downstairs and opened the front door for Tony, now almost out of his skin with impatience.

"Be quiet, don't wake her," I muttered, surprised that he understood me immediately. Need does strange things to one's character. He went into the kitchen and got the other book, and the envelope from Merrill's Drugs with the blue stickers. These he proceeded to affix in the designated places on the phone books, extremely neatly. I had never seen my little brother act to such purpose before; he had always been a ruminative little cuss, or so I'd thought. Now he was unswervingly direct. He hoisted his burden in his arms and left the house at a semi-canter, an interesting lurching gait, down the verandah steps, brisk turn to the right and out of sight. I began to laugh. I understood so well what was moving him. I heard my grandmother stirring upstairs, and I tip-

98

toed out the front door, genuinely unwilling to disturb her, from various motives.

It was now mid-to-late afternoon. My mother had just alighted from the bus at the corner of MacLennan, then strolled back along the street to the drugstore, where she decided to drop in and have a look around, make a small purchase or two and get acquainted with the layout of the store and the looks of the staff; she always liked to know something about the people she dealt with. She knew volumes about our breadman, Alfie Strutt, quite a lot about the Hollingshead family who ran the grocery store, and enough about the milkman to lay a charge. She never made any use of information collected in these researches. That day she introduced herself to Miss Clarkson, who was to work in that drugstore for 35 years, and to bland, balding, pleasant Mr. Halifax, the junior pharmacist, and naturally to Mr. Merrill, still a practising pharmacist with three stores in operation in widely separated parts of the city, a very sound businessman.

This little group, together with three or four neighbourhood ladies, were beginning to exchange information on really confidential matters—the credit status of certain out-of-work persons in the disrict, the efficacy of Castoria, affairs of that stripe. All at once the heavy plate-glass door was laboriously pushed open and Tony struggled in, his face flushed with emotion and exertion, cheeks distended as if stuffed with tennis balls, arms locked around the two large volumes which were showing a tendency to droop and lose their pages. He had his mouth clamped shut, for some reason, and was breathing heavily through the nostrils. My mother stared at him in surprised amusement, while a chorus of ladies fluttered in the background. "Isn't that too cunning?" "The cute little thing." "He can just barely manage."

Tony now advanced into a wide space between showcases in the middle of the store, then seeing that the floor was clear and feeling his powers attenuated, he suddenly let his distended cheeks collapse, blowing out a great noise between compressed lips.

"Ppppooooooooooooffffffffffff!" Feminine giggles.

"I've brought them," he said, letting the books fall from suddenly nerveless arms. Flop, they fell on the floor, and little Miss Clarkson rushed forward like somebody with a small part in a play, to pick them up. "They've got the blue sticker," she cried out, like a carnival pitchman announcing a lucky winner. And at the back of the store, Mr. Halifax and Mr. Merrill nodded at each other like clockwork toys, repeating, "the blue sticker."

Mr. Merrill, not displeased by this occurrence, said, "Give that lucky little guy his choice of any two five-cent candy bars. Hold him up, Ruthie, if you have to."

"I want a Sweet Marie and a Wildfire." Tony always liked bars with nuts in them, something I couldn't abide. I think he thought he was getting fuller value for his phone books, when the bars were mixed in texture. Miss Clarkson handed him the candy.

"Whose little boy is this?" somebody demanded; everyone was behaving, as my mother observed later, like the cast of an optimistic Hollywood movie of the period. Lewis Stone or Jed Prouty, possibly Spring Byington or Fay Bainter, might make an entrance from moment to moment. One does still, I suppose, strike those moments of feeling that everything is all right with society, that the sinless facade of middle-class life only conceals depths of the same innocence. These folk in the drugstore were cooing at a cute kid, when I came in.

I said sourly, "That's my kid brother, and, oh, hi Mom."

"Hello, Matt," she said, a little negligently I thought.

"Such a brave little boy to carry them all that way," said a lady.

Jeeze, I thought, he only lugged them from the house. I could tell my mother was thinking the same thing because her eyelids flickered in a certain way they had, when she was secretly amused. It's possible I was her favourite. I know I noticed that facial characteristic long before Tony did, and I had to point it out to Amanda Louise years afterward, and even at that she had trouble remembering.

"What are you talking about? I don't remember that."

"You don't? I could always tell when she was killing herself laughing inside."

"Oh, foo. Foo!"

"Foo to you, hep cat."

We left the store, vows of future association rebounding from side to side. These promises were kept. The drugstore flourished through four decades and is still functioning under new management, only the second owners in its history, who took it over at the tail end of the nineteen-sixties. Miss Clarkson then terminated her 35 years of service, having remained in the store through the principal events of recent history: the great economic slump, the onset of world war, the decade of the cold war, the enormous cultural transformation of the nineteen-sixties all over the world.

During successive ages of unrest, conflict, near apocalypse, final rapprochement, there stood Miss Ruth Clarkson, behind the counter in Merrill's Drugs, Summerhill Avenue, aging imperceptibly, such that her lovely hair, a reddish blonde at the inception of her tenure, which impressed all the men and some of the boys on Summerhill in the thirties, turned without anybody's noticing it to shining silver, glorious testimony to the virtues of the shampoos and sprays in which she dealt so liberally. When she retired, she was old, but nobody noticed it. She saw the same clientele day in, day out, for three and a half decades. An immensely able woman, she did the inventory, the ordering, reviewed the books, was in effect the store manager, except for the prescription department. Such a life may do more to ensure permanence and continuity in the experience of, say, 500 or 600 regular customers, than almost anything else that impinges on them.

The directly experienced structure of an individually lived life depends enormously upon repetition of encounter, not simply with physical objects, but especially with other persons—persons to whom we may be emotionally indifferent, but who function nevertheless as the psychological surroundings in which we make our choices. Our moral landscape. When we see Ruth Clarkson from one day to the next over three years, then over seventeen, we come to imagine that she is necessarily in the drugstore, smiling and alert, perfumed, when we are not there ourselves. We expect to see her as we push open the door, and ask if she's on vacation when she isn't visible. And we're relieved when she pops up from downstairs where she has been storing newly received stock. The fatal onset of change has been deferred by this belated appearance. We say, ''She was a fixture in the neighbourhood.'' Our lives cluster around her and those other few who are the key points on the grid of social relations that we know.

Perhaps this is simply to say that we all try to impose permanence on change; perhaps not all of us do. Perhaps I am running a wash of illusory duration over a flux that cannot be contained; but my intelligence, what I have learned and what it is possible for me to think and feel and imagine (and intuit) won't allow me to function on any other premises. When I move into a neighbourhood, whether by being born into it, or coming there on wheels in maturity, I begin at once to familiarize myself with it, as we say. And the idea of the family is locked inescapably into the idea of the familiar; one notion requires the other. Attack the family and you attack the familiar, the expected, the sure; in the end you do yourself fatal harm.

I wish I could rid myself of those four or five bloody paired sets of metaphysical states or forms with which my father saddled my thinking. Permanence and change; sameness and difference; being and becoming; form and matter. Aha, you say, he was an Aristotelian, your dad. Well, he was and he wasn't. Technically he was an existentialist axiologist, whose thought derived from the idealistic-experimental psychology of the twenty years prior to the Great War, the years of Brentano, Scheler, Meinong, Weber, Hüsserl and in North America of W.M. Urban, almost the only philosopher born on this continent whom my father spoke of with invariable respect.

"Powerful mind, Urban. *Vox Clamantis*," he would mumble, as if to himself, *"vox clamantis."*

Still, phenomenology or no phenomenology, Andrew Goderich *was* in some sort an ontologist in the line of descent from Aristotle, and he endowed me with a habit of mind I've never been able to modify, the wish to see conflict between dialectic poles resolved. I like to see permanence coexist with change, one moving in the other. I think that that is how being is. And there is some sense in which a thing never ceases to exist, when once it has begun to exist, a law of the conservation of existence. Ruth Clarkson is still behind the counter in Merrill's Drugs, and that is the significance of history, the conservation, better the preservation, of existence.

Farther up the street toward the level crossing was Hollingshead's Grocery Store. The storefront is still there, and as I look at it I behold George Hollingshead, his stained apron stretched tight across his ample middle, tied behind with long cloth tapes, like the ties on a priest's amice. He carries a book or pad of grocery order blanks, with red numbers on successive blanks and sheets of carbon paper between each set of blanks. He has a large block of accounts receivable. Nobody pays cash for a week's groceries; it is the nineteen-thirties and Mr. Hollingshead remits to the wholesalers on a 90-day basis, and sometimes over a longer term. Payments trickle in. He can just stay in business, and his white moustache luxuriates. He will sometimes sell us six one-cent items for 5¢, if we buy what we call a bag of candy.

"Can I have a nickel for a bag of candy?" We hand him the nickel; he nods cheerfully and we understand that we can pick six items from this extensive prairie of possibility:

Licorice whips, red, black. Licorice plugs, with Indian Head in red or white or blue or gold, affixed to each plug. Licorice pipes with tiny red candy balls clustered on top of the bowl to simulate flame. Licorice cigars. When fresh, the licorice is strongly laxative, black on the outside, faintly oily, and a memorable brownish-green when bitten into, a colour unique to itself.

Butterbars. Strips of caramel taffy about the size of a small wooden ruler, dusted with faint traces of flour, doubtless to obviate stickiness. Wrapped in oily yellow wax paper with the name lettered in pleasing light red.

Milkmallows, the product of Paterson Limited. Little rolls of caramel with firm white nougat inside, wrapped in bluish-white wax paper. My favourites. Hard on the fillings in people's baby teeth.

Blackballs, three for a cent. Suck them further and further down and they keep changing colour from their original deep black to an ultimate hard little speckled nubbin of white: allegories of sin and redemption, they seemed to me; they were black enough, to start.

Hard hats. Two for a cent. Shaped like brimless derbies. Hard taffy that requires plenty of sucking. Cocoanut embedded in the taffy and a good thick chocolate coating overall.

BB Bats. Suckers on sticks, made from chewy taffy of a rich mocha tone. Oil paper wrapping with a highly coloured illustration of a ball game in some never-never land of weirdly Japanese baseball.

Sherbets. Not frozen sherbet like ice-cream, but small triangular coloured bags filled with a mass of tartly sweet whiteish powder meant to be sucked from the paper bag with a straw made of hard licorice. Fruity flavour. Eat the licorice straw when finished.

Gumballs. Bubble-gum. And marvellous flat rectangles of gum in a faint light dusty coat of that recurring sweet flour, backed by cardboard pictures—the celebrated "gum cards" of that era—tightly and neatly machine-wrapped in coloured wax paper. Thinking of those series of cards, baseball players, hockey players, kings and queens of England, causes combers, breakers, of recreated feelings to roll over one in vertiginous waves. There was one series of hockey cards in particular that made every boy along the street dizzy with the desire to possess a complete set. The designer had managed to fit the photograph of the athlete into the middle of the card, so that his silhouette could be half punched-out, making a partly detached figure of the upper torso, arms and shoulders. You punched this part of the picture loose from the bottom half of the card and folded the top part backward to make a little stand; what you had was an erect head and shoulders and torso supported by the back and the bottom of the card, which showed the legs and skates. Paul Runge. Joffre Desilets.

Joffre Desilets. Jesus! I'm calling to all of you out there, members of a putative Joffre Desilets fan club. Can you hear me? Were you, like me, a child of the starveling thirties? Are you perhaps a wholly francophone son of St.-Pachôme des rochers, or St.-Joachim du bord de fleuve?

Who pines for Jimmy Ward of the Maroons, for Elwyn "Doc" Romnes, for "Buzz" Boll? Where is "Buzz" Boll? Where are the star-bespangled New York Americans who had the most beautiful hockey sweaters ever conceived? I ached with longing all my childhood for an Americans' sweater and all I ever got was a Leafs'. And with a turtleneck at that. The first NHL hockey game I ever attended was at Maple Leaf Gardens one curious Saturday evening in the late thirties, when the Chicago Black Hawks decided (from nationalistic political motives) to ice a team composed entirely of US-born players, an experiment never since duplicated. I couldn't tell you the names of any of the Chicago players except the netminder, Mike Karakas, if memory serves. But I can state with unmediated satisfaction that Frank "Buzz" Boll was one of the Leafs' forwards, a winger, not a great scorer; he was later traded to the Bruins, where he enjoyed some success around the nets as a wartime player.

Gum cards. There was hockey, to be sure, but there was also, maybe more important even, baseball, a major sport in our eyes, even *the* major sport for gumcard collectors. The major leagues were composed of two sets of eight teams, all in large American cities of the northeast, none very far from Toronto. For some profound reason we all considered baseball a native game; maybe we thought of ourselves, and baseball, as part of a continental system. Something serious is mixed into this question, and it will take plenty of working out. Mike Pearson played baseball both before and after his time at Oxford, and his brother Vaughan might, in the late Prime Minister's opinion, have made it to the majors. There have always been excellent Canadian ballplayers, though not in extremely large numbers; there have always been Canadian cities in professional leagues: Québec, Trois Rivières, Montréal, Toronto, Ottawa, Hamilton, Winnipeg, Vancouver and some other cities have enjoyed franchised representation in leagues most of whose other members were located in the States. Even this was not invariable. Havana was represented in the International League (interesting name) when Toronto still had a franchise, so league ball was genuinely international.

There were the great Canadian players, whose careers encouraged us, from the eighteen-seventies onward: Napoléon Lajoie and Phil Marchildon, to name two athletes of francophone background. There were many others like Jean-Pierre Roy, Stan Bréard, Ron Piché and Denis McSween. Goodwin "Goody" Rosen came off Spadina Avenue, Toronto, to play for the Dodgers. Oscar "Lefty" Judd came out of Ingersoll to make it in the majors with Cleveland. It seems that the mythology of baseball is truly international, a circumstance that has sometimes puzzled Québecois writers who enjoy the game as folk ritual ("the management will not be held responsible for batted balls projected into the stands") and wonder about its relations to their conscience and their politics.

It was the framing *distantiation* achieved by the gum cards, their status as pieces of art, that hooked me. I was never all that much interested in the endowments or achievements of the players, as players. What I cared for was their magical names: Goose Goslin, Kiki Cuyler, Zeke Bonura, Luke Ap-

pling, Harry "the Horse" Danning, Spurgeon "Spud"
Chandler, Marius Russo, Ossie Bluege, "Arky" Vaughan,
"Pie" Traynor, Billy Jurges, Tex Carleton, Lon Warneke,
Paul Derringer (usually known as Oom Paul). It was Paul
Derringer who, upon entering the clubhouse after his
twenty-first consecutive defeat, said, "You can't win 'em
all."

Hank Borowy. Bobo Newsome. Eldon Auker. Bucky
Walters. Babe Herman. Johnny Rizzo. Gabby Hartnett.
Catalogue of the ships and heroes. The Boston Bees!

"Sibby Sisti guards Hive hot corner."

The Hive, naturally, were the Boston Bees, who bore that
nickname through three or four seasons in an attempt to
evolve an attractive box-office image. Later on they reverted
to being the Boston Braves, and later still the Milwaukee
Braves, the name conjuring up a surreal phantasy of some
beer-swilling German American Iroquois or Narragansett.

"Denny Galehouse, acquired from Bosox, has been no
ball of fire in St. Lou."

Complaint of a sportswriter condemned to follow the St.
Louis Browns from city to city in the infernal midsummer of
an American League pennant chase, when his club was
powerless to intervene in the race except to get beaten with
dismal regularity by powerful contenders, the Yanks,
Tigers, Red Sox. Never mind, the Browns, like those other
chronic losers, the New York Americans, had really terrific
uniforms, with the most interesting baseball caps prior to
those of the Montréal Expos, caps less affected than the
Montréal team's by modish views of good design, more
authentic caps perhaps. I wish I had one.

For a decade after their ultimate transmogrification into
the Baltimore Orioles, the old St. Louis Browns were the objects of a devoted cult whose acolytes were the members of
the Browns Fan Club. This organization devoted itself to recording the feats of former Brownies now with other major-
league clubs, and to preserving the records of the St. Louis
American League Baseball Team, Inc., from the eighteen-

eighties forward. A useless enterprise, serving no discernible social end, unacceptable in a Socialist community, trivial bourgeois tomfoolery? Perhaps, but how intensely human. My dad took a lenient view of the impulse, on the whole. He riffled through a few packs of gum cards, stood looking out the window at the pedestrians on Summerhill, came to a decision. "It's an impulse like that of an antiquarian or an archivist, a fundamentally preserving act. Do you notice how all those cards are concerned with scoring records and batting averages and dates? There's more to it than appears on the surface."

He mused in silence for perhaps half a minute.

"It's like an epic," he said. That's where I got the idea originally, from my father. "An epic doesn't have a tragic action; certainly the epic of baseball is beyond the dramatic categories of tragedy and comedy. If it were either, it would be comic. But the epos of baseball has no end; it renews itself continually. I'll have to think about it. Anyway, Matt, no activity carried on by very large numbers of people can be inhumane tomfoolery. Only foolish people fly in the face of widely observable human longings, or what moralists call 'general consent.'"

He added comments and notes on the matter over the following two decades; it was one of the problems of intellectual history we discussed most often—the collecting and recording impulse, so intimately tied to calendars, the methods of historical chronology and the impulse to articulate a connected account of the past. My father was not at bottom an historian like me; he was really a critic of moral style. When he spoke of Adam Sinclair as "yon wee Scotch farrrrtttt," he wasn't labelling Adam, he was framing a sentence, making the kind of existential *epoché* or "putting in brackets" recommended by his intellectual masters for extracting a portion of living being from its phenomenal context, so as to be able to observe it supra-phenomenally, phenomenonologically, or, to drop out a syllable and speak technically, phenomenologically—that was the name of his philosophical school.

If there had ever been a scientific ethics of gum-card collecting, my father would have been the first to extricate or
isolate it. His phrase for Adam Sinclair put in brackets the
kind of people who use such phrases. This was plain to some;
we have to except persons impervious to the analysis and
criticism of style, like Mme. Archambault. On the whole my
father's humour made its point fairly regularly, without
causing distress or giving offence.

We had in common our fascination with the forms of
behaviour, and with the physical forms of things. When Dad
found out—when I was still not quite an adult—how totally
questions of style had come to absorb me, it was suddenly as
if a whole new ground for communion had established itself
beneath us as support. As a child, all I could really take in
about him was that we had common interests approached
from different avenues of investigation.

It may be that to propose a scientific ethics and rational
models for conduct, as he did consistently, especially in *The
Place of Conceptual Thought in Ethical Judgments*, is to attempt
the impossible task of throwing the net of logic over feeling
and instinct. I know that this is an ancient crux. I know that
my father was foolish to write such a book, in the sense that
any attempt at a solution of a primary philosophical problem
is foredoomed to failure (at least the testimony of many generations suggests it), but he felt, and I feel, that it is better to
be a fool after hard thought than wise before it.

Tony felt the same way, as he has shown clearly in his later
adventures; perhaps of the three of us Tony has come nearest
to an achieved philosophic folly. That may seem a slur on my
brother, but of course I don't intend a slur. Anyway you
can't cast a slur on Tony. The world recognizes him as far
too agreeable, far too richly endowed by fortune and self-
discipline, for any such wounding glance to have effect. Old
Big T.

He and I would swap gum cards cheerfully, as soon as he
was able to read, maybe around 1938. We had visited Hollingshead's to buy gum, then sat outside the store beside an
oblong tin sign with feet, which praised Acme Farmer's

Dairy Ice Cream, comparing the cards that came in our gum. Before Tony could read well, he could compare the pictures of ballplayers; he knew when he had two Joe Vosmiks and how much a Vosmik "trader" would fetch on the card market. Joe Vosmik cards were extremely rare one whole summer, and a thriving market in traders could have been worked up, if a way to counterfeit images of the popular outfielder could have been found.

We were going to Hollingshead's together well before Big T went to school. I'm not sure whether we patronized the place before he could read—that would have been the year before he went to school. I do know that we moved away from Summerhill toward the end of 1938, which gives me a fix on it. Tony went to school for the first time in my company in the fall of 1938. He was five and a half. My father had decided to let him go a year early, rather than a year late as in my case. Did he and my mother consider Tony more stable, or simply more advanced physically? I think—I hope—it was simply the latter, for goodness knows I was a balanced and controlled little boy, probably too stable. Anyway, our parents had abundant reasons, more and more serious reasons, for wanting to have their youngest child safely in school through that autumn. It guaranteed our absence from the house all day, at a time when their lengthening debates over potential avenues of conduct were elaborating themselves into a labyrinth of perplexity. Debates, debates, never conflict, never at any time argument; they were a most precious pair.

"Look at everything as it comes along; first it was in Spain. Oh, wrong, why do I say that? First it was in Munich about 1922, when this vicious man began his talk. Perhaps even earlier. What was he doing from 1918 to 1922. And when did the Italians move to the right? 1919? I suppose it was 1919."

"Andrew, do the Italians matter?"

"In modern history, the Italians always matter. In literature, in music, in art and architecture."

"In politics?"

"My darling girl, have you never read the *Commedia*?"

Of course she had; that was a conversation I overheard one Saturday afternoon, on my way out of the house with Tony to play baseball at Rosedale Lacrosse Grounds, which we rarely called by its proper name. We called it the park, just as when the time came we never referred to Moorevale Park by its correct name, though we might play there on Saturday from early morning to dusk. Leaving the house that Saturday, I heard my father say dolefully, "It's called creeping fascism," and I hadn't the faintest notion what he was talking about. Directly after he said that, I heard my mother begin to chuckle in a peculiar and distinct way, and I knew that they were embracing one another.

They would not let politics interfere with lovemaking, but they kept politics high up, maybe in third place, behind the loving caress and hard thought. In 1937 the Moscow purge trials were terrifying people like my father, who had hoped to see the socialist experiment in the USSR issue in a triumphant illustration of the workers' communal state, whose sway might extend itself peacefully throughout Europe via the Communist International. "The peaceful evolution of socialism." We used to laugh about it around the supper table, we children, having no notion that the ideal of a peaceful and loving reconciliation of Marxian and other socialisms in an international community was a cherished dream to people like Keir Hardie and J.S. Woodsworth. Where do they come from, these men, how do they evolve so peacefully themselves, these saintly socialists? I remember pictures of young Tommy Douglas and the only slightly older Major Coldwell sitting on either side of Mr. Woodsworth in somebody's kitchen in Regina. I have myself been in the kitchen of a Regina household not two blocks from there, on Connaught Crescent, where often and often Mr. Coldwell would sit for hours discussing spending for social services, or campaign methods for the party in Saskatchewan.

They laboured in the wilderness, and they were so *nice*.

They weren't Trotskyites. They weren't Stalinists nor were they at that date Maoists, though Mao was known to them by reputation from his struggle and his agony in China in the mid-to-late twenties, and was at that very time labouring in his own wilderness. They weren't Fabian Shavian socialists nor Marxian revisionists like Laski, not Ernie Bevinites with both feet planted squarely on the backs of the trades unions and their membership. Oh, I know they were genteel. I know that they emerged from the small professional class, as my father did, the son of a village lawyer who became a professor for a while and finally felt himself to be driven out of the professorate. Think of them then, in the mid-thirties in remote Canada, far from Catalonia and the glamour of the much-publicized Orwellian struggle over the POUM and all that, far from the death struggles of the absurd Carlism portrayed as late as 1932 by Graham Greene in his novel *Rumour at Nightfall*, later suppressed by its author for its excessively Conradian flavour. Few now living have read this book; after Greene published it he decided that it stank of Conrad's mannerisms and had to be put down, and from that day it has never been reprinted. The book shows Spain as an evil, swimming, political dream—the same romantic flow of dreamed edgeless imagery, all running and coloured, like the split yokes of fried eggs in a tilted pan, as gave Green the impulse for *The Confidential Agent*, a book in which the feel of political dreaming is so explicit that the writer gives his main personage an initial only, on the model of Joseph K.

Graham Greene's Mr. D, the confidential agent and much-fooled, much-perplexed amateur of politics, is a cousin of Andrew Goderich, fooled and puzzled in Toronto and Regina in 1935, 1936, 1937, 1937, 1937, terrible year, by the purge trials, by broken strikes in Oshawa, by the consistent vicious reactionary behaviour of the RCMP, in face of social unrest in the West, by the political character of Ontario puppets like Mitchell Hepburn, nominally a Liberal, far far to the right of any sane liberalism, and George Drew, nominally a Conservative, far far to the right of that classical political attitude. George Drew repudiated trades unionism as radical. In this century. In 1940. Can you tie that? My father couldn't. He began to realize that the universities were the captives of the provincial governments, and would become more and more so.

He couldn't quite foresee the situation of the following generation in which the universities in the Canadian provinces became, not the captives of governments, but wholly-assimilated limbs of the provincial civil services, where the professorate, so long ago abandoned by him, became a legion of middle-grade government hirelings, something like the officer corps of the armed services, a shade higher in the freedom-of-utterance scale than clergymen in the English Church. The scholar, the professor and defender of a learned discipline, was a creation of the European Renaissance and had no place in this former colony. The professor in Canada had much the character of the high-school teacher, except that his salary was perhaps lower. In the end, the universities became institutes for the forwarding of research programs of use to governments, with the elegancies of liberal education each year more attenuated.

In 1937 my father had not witnessed these things in lived history; he guessed at them. And he could certainly see that the provincial government of Ontario was not so much hand-in-glove with reactionary finance as owned by it outright. The government of the province under Drew, Frost, Robarts, Davis, has been an administration without personal character or enterprise, dictated to by investors. The government owns and engrosses the universities here as everywhere, and allows the free intelligence to reside there as long as boundaries are not transgressed.

In 1937 my father decided not to wait for the definition of these boundaries. Their slow manifestation from the indeterminate haze of Ontario society was going to be too long drawn-out. Creeping fascism was all around, in Ontario in 1937 and 1938, but nobody called it that; nobody took politics seriously except those ideological cenacles of a few here and there whose names are so easy to remember, though almost none has ever held power. Safe seats for socialists—no, there were none. It didn't worry me. I was left with a mental image of funny little bugs walking on many legs in corners of unclean houses, places like the McNallys' house. Creeping fascists would be green, the size of silverfish or cockroaches, slow moving, no threat. I went with Tony to the Lacrosse Grounds, when he was five and I was eight, without a care in the world. That spring the Coronation took place, and in honour of the royal occasion the Ontario Government had decreed that the licence plates for the year should be coloured an unusual combination of powder-blue and orange-pink, a boon to drivers of getaway cars. Never mind that the pink sank into the blue at any distance over ten feet so that the numbers were unreadable; certain loyalties must be perpetuated. At the park that Saturday afternoon a cricket game was in progress.

That sounds as if I'd invented it to reinforce my declarations about the colonial mentality. No so. The cricket pitch deployed below and before the clubhouse wasn't my invention, nor was the giant roller that stood nearby, nor the Toronto Cricket Club, whose home grounds these were. Additional paradox: immediately next to the cricket pitch stood a wire batting cage or backstop for baseball and softball, and an infield diamond. Along the third-base side there were a couple of bleacher-type benches. Organized softball leagues used this ballpark on week nights; there was a Bank League in which a friend of my father's played second base for Bank of Commerce; we used to root for his team.

Nobody at this date played lacrosse in the Rosedale Lacrosse Grounds. That activity must have gone on before my time. In the thirties the maintenance of lacrosse grounds cost too much, and the game declined somewhat in popularity, or at least in viability; the number of active players diminished. Finally a truncated form of the game was devised called "box lacrosse" or in the jargon of the sports page simply "boxla." Six men to a side played on a species of court or rink, the "box" of the game's name. There were famous teams competing across the country for the Mann Cup. Mimico Mountaineers. Who can have invented that picturesque nickname? There are no mountains within 500 miles of Mimico, none that I can think of anyway.

The Mimico Mountaineers were perpetually playing off for the Mann Cup against a team which had, in my opinion, the most pleasing team-name in all of organized sport, excepting perhaps the ladies' hockey team called the Preston Rivulettes; this was, if you can imagine, the New Westminster Salmonbellies. I used to make up sports-page headlines to chronicle this club's victories and defeats, thus:

"Salmonbellies Spawn Mann Cup Victory."

"Mountaineers Find Crevasse In Salmonbellies' Defence."

"Upstream Struggle Ends Salmonbellies' Slump."

"Fins Finish Mimico in Boxla Swim."

These never appeared in print, only in my heated verbal imagination.

At other times I might do the same exercise in behalf of the storied ladies' hockey team mentioned briefly above, the Preston Rivulettes. Their wins could be reported thus:

"Trickle Of Wins Brings Rivulettes Triumph."

"Rivulettes Babble, Gurgle, To Series Loss."

Those cricket players had the almost ladylike deportment of the fabled Rivulettes in the solemnity with which they acted out, during Saturday afternoon matches at the Lacrosse Grounds, a fake-English ritual that included delicately nurtured gentlewomen's discreet applause, and tea and buns in a tent. We all used to laugh at them, even hoot rudely; we had names for them and their society which, though rude and wounding, were neither indecent nor obscene, merely enviously scornful. We knew perfectly well that the playing of cricket had a definite place in Canadian life, that it was practised by people of a distinct stripe who were a lot richer than our parents were.

People with names like: Scaife, Twaits, Strathy, Skace,

Skaithe. Members of the RCYC, and the various gentlemen's clubs around town, the Albany Club, the Toronto
Club, the York Club, the National, the Carlton, the various
hunt clubs. Ah yes, the hunt clubs. There galloped the colonial mentality in its most intense expression. These squires
of Forest Hill and Armour Heights, galloping across their
fairly broad acres somewhere up around Maple or King in
search of Jalna. Can that truly have been their imagined
goal, Jalna? Had they read any book at all? Blood sport with
neither blood nor even fox, unless it be fox trapped elsewhere
and held in box, then brought to hunt in someone's Buick.

I used to laugh at these people, sure. I saw that they were
ridiculous, but I was impressed by them all the same. I
didn't go to the Lacrosse Grounds to play either lacrosse or
cricket, I went to learn to skate, aged four on cheese-cutters,
and to play football in the helmet I won selling magazines. I
went a bit later to play shinny on the cushion. Can anybody
tell me why an outdoor hockey rink with wooden boards
around it supplied by the park men is called, or was called, a
"cushion"? Was it that the boards would cushion you from
the effects of a heavy bodycheck?

I went to the park in the heavenly hope of seeing Bea
Skaithe who lived on upper-class Highland Avenue and was
therefore, in some infinitely obscure way, I thought then,
above me. Origins of courtly love. I had found out who Bea
Skaithe was when soliciting customers for my *Saturday Evening Post* route from door to door, riding along on my CCM
sidewalk bike, a recent birthday present. Knocking on front
doors, attempting to look like the friendless, homeless raga-
muffin I had seen described in Alger's *Bound to Rise*, I
managed to work up a mighty extensive magazine route, and
in weekly calls at the Skaithe home on Highland Avenue I
had seen enough of the young Beatrice to wish to lay my little
heart at her little feet. She banished the last lingering traces
of the image of Letty Millen from my childlike sexual con-
ceptions, and made Alanna Begin seem trivially my own
sort, by her distant superior status as classical *princesse loin-*

taine. I had no formed plan of what I would do to or with Bea Skaithe, when I was getting to be eight years old, except that I would tell her that I was her *Saturday Evening Post* boy, that her mother also took the *Journal*, that in this capacity I would serve and protect her. No issue of those magazines would fail to arrive at her Highland Avenue door while I was on the job. Would this have drawn her toward me? I haven't the faintest idea. I never spoke more than five consecutive sentences to Bea Skaithe when we were children.

Besides the hockey cushion, from which on week nights you heard boys and men hollering at Georgie-Balls Bannon to give up the puck once in a while, there was a large sheet of uncushioned ice for pleasure skating, *patinage de fantaisie*, fancy skating, and also for simply stumbling around, lighted by half a dozen tall lamp standards. Here men and women, large flocks of girls, boys of the general stripe of Adam Sinclair, and a few others worn out from pursuit of the flying Bannon, might be found circulating counter-clockwise at leisurely pace. On a Tuesday or Wednesday night I would run into Bea Skaithe, member of a little band of persons of the female sex, who would occasionally cast a deliciously offensive glance of superiority at me or Monty or Jakie. They knew they were better than we were, as class and money lines were drawn then; they had no doubt of it. But still, very occasionally, a little girl unsteady on her blades might wobble across our way, smile winningly, give her name.

I did in fact introduce myself to Bea Skaithe and tell her my father was a professor, by implication in some sort superior to her father who was a stockbroker, and not one of your penny-stock operators either. A respectable dealer in bonds, debentures and shares, who had suffered losses during the depression of almost the same proportions as some of his customers. Alfred Skaithe was not the man to place his customers in the forefront of the battle, then refuse to join them in the imminent deadly breach. He put his own money where his newsletter was, and actually lost a lot of it.

Not all. A colonelcy in one of those comic-opera regiments which flourished for so long in the city, perhaps that of the

Queen's Own Rifles, and membership on the boards of seventeen companies, were two of the badges of Alfred Skaithe's continuing solvency and place at, or somewhere near, the head of the Toronto financial community. Like so many distinguished members of that community, his fortunes were founded on those of a wholesaling house, in the case of the Skaithe family a houseful of drygoods located in a superb old red stone multi-storied loft building near the corner of Front and Church, almost exactly where the St. Lawrence Centre stands today. Photographs of the city in the eighties show how imposing the front elevations of these commercial buildings were, massive, surprisingly large-windowed, reminiscent of the superb work done in warehouse building near the docks of London by Telford, and in their use of large, rusticated, rectangular blocks, of the early work of Richardson, whose G. Fox Department Store in Hartford, Connecticut, will serve as an illustration.

Wellington Street from Church to York, and Front Street, and their environs, were the seat of these merchants, whose use of loft space in their heyday, from immediately after Confederation through the war of 1914–18, was on an extraordinarily generous scale. The reason for this was, of course, their need to stock goods for quite long periods. The highway network that permitted ready and easy stocking of local entrepôts didn't exist at that time, nor did the gasoline-powered transport truck-trailer unit. The rail system was flourishing, but freight rates for local service fluctuated; on the whole transport and delivery costs were a persistent headache to jobbers, and their instinct was to receive goods during two major periods of shipment annually, then hold them over a longish stretch for graduated feed through to retail outlets. The really great achievements in Canadian public life have not been those of industrial management or the organization of labour. They have been those of the wholesale distribution of goods. The true epic of Canadian life might be told in the story of the Hudson's Bay Company or the Eaton's catalogue.

Modes, designs, the consequent shifts in demand, were

slow to evolve. It was the age, in short, of the great warehouse. The proof of this is the huge central warehouse district which then dominated Toronto commerce, down near the railroad and the lake, extending from about Parliament Street, at the most easterly, to Bathurst or perhaps even Dufferin Street in the west, with Front, Wellington and King Streets as the crosstown defining arteries.

The great wholesale stationery and office supplies house, Warwick Bros. and Rutter, had their warehouse at the corner of Bathurst and King, and I think of other more central establishments like Gordon Mackay, A.A. Allan, Barber, Ellis and Company, all close to the corner of Front and Bay. These family-held companies, like Skaithe Drygoods, were not owned by "merchant princes" nor any kind of true mercantile artistocracy; they were a class of merchant-jobbers, in the eighties usually at most two generations removed from Britain, sometimes themselves immigrants to Canada at the end of the "hungry forties." A man who had come to Toronto in, say, 1852, and begun to work his way upward in merchandising, might have begun by accepting bartered produce in his retail outlet. The strictly cash policy in retailing was the principal effect of the stable economic conditions after Confederation, when the national currency began to be widely circulated and a network of financial houses—banks, trust companies, insurance companies, and finally a strong commercial bourse and its attendant brokers—came into being in the nation's midland. All these things were happening to folks like Alfred Skaithe's grandfather, Peter Skaithe, who was born in Falkirk around 1840 and came to Upper Canada, or Ontario if you prefer, as a boy of twelve, accompanying his father, who had early lost his wife. Nothing much is remembered of the father, but the Skaithe family remember perfectly what happened to young Peter. He did his short term of service as a shopkeeper's boy assistant, sleeping in the store under the counter, rising at dawn and retiring just after dark, through the eighteen-fifties.

By the early eighteen-sixties, Peter Skaithe owned a horse

and wagon which he loaded several times a year with bolts of suitings and dress materials, sheeting, blanket materials and so on, to make a circuit out from Toronto around a radius of 40 miles, supplying general stores with a complete range of drygoods, though with no very wide selection within each kind.

After Confederation the new Ontario began to breed a generation of bankers who came speedily to rival those of Montréal; these were men who came on from Nova Scotia, for the most part, to staff and develop the nascent system of credit-management and financing of small business. The Bank of Commerce, a Toronto bank from its beginnings, was founded (not accidentally) in the year of Confederation, 1867, and reflected in its founding the general optimism among businessmen at the birth of the new nation.

It remains matter for quiet, dignified family pride among the Skaithes that Grandfather Peter received the second loan ever granted by the Bank of Commerce, which he used in 1867, when he would have been just under 30, to rent warehousing premises on Duke Street in Toronto, and to provide himself with an expanded stock for sale the following season. He married the year after that, and his son Edward was born in 1870, surviving to become the *and Son* of the legend "Peter Skaithe and Son," which was lettered in spidery gold script on a black ground on the long signboard over the ground-floor windows of the big warehouse on the south side of Front Street, just east of Higgins and Burke.

It was the third generation of this clan that permitted one of its sons to hive off from drygoods wholesaling into finance. Alfred Skaithe, born in 1899, my Beatrice's father, just too young to be in the Great War, entered stockbroking in the nineteen-twenties bearing the unfortunate tag of younger brother, but his acumen and energy were such that he rapidly took administrative control of the conservative brokerage house into which he obtained entry in 1922. By 1929 he was a full partner in Taverner, Skaithe; the company acquired a seat on the New York Stock Exchange that year at an inflated price which shrank grotesquely over the ensuing five years. This calamity, and the others which came with it between 1929 and 1935, those years when the choice was among Bennett, chaos and King (and what a choice), gave Alfred Skaithe a shocking case-hardening, and brought out his professional mettle. Strengthened him, whatever they did to the nation and its people. Bea Skaithe was born in 1930. So was I.

She was one lousy skater, whether on the primitive cheese-cutters, sometimes also called bobskates, or later, involved with the complex manoeuverings of the figure-skater, like those displayed years afterward by certain members of the Minto Club who wintered in Stoverville. Bea Skaithe would come toddling up the wrong lane of the pleasure rink, skating clockwise when everybody else was trying to turn time backward. She would walk over from her house on skates, a shameful thing to do to her excellent blades. I guess her parents didn't want her hanging around the clubhouse, commodious and strangely clean-smelling though it was, and strictly separate as to sex.

I loved that clubhouse, especially the specific, never-elsewhere-duplicated texture of the verandah and the wide front steps, splintered by thousands of skate blades. The dressing rooms had long benches carved with thousands of initials. There was that funny clean smell, like toilet disinfectant or perhaps Dustbane. The Silcoxes were always there; you'd have thought they owned the building. One of them later went to St. Andrew's College and became a company commander in the cadet corps. That impressive paramilitary unit, complete with incredible pipe band, used to parade on the Lacrosse Grounds, when Bob Silcox would be in his glory. Sunday mid-mornings, that would be, in the spring.

Before St. Andrew's College moved to a new campus near Aurora, they had successive locations in Rosedale, and cultural connections with the district going back to the date of the college's foundation. This assertion fills me with an almost insane joy because I can document it with unbelievable, purely accidental, precision.

My Uncle Philip was a great reader, and my grandparents
were insufficiently assured of the post-colonial status of the
new Dominion to put into their sons' hands books not of
soundly British origin. One of the presents my father and
later my uncle used to value most was their annual bound
volume of the *Boy's Own Paper,* which came to them at
Christmas for decades. My father had in his possession as
late as my teens the bound annuals for the years between
1904 and 1914, the decade when he was a child beginning to
read.

My uncle Philip, a clear half-generation younger than his
brother, and slower to mature, collected the *Boy's Own Annual* from the year 1916 through 1927 and I have the latest
volume of his collection before me as I write. The *Boy's Own
Annual* for the year 1926–27, the individual issues running
round the calendar from autumn 1926 to summer 1927. And
in this large, handsomely bound book, presented to my uncle
Philip with the affectionate inscription, "Philip Bentinck
Russell Goderich from Mamma and Dad Christmas 1927,"
there appeared a series of articles, very abundantly and accurately photographed, called "Some Canadian Schools."

Schools so enshrined were: Trinity College School, Port
Hope, Ontario; Upper Canada College, Toronto, Ontario;
St. Andrew's College, North Rosedale, Toronto and
Aurora, Ontario; King's College School, Windsor, Nova
Scotia; St. John's College School, Winnipeg, Manitoba;
Bishop's College School, Lennoxville, Québec; and finally
Appleby School, Oakville, Ontario. There are elements of
providential aptness in this series of articles. They were written 50 years ago; they appeared three years before my birth,
the year my sister was born, the year following my parents'
marriage. The bound volume of 1926-27 demarcates the
earliest backward reach of my memory and existence. I can
guess back to 1925, 1926. Before that is history. And these
articles depict as almost nothing else could the situation of
the Dominion just before the Statute of Westminster.

One school from the Maritimes, a school which my pater-
nal grandparents considered and rejected for both their sons,

perhaps to their cost. One school, an anglophone and Protestant institution from Québec. No school from farther west than Winnipeg. Four Ontario schools, all from around Toronto, including St. Andrew's to represent the Scotch element in the life of the colony. Six out of seven describe themselves as "College" or "College School" when in fact they were secondary schools like most others, as far as curriculum and class organization go. No Catholic school, almost no school with lots of Jews in the student body. No French school.

St. Andrew's comes third in line in this series. The Scots were after all only the third most important cultural presence in the colony:

> The success of St. Andrew's College has been due to a variety of causes. It was founded in 1899 at a time when the Dominion of Canada, after many years of arrested development, was entering upon a period of unprecedented growth and prosperity; between 1899 and the Great War there was a great influx of population; new railways were built, financial enterprises of all kinds were undertaken, new provinces were set apart and Canada attained a new and vigorous consciousness of geographical and commercial unity. The optimism of those years of growth was reflected in the life of St. Andrew's, which from the first enrolled boys from all parts of the Dominion.

Only two years after this optimistic piece appeared, Taverner, Skaithe, Limited, bought their inflated seat on the New York Stock Exchange.

> The first home of St. Andrew's was Chestnut Park, the residence of the late Sir David MacPherson, an ornate and elaborate estate then on the outskirts of Toronto, consisting of a rambling old mansion surrounded by gardens and orchards tastefully arranged.

This explains why MacPherson Avenue runs west from

Yonge Street just above that lazily winding thoroughfare still known as Chestnut Park, the street with the pretty yellow lantern-globes, two minutes' walk north of the Rosedale subway station on Yonge Street. There's nothing surprising about the evolution of a rich man's estate into a school foundation. Both of the Catholic boys' secondary schools in the Toronto of that epoch were located on what had been the estates of rich families: St. Michael's at Clover Hill, formerly the residence of General Elmsley's family, and De La Salle at Oaklands, which had been the property of the McCormick family. It is an old, old story in the history of education.

At the end of six years the School migrated to North Rosedale, then a suburb of Toronto almost in the country, where a commodious and modern building was erected. . . .
   Among other distinguished Canadians of the earlier generation of Andreans may be mentioned Mr. Vincent Massey, so closely associated with the gift of Hart House to the University of Toronto . . . and Mr. Lawren Harris. . . .

Mr. Vincent Massey and Mr. Lawren Harris: the ploughshare, the sceptre-viceregal and the artist's smock and brush! This providential linking of finance, business, industry, the public life and the art of painting, in the innocent observation of the imperialist observer of half a century ago, does much to explain the climate of experience in the adolescent Dominion.

. . . plans were prepared for a new site and a new building. Aurora, a village some twenty miles north of Toronto, was finally selected, and there amid surroundings of much beauty, extensive buildings are now (in 1927) in process of erection. This new era has been made possible by the unbroken success of the last 25 years, often amid many obstacles, by the untiring efforts of Dr. Macdonald, and by the munificent gifts of such benefactors of the school as the late Mr. D.A. Lowther and Sir Joseph Flavelle, now Chairman of the Board of Governors.

Originally organised as a joint-stock company, St. Andrew's College became in 1911, under a special Act of the Legislature of Ontario, a public trust administered by a Board of Governors. . . .

In the *Boy's Own Annual* there are photographs of the old and new college buildings, and a clear wide-angle shot of the pipe band and cadet corps on parade in the Lacrosse Grounds. Mr. D.A. Lowther, great benefactor of this curious school, was of course the head of the great Lowther family of south Rosedale under whose patronage the Farquhars, Cloughs and Sinclairs mimed the role of grateful retainers, in their row of dormitory dwellings halfway up the block from us. Sir Joseph Flavelle, a meat-packer by original impulse, was a giant of corporate finance during the first four decades of the century, an organizer of the Robert Simpson Company, Limited, one of the great department stores whose essence so finely expresses Toronto life over almost the entire course of modern Canadian society. He was a high corporate officer of the Canadian Bank of Commerce, active in meat-packing and food distribution, created a baronet for his (perfectly real and valuable) services in this connection during the Great War.

Silkscreen prints of the works of Mr. Lawren Harris adorned banks and boardrooms the length of the Dominion for many years, happy Old Andrean! How oppressive were these images in their obsessively repeated domed shapes and greyish hues.

This is a complex web.

The process by which a cannily organized and patronized small private joint-stock company—a school, as it happens—acquired a special public status by act of the provincial legislature, and rose into being a public trust administered by a Board of Governors, reminds us pretty insistently of the way in which the universities "went public." Canada has never been an achieved democracy nor a socialist state. In those days finance owned the legislature and created what educational institutions it desired, giving them what legal status it wished.

When I was trying to put my hand in the hand of Beatrice Skaithe, in 1938, as she wobbled around the pleasure rink on expensive white bootees and blades, I was attempting a touch, a gesture, that society and history refused to permit. I wasn't simply Matthew Goderich, son of a radical philosophy professor, not very rich boy about to become, suddenly, much poorer. Nor was my admired little friend simply a sweetly pretty little rich girl from Highland Avenue. The Canadian Bank of Commerce oversaw our acquaintance, and the CPR, and the Robert Simpson Company, Limited, and Sir Joseph Flavelle, Bart. What could I do?

I wondered why there was this preoccupation with Scotchness, or Scotticism if you prefer, in the post-colony of my boyhood. Why were prefectly un-Scots boys like Bob Silcox strutting up and down on the greensward of the Lacrosse Grounds in kilts, to the truly dreadful sound of badly played bagpipes (think of Haydn's use of the drone bass in his *Bear* symphony and then think of the St. Andrew's College Pipe Band), with sporrans and some sort of ludicrous large safety-pin affixed to the material of the plaid? Why were the leading militia regiments of the city apt to be kilted, as were the Toronto Scottish, the Forty-Eighth Highlanders, even the Irish Regiment? Why, for that matter, was the annual display of military pomp in Toronto called the Garrison Parade? God knows, the garrison mentality has been often enough attributed to the small ruling class of Ontario society as it then was, beset by Indians, and worse, by French. The name of the parade betrayed the reality of the syndrome.

Tired of trying for a word or a smile from Bea Skaithe, I would go back to the hockey cushion and watch the graceful motions of Georgie Bannon, now aged thirteen or so, already marked out for a career in the pros. In another year George was playing with St. Mike's "Buzzers" and by the time he was sixteen he was with St. Mike's "Majors" in Junior A, and had signed the notorious "C-form," which bound him forever to the peonage that a professional contract enjoined at the time, and was being groomed to graduate to the NHL (that happy haven of corporate finance) as a very young, wartime rookie like Tommy O'Neill, Jackie Hamilton, Jack Ingoldsby or, in Montréal, a silent dark lad, not known for his backchecking ability, with a tendency to leg injuries, which crippled him at the beginning and end of his career, young Maurice Richard.

Watching George move the puck around, or in spring and summer swing a golf club, I realized early that the grace of art shows itself in multiform masks. I could not, nor could any of my friends, do the things George could do with stick, puck, ball, club. He wasn't a big boy or specially impressive physically. I remember he had strangely shaped muscles in his upper arms, long and flat, which reminded me of the shape of certain large lake fish—the ellipse described by the mass of flesh in section would have been the same, as would the length of the objects. Arm muscles like pike!

Of the eight or nine Canadian painters more or less loosely lumped together under the rubric "Group of Seven," Lawren Harris would carry all before him, without possibility of dispute, as the worst. Just as indisputably, Fred Varley takes rank as the best. Varley after all could draw, could define a mass in his pictorial space and make it signify, in a way that none of the other seven or eight people in the group could. It might reasonably be alleged that Lawren Harris—as bad painter—carried all before him. It would however at that epoch, and for a long time afterward, be thought inexcusably bad manners to mention the matter.

The point was not that Harris was a consistently awful painter, that his colour was vomitous, his line obsessively repetitive, his understanding of the problems of abstraction hardly begun. He was an Old Andrean. The Bank and the CPR made wide use of those terrible silkscreens. And George Bannon had been persuaded to sign the "C-form." In either case, as also in the case of my mildly disappointed liking for Bea Skaithe, the real and true issue wasn't the strength of the affection, the hockey player's elegance, the painter's incapacity. It was the form and pressure of class and money that hemmed us all in: Lawren Harris, who can't after all have wanted to paint as he did; George Bannon, whose career was wholly out of his control; even Bea Skaithe, who might otherwise have cared for me as early as 1938.

When I walked up the curvy front walk through shady shrubbery to ample verandah and lacquered black door, brass knob, brass knocker, of the Highland Avenue retreat of the Skaithes, I was assailed by inferiority-feelings of a specific flavour, not to be paralleled in any other country, because of the delicate poise of our system of social differences, or any such system. A society seems to be a kind of organism for webbing-out, outlining, highly specific collections of differences between smallish groups. When Chekov begs that the story be told of a poor youth who has grown to young manhood in near-serfdom, somehow scrabbled his way through a petty education, then begun to feel faint stirrings in his breast of the wish to be free, he is speaking pretty directly to me. I understand the emotion and the nuances of the story so outlined. It is not, however, exactly my story. I have never been a serf, never a cotton-chopper or migrant worker.

Later on, when I held one of the innumerable temporary jobs I took to help pay for my education, handing out uniforms to high-school kids who were coming to work at the Canadian National Exhibition, I performed a slave's act. There may be grovellings to come; this was my only grovel so far. A boy not much younger than I came into the uniform room to collect a parking attendant's striped shirt and peaked cap. I compared his name, on my list, with that of a famous local family of merchants, the same name. I made some fatuous remark about the noted head of the family, at that time much in the news because of a book he had written, or caused to be written.

This boy said, "That's my grandfather."

"Oh," I said, and then by some mean, self-betraying reflex, "does your shirt fit, *sir*?"

The speech wasn't sinful, nor the motive that produced it;

but my feelings about it were—of wounded self-esteem, rage, wish to even the score. I don't think that kid even heard my corrupted monosyllable, but I heard . . . I hear it still. I can't explain how that servile impulse crossed me unawares. I've never called anybody ''sir'' except out of politeness before or since, certainly not some adolescent working at the Ex. One of the most puzzling and subtle things that's ever happened to me. I was ready to act like a servant, however briefly, in front of this kid because his grandfather was head of a big store. Not at all the same sort of class-distinction as the one Chekov had in mind, not nearly so profound or touching.

Emancipation, the flutter in the rib-cage of the bird, freedom, was for Chekov's young former serf a matter of flying from the blows of the knout, of having cringed for years in humiliating postures before people unimaginably one's superiors. I, on the other hand, have once in my life half-involuntarily accepted the role of menial, and been guiltily ashamed of it ever since. What it is to be a Canadian! Few who have gotten as far as a Collegiate Institute, no matter whether they have had to hoof it into Stoverville from Lyn, or live in a roughcast smashed farmhouse somewhere up the North Augusta Road toward Spencerville, have felt at all like servants or serfs.

I have held jobs where I had to do as I was told. I don't much object to that. Obedience isn't a bad sort of experience; it encourages a useful civility before, say, legal institutions. I'm not committed to violently revolutionary politics, nor to anarchism. But I am opposed to every form of humiliating oppression and to all servility. The thing is, I only ever felt it that one time. I didn't feel servility toward the Skaithes. I felt that we lived in about the same kind of neighbourhood, a few blocks apart, though I could judge the difference between Summerhill and Highland. Mr. Faucett's notion of home construction was more modest and less elegant than what appeared along Highland behind the shade trees marking the southern boundary of the Lacrosse

Grounds. Highland had mighty nice houses, and the Skaithes' was clearly the nicest. I arrived there each Tuesday around twenty after five, almost the last call on my wide-coursing magazine route.

I had to make my best speed home from school on Tuesday afternoons, arriving on our verandah at half past three, when I would find a large, heavy bundle of copies of the *Saturday Evening Post* lying at the door, tied with twine. I had two heavy canvas bags that I slung over either shoulder, sliding perhaps 30 magazines into each bag, which made a cumbersome load. I would pick up my little bike from the garage and set off. This wasn't a full-sized wheel, but a tiny thing of a type you never see any more, called a "sidewalk bike." It didn't, for example, possess a regular brake and hanger. The pedals kept going round no matter how, or at what speed you were pedalling, uphill, downhill. It wasn't a bad little contrivance at all. I rode it for thousands of miles, and it did me good.

I bicycled all the way back up to school to begin my deliveries on Garfield Avenue at the home of some ladies of the parish, friends of my mother, perhaps family connections in some obscure way, perhaps only companions in the Altar Society. They took both the *Post* and the *Journal*, but I only had to make *Journal* deliveries one week in four, to about twenty customers. From Garfield I swung up to Inglewood, and eastward along Inglewood to Hudson Drive where I had to negotiate a short steep ascent on the little bike, which had a very small sprocket, up to Rose Park, home of Mrs. Wickett, mother of nasty stinky Paul Wickett, the class tale-bearer, my customer farthest north. Back down Welland to Ingelwood, jog right to the top of MacLennan and thence southward to the hill, riding on the sidewalk except at intersections, where I used to shoot down the nearest driveway ramp and dart across the street without dismounting as I ought to have done.

I crossed the tracks at the foot of the hill and went east along our street, disposing of five customers along our block;

by now the bags would be lighter on my shoulders. I used to jettison one bag when I passed our house, over half the route completed. On Jean Street the Forbes family took both *Post* and *Journal*, though Jakie used to complain sourly that he meant to go into magazine sales at any time and take the business away from me. At the corner of Glen Road, in former times, I had been wont to ring Mrs. Millen's door-bell, thinking that I might persuade her to take the *Post*; this gave me a chance to take a peek at Letty, who often sat in their living-room before a glass-fronted desk, doing her homework. Mrs. Millen took no interest in the periodical press of the day and never became a customer. I suspect that my gradual loss of interest in her fair daughter was mainly because of this obduracy; entrepreneurial instinct often supersedes passion.

I hustled south along Glen Road almost to the bridge, where I reached the southernmost point of my route, quite an extensive circuit, you see, from Rose Park Drive to Beaumont Road on the north shoulder of the tenebrous ravine that gave Glen Road its name. My grandfather Goderich and my uncle Philip were then sharing rooms in a big old house on Beaumont Road; they had the third floor to themselves, sitting-room, two comfortable bedrooms, kitchen of a sort, bathroom. I looked forward to seeing either or both late Tuesday afternoon; they paid promptly for magazines and were otherwise kind, giving me a chance to rest for a bit, asking how things were over on Summerhill. After this respite, very late in the day, I pedalled hastily westward along Highland Avenue, sometimes passing Mr. Busdriver Smith as I sped along on the last bit of my route. I had a customer where Binscarth leads off from Highland, and another down in the valley on Roxborough Drive. Finally I'd climb back up the side of the ravine, on foot, pushing my little bike. I would turn in toward the west end of Highland, which wound in above Roxborough along the shoulder of the ravine, shaded by the graceful oaks that screened the house from the stares of softball players and cricketers in the park.

The Skaithe house stood well over toward the edge of the ravine. I had only one other call to make on my way home—at my best customers, who lived on St. Andrew's Gardens—and my feet would be moving slowly as I came to the polished weighty brass-and-black door.

The Skaithes were slow payers, would accept magazines for weeks, a maid coming to the door and receiving a *Post* and a monthly *Journal*, occasionally fumbling in her pocket for change, more often retreating into an invisible parlour to ask her mistress for silver if convenient. When I gave up the magazine route the year we moved to Moore Park they still owed me seventy-five cents; the sum is engraved in my memory. More indelibly marked there was a series of apparently chance encounters with Bea, cagily planned by me. It was no accident that I called on the Skaithes when I did. I knew young Bea would be hanging around outside at 5:15 or so, when it was warm spring.

On one particular afternoon, I sauntered up the walk on the alert for Bea; sure enough there she was, sitting with a tea-set spread out on the lawn beside a big shrub. I noticed that the lid had come off a tiny teapot and hidden itself in a depression beside the sidewalk. I picked it up and handed it to her with a flourish. I was almost nine.

I said, "Don't you ever go to the Beverly on Saturday? I never see you there." All at once I was overcome by a vision of Bea Skaithe running up the gangway with sponge taffy stuck in her lovely tresses, and I knew why she didn't go to the Beverly. She was too good for the place; this was inescapable.

She knew perfectly what and where the theatre was. "My mother would *never* let me go there," she said disdainfully. "Nobody on our street goes to the Beverly. It's just a *neighbourhood* theatre." Suddenly I could grasp that the Beverly smelt bad and didn't run the newest of films.

She said, "Sometimes my mother takes me to the Hollywood." A maid appeared in the doorway without my knocking.

"Time to come in now, Miss Beatrice," she said. This silenced me, and I followed her to the doorway, sliding a magazine out of my pouch and handing it to the maid. I didn't wait to try to collect. I felt obscurely crushed.

But there were always the kind, prompt-paying Angstroms who lived a few doors east of MacLennan on the north side of St. Andrew's Gardens. They often gave me a cookie or offered a glass of milk. They had no maid; their street was leafy, relaxing, and all that time I half-sensed what I see so clearly now—why that peaceful treed street described the strange circlet with Douglas Drive that it did. St. Andrew's Gardens, which housed the friendly Angstroms and the red-haired Esther Bannon, must have been the primitive site of St. Andrew's College. Certainly. Of course. Removed to Aurora in the season of my birth, the school haunted the district in the name of a realtor's development. MacPherson. Chestnut Park. St. Andrew's Gardens. Highland (because lying above the ravine), Sighthill (because it ended at the brow of the hill above the tracks), they all meant something, concealed some historical secret, if only I knew where to look and what I might expect to find. Glen Road. Edgewood Crescent. Suddenly the names of streets I walked on daily took on resonances and tinklings, ringings, I would say tintinnabulations if it did not seem affected, of historical significance. Why Rowanwood? Why Douglas Drive? What allegiance to legendary Scottish hero was figured in the innocent suburban name? I am perhaps the only living man who remembers why Rumsey Road in Leaside is so called. What is happening to the city?

The day after *Post* delivery day, Mr. Bottome called for the receipts and for any magazines left over. Poor Mr. Bottome, like the men at the Beverly he was eking out a thin livelihood in a job that would not have supported a married man with a family at any recent time except during the years from 1931 to 1939. He was supplied with a car, an abashed Hudson two-door, and was an assistant circulation manager for the enormous distributing near-monopoly that handled

the Curtis publications among many others. He would dole
out to the route boys the semi-annual prize catalogues showing remarkable premiums to be exchanged for our ac-
cumulated greenies and brownies, our capitalist indoctrina-
tion, our training in small business.

Greenies and brownies were the small, currency-shaped
coupons allotted to us boy magazine salesmen in addition to
the small commission on each sale, a cent and a half for each
Post, and two and a half cents for each *Journal*. I could earn
up to 75¢ a week if everybody paid me on time, and an extra
50¢ on the monthly delivery of the *Journal*. Hardly anybody
paid promptly, but my magazine earnings supplemented my
irregular allowance and the occasional quarter from Grandpa Goderich or Uncle Philip, so that I usually had money for
the movies and a glacial balance in a savings account administered for me by my father when he went downtown—
less and less often now.

The real prize for the *Post* boys was the premium catalogue
and the greenies and brownies—they were fun. You were
supposed to get a greenie for every five magazines sold and a
brownie in exchange for every five greenies, but this crypto-
currency had like every other money much depreciated as
time went on, and Mr. Bottome handed the coupons out
much more generously than these fiscal and monetary fiats
allowed. The practice later on brought him into conflict with
his bosses. As long as he was the route-man, my pile of
brownies built up quickly, and I was always ordering
something from the premium catalogue or waiting for
delivery. *Gantner Wikies*. What were they? The name figured
largely in the catalogue pages but what they were never
registered with me. *Wikies. Wikies?*

I acquired from the catalogue, after the uneasy rapture of
the six- to eight-week interval of waiting, a stamp album and
beginner's collection, with stamp hinges and perforation
guage, and watermark detector with which I failed utterly to
detect any watermarks. Football shoulder pads and a helmet,
which was always half a size too small for me and gave me a

headache, but which I wore anyway till it came apart. A haversack. A most magnificent huge chrome-plated battery-operated lantern. Sure we were being trained to think like little businessmen, but when I recollect that gorgeous lantern I can't object to the practice, which slowly inched my bank account up to the $50 mark.

After three years of uninterrupted tiny deposits, my passbook suddenly showed an inexplicable, unauthorized withdrawal of $50, which just about bankrupted me. Made by my father because $50 was exactly the sum needed to placate Mr. Faucett, exigent about that month's rent, and buy groceries for the weekend; you could get three bags full of groceries for ten dollars at that epoch. I wasn't too put out by the surprise of the missing money, certainly never felt that my father had acted irresponsibly. I just felt slightly puzzled that he hadn't mentioned it to me, had had the deduction entered in my passbook and returned the book to me without a word.

I began to connect certain phenomena: Mr. Faucett's frequent visits, more and more often with the air of a man inspecting the property with a view to selling it or finding a new tenant. He was never unpleasant to me, but was sometimes impatient with the Goderich family as a group, and especially with my father who seemed to him to lack the elements of basic good sense. This was clear from things said in front of me, disconnected mumblings standing in front of the house, looking up at paint flaking from eavestroughing.

"There's a lot of money goes into maintaining a house, Matthew, for paint, wallpaper, shingling. When I built this house I put only the best materials into it, on the flashing, the sills, the wiring. This house is only ten years old. I could sell it today for a thousand dollars more, a thousand more than it cost. This is a $7000 house in the market of today."

"How do you sell a house, Mr. Faucett?" I had the idea that he meant to sell it to us, which was very wide of the mark. "Does Dad want to buy the house?"

He looked at me for a long time without saying anything,

very kindly and quietly, as if he felt sorry for me. That alarmed me much more than if he'd shown dissatisfaction or anger. I couldn't think of any reason why anybody should feel sorry for any member of the Goderich family. Everybody was well. My father had a good job, and Grandpa Goderich was after all a KC and a lawyer. Once you were a lawyer, I knew, you never stopped being a lawyer so you always had ways of making money. My mother looked inordinately healthy; even her freckles looked healthy. She had smooth brown skin liberally freckled, and pretty little ankles. I knew she was all right. And it appeared that my grandmother too enjoyed the best of health—in fact she lived another 25 years, dying in her tenth decade—and was therefore no cause for childish insecurity. Why then should Mr. Faucett feel pity and kindness toward me? I rejected these feelings quite involuntarily, turning away and walking toward our front door.

"You'll understand when you're older," Mr. Faucett said to my retreating, perhaps slightly insolent back. I went inside and into the living-room, from where I saw Mr. Faucett on the street, staring at our door with a perplexed expression. He took a small note pad and a pencil from his breast pocket, licked the end of the pencil and began to write, first spoiling a sheet or two, crumpling them and sticking them in his coat pocket. He was looking at the roof. Then he came up onto the porch, took out a good-sized pocket knife, opened the largest blade and stuck it between the bricks near the window where I was concealing myself. I could hear through the glass, and perhaps through the walls, a funny scrabbling, scratching sound, the knife-blade scraping the mortar. I wanted to go out and tell him to stop it, but knew perfectly well that the building belonged to him. I swallowed several times very fast. I felt sniffly and choked up. I was frightened and couldn't detect the reason. Mr. Faucett was a fine man, very friendly. Why was he doing that?

The following week Grandpa Goderich spent the evening with us. Uncle Philip had been here for dinner and gone away to an appointment he claimed to have, somewhere downtown. His appointments were innocence incarnate; he was always going somewhere to see somebody about a possible job, and when the depression finally lifted with the onset of war production he actually got a job, a pretty good one, which he held for many years. There was nothing tragic or funny or in any way extraordinary about my uncle; he was well educated, sober, agreeable, polite, honest, and had suffered much from the wounding nature of his start in life. Twelve years younger than my father, he had from early childhood to contend with two grown men of extremely strong character and definite personality. He depended for solace and support upon his mother, who died, as I have already noted, when he was still in his teens. He never found that elusive permanent job till he was almost 30. This warped his youth and young manhood, certainly affecting his self-conception permanently. He didn't, for example, serve in the 1939–45 war although of an age to do so, having had a bout of rheumatic fever as a boy, which left him with a somewhat weakened heart muscle. His employment, when he finally discovered it, had nothing glamorous or exciting about it, but it was steady, not taxing to the emotions, gradually more responsible. One of the really admirable things about this uncle was the way in which he reconstructed his person, point by point, on the ill-laid and irregular foundation originally laid down for him by life. Maybe the unspecified appointment of that evening was one of the first blocks in the readjusted foundation. There is no way of knowing.

My grandfather and father passed the evening in persistent mild quarrelling. Of the two, the older man was the more aggressive personality, ready to flare out into genuine animosity, even with the son whom he admired so greatly, though half-unwillingly. My grandfather was intensely aware of my father's mental endowments, which greatly exceeded his own—and God knows exceeded mine—and strangely enough didn't resent them. I think he felt that his own prudence and knowledge of how affairs are managed, as he considered them, gave him a practical advantage in daily life—traditionally the attitude of the legal mind toward the philosopher. They argued the whole evening, long after I had retired to bed, sometimes noisily, about some course of action proposed by my father which involved our moving away from Summerhill. This came as a revelation to me. I had never entertained the idea of living elsewhere. I lived here.

I was falling asleep as their discussion drifted up the stairs sharpest and clearest. I vaguely took in the conception of the proposed move. I thought dreamily of some residential area nearer St. Clair and Yonge. I would stop going to the Beverly and start attending the Hollywood. I would better my circumstances and appear mysterious to Bea Skaithe. Perhaps our new house would have glass doorknobs.

3

Sitting in the Senior Second classroom at OLPH school in September 1938, at the end of the week in which we moved to Cornish Road in Moore Park, proud in the possession of (rented) glass doorknobs, slightly irked at having to conduct Tony back and forth to school and eager to be home through lunch hour so as to hear Singin' Sam at noon, I drowsed through a talk on the work of the Scarborough Foreign Mission Society and its policy for China on the question of a native clergy and episcopacy, given by fairly recently ordained Father Feeney McCoy. At the back of my imagination there ran slowly in confused windings the musical complexities of the school's grade system. Was I or was I not in Grade Four? This was my third year in school. I could read extremely well, spell accurately and use my father's collection of dictionaries correctly. My penmanship was poor, mainly because of my left-handedness, which caused me to arch and twist my wrist in an arthritic way when writing, and also to drag my arm across what I had written. There ought to be a league for the defence of the sinister, who should refuse to write as the dexterous do; we ought to write across the page from right to left; there is no reason why things should go the other way, except the tyranny of the 80 percent majority. I was an early exponent of southpaw power. The Chinese, after all, read from top to bottom instead of from left to right. I had a vague notion that the Jewish newspapers one occasionally saw on the streetcar were laid out similarly. What was the typographical connection between Chinese and Jewish?

A class monitor passed down the aisle, and plunked a free copy of the SFMS magazine, *China*, on my desk. I noticed that the name of the magazine was run across the top of the front cover in very large letters looking like Chinese ideograms, the A resembling a little house, the C a crescent moon, and so on. Brushwork! They used brushes to do their writing, didn't they? I might be a better penman if I used a brush and stood off from the paper at a little distance. Or I might not. I had tried and tried to handle a brush in our rudimentary art classes, which naturally did not, in those days, aim at a true marriage of the child's imagination and the realm of art. These classes were given by the same teachers who taught everything else. Sister Matilda, who was taking Senior Second this year, knew nothing whatsoever about any form of art, though under her direction we were already beginning to make rude pencil sketches of pumpkins, against the oncoming Hallowe'en. Black cats. Stooks of wheat. Witches. Jack-o-Lanterns. There was a charming story about a Hallowe'en party in the Canadian Catholic Corona Reader, Book Four (ha!), which had orange-and-brown illustrations of autumn landscapes, and ingenious invitations to the party, plagiarized from Katy's birthday party invitations in *What Katy Did*. Our class specialized all the way through OLPH in cutout window illustrations of the various holidays and festivals: Hallowe'en, orange and black; Christmas, red and green; Valentine's Day, white and red; St. Patrick's Day, masses of shamrocks in green, clay pipes, golden harps; Easter, purple and yellow. There were no special celebrations on May Day, but the month of May was blue, Mary's colour. We were not in school on Labour Day; this eliminated a touchy problem.

Every Friday afternoon the art class would start. The girl monitors would hand out round small glass jars. We would fumble around in recesses at the bottom of the pile of books in our desks and find the book of art paper with each leaf perforated at the left margin for easy removal. The paper was a coarsely woven, scratchy light brown, unattractive and putting you in mind of all nasty elements of school. I never saw any really good work done on this paper.

We dug out our watercolours. As early as mid-September my paintbox was a chaotic mess. Water would be poured into each jar. Jim Barrow would contrive to joggle Eleanor Nugent's elbow and a puddle would begin to spread down the aisle. Work in watercolour now began; brows knitted, silence descended. I would start to mix colours in the little wells formed by the lid of the paintbox and inevitably, as surely as sunrise, my mixture of pigment and water would turn a deep muddy grey. It always did that, no matter how I varied my choice of tints from gamboge—a name I felt obscurely drawn to—to ultramarine—another delightful word. I think this early bewilderment at the refractory behaviour of pigment, coupled with the discovery that I had no capacity whatsoever to form pleasing or interesting lines and shapes, and my ingrained love for exotic names (ultramarine, gamboge, burnt sienna, ochre, chrome yellow, crimson lake), founded my attachment to the methods of the arts. If I couldn't manage them myself, I might nevertheless learn all there was to know about how those others did their trick.

I would sit with my sheet of cheap drawing paper propped in front of me, with a badly traced silhouette of, say, a pumpkin on it. Triangular shapes indicative of eyes and nose. Slit for a mouth. I would now ponder the artistic problem of representing a carrot inserted between the irregularly formed teeth as a cigar. I couldn't see how to do this.

Sister Matilda thought me obstinate in this respect, disobedient. She had said we were to do watercolours, and Matthew wouldn't! Plainly I was being lazy and idle in art class. I would simply sit and stare at my paper, instead of producing those tasteful representations of celebratory icons necessary to successive seasons. I would get two marks out of ten for my art work. Mind you, I got ten out of ten for com-

position, and so managed to obtain passing averages as between the rival claims of the sister arts. Sister Matilda never
showed me anything. I never thought to ask her why the
water ran all over my page, no matter how little was applied.
Why did my paper plump up here in a disagreeable swelling,
there lie wrinkled and flat and desiccated? I didn't know.
Sister Matilda didn't know. She wasn't a malicious woman,
and if she had had a secret to communicate would have
shared it in the most Christian manner with us all.

Eleanor Nugent was best in the class at art. Frankie Walsh
was probably next best. Jim Barrow was really disgusting,
even worse than I, although my handwriting was worse than
his. Jim's pictures had a leering, aggressive air. Alanna
Begin was surprisingly bad at art for a girl, and this, together
with other faintly disturbing surprises in her personality,
gave her a rakish air and a reputation among the boys in the
class, wholly unfounded I have to admit, for looseness of
deportment. Her French surname reinforced these nuances,
although it was at no time pronounced by any person in the
school as a French name. The indubitable Irishness of
"Alanna" saved the child from the opprobrium often then
visited upon too foreign character. I said nothing at OLPH
about my grandmother Archambault and her exasperated
frequent floods of well accented and articulate French.
Nobody's business, I fancied, and acted religiously upon the
assumption.

My unhandiness with the watercolour brush, I concluded,
looking at the cover of *China*, would rule me out as a
calligrapher in the ideogrammatic tradition. I didn't use
those words, nor any that I can call to mind. I just felt put-
upon and bewildered by art class, and by Chinese affairs as
Father Feeney McCoy continued to expound them. He had
been ordained a year or two before; a collection had been
taken up at school when I was in Junior First, to buy him
a Mass kit; chalice, paten, ciborium, Communion stole,
packed in neat leather satchel with red watered-silk lining,
from Desmarais and Robitaille, Canada's leading ecclesias-

tical outfitters. It was felt in the parish that in making it as far as China Feeney McCoy was disseminating the presence, the being of OLPH, very widely.

His folks lived on Inglewood Drive and his younger sister Joan was a classmate of Amanda Louise; she was a black-haired girl with a pronounced squint. This was one of the best known families in the Toronto Catholic community, one son a priest in the China missions, a daughter one of the Ladies of Loretto, their father a thirty-third degree Knight who carried the canopy over the Blessed Sacrament, together with five other knights of high degree, when the ciborium was moved from the high altar to the repository on Holy Thursday. I remember seeing him in his evening dress and sword the same day I got the strap from Miss McHale, during the morning service for that solemn fifth day of Holy Week. It was that particular visit to church that later on made an altar boy of me. I noticed, as the Host was being borne to the temporary resting place symbolizing the three-days' harrowing of Hell by Our Lord, that the altar boys in the procession all wore red soutanes with little round buttons all down the front instead of their ordinary black. I found this most intriguing when added to the fact that some carried funny little swinging lanterns suspended from long forked poles—it was a gorgeous spectacle, much affecting my later decision to "go on the altar." There were also repeated tales of "the Altar Boys' Banquet," which laid hold on my curiosity. I knew that these were forms and institutes where the disturbing memory of Bea Skaithe would never supervene, she being wholly Protestant in allegiance. Being an altar boy had none of the flavour of being a *Saturday Evening Post* boy. It was to make of oneself a useful and dignified participant in a great, holy, public and institutional scheme. To belong, in short. I felt in need of assurance that I belonged. Once or twice during this fall term in school reference had been made by one of the sisters to the strange fact of my father's resignation from the university, which had taken place the previous June and had attracted considerable attention from the newspapers, who began to refer to Dad as the "red philosopher."

VARSITY PROF RESIGNS ON PRINCIPLE

I could see the implied joke even then, the suggestion that a professor's acting on principle rated a three-column head. The *Star* was inclined to treat the matter as a joke, the *Globe* was not, and the *Catholic Register* was frankly thunderstruck. Before my father had quit his job, declaring that he could no longer profess philosophy in an institution that served reactionary, arch-conservative interests, he had been the darling of the city's small covey of Catholic intellectuals, though never in any way one of them. He had nothing to do with the Basilian fathers at St. Michael's except through his friendship for M. Maritain. My father's philosophical training and opinions were very remote from the Neo-Scholasticism of the ordinary Catholic intellectual of the period; he had no taste for party lines in philosophy, but was tolerated and even covertly admired, somewhat as John Henry Newman had been, as an example of the oddball eccentric whom the Church could tolerate and even welcome. A persistent analyst could show a kind of distant cousinship between his views and those of orthodoxy, which would do to go on with.

A public self-identification with formally socialist politics, a declaration that the emergent Falange in Spain was dangerously reactionary, that Francisco Franco was the enemy of intellectual and moral freedom, a readiness to point out in Ontario life certain clear falangist tendencies and fascist leanings—all that was quite sufficient in June 1938 to make that little covey of Catholic intellectuals shake in their shiny black boots and wish that my father would either hold his tongue or reveal that he was actually a High Anglican like the Very Reverend Hewlett Johnson, the notorious "Red Dean."

My father was simply a young man from Nova Scotia who was a serious and able student of ethics and social philo-

144

sophy, indeed a man of talent verging on genius, who could
see in 1938 what everyone could see in 1968, insufficiently
pliant to keep his opinions to himself and hang on to a
starveling academic post. By the middle of that year he had
come to believe (after observing the antics of the dictators
and the profound slumber of the Atlantic nations) that his
own job-security and his family's welfare had to take second
place to the need for an abrupt public gesture in the interest
of radical socialism. The late thirties tortured my poor
father.

One after another his political illusions were swept away
by events. The Moscow trials *could not* be explained away
convincingly by certain of his correspondents in New York
who were teaching that year a pure unadulterated Stalinist
cult-of-personality doctrine. He saw that Stalin was not a
hero of the revolution, that Stalin was becoming more and
more like his mirror-image in Germany, an absolutist dictator sustained by a ruthless secret police.

The Republicans were losing, had now clearly lost, the
Spanish engagement, Chinese socialism had passed underground and been dispersed, as Chiang's militarist-conserva-
tive sect gained ascendancy. Japanese militarist finance was
preparing some sort of catastrophic thrust in the Pacific,
most likely, my father thought then, as I learn from his cor-
respondence, in the area of the Philippines or in an assault
upon New Guinea and Northern Australia. He had a low
opinion of Japanese aircraft carriers and their fleet air service, and was unable to imagine an attack upon heavily
guarded Pearl Harbor.

One circumstance helped cheer him up after he quit.
Stalin or no Stalin, the USSR was in fact what those initials
said it was, a federated body of soviet socialist republics.
Such a federation, he knew, would never come to terms with
Nazism. The thing was inconceivable. As long as Russian
power effectively counter-balanced the expansive German
imperialism to the east, Hitler would never mount an attack
in the west, feeling himself too seriously threatened to the
rear. My father believed that there would be no second

general European war in his lifetime, the first having been so devastating.

Like so many Canadian socialists, he had that strain of pacific, idealist, wish-fulfilment fantasy which Orwell used to inveigh against. Perhaps that is why they are, as they are, so nice. Nobody in Canada seemed able in 1938 to take politics seriously, a consequence of the colonial mentality, which sees no connection between its local concerns, which it feels to be trivial, and the grand affairs of France and Spain, courts of emperors and czars and popes and unreliable people like that. I used to wonder how my father got himself so involved in the ethics of socialism. I see now that study and reflection did it to him. He had no familial connection with the world revolution, yet he knew about Mao long before Father Feeney McCoy, old China hand of some months' standing, and might have told that kindly missionary a thing or two about modern Chinese history, about what had passed between Mao and Chiang in 1928, how the people's party in 1926 and 1927 passed for heroes with Chiang's men and for villains a year later. I don't yet understand how he found out about these matters so early; they weren't current in Canada at the time. He certainly didn't hear about them from the priests of the FMS, who were occupied in soliciting funds to buy food for newly christened babies.

The sisters used to set up cardboard collection boxes on the classroom window-sills; for $5, they declared, you could buy a Chinese baby. They meant that a subscription of $5 would buy enough food to feed such a child for a year or more. I can remember thinking what a lot of Chinese babies there must be, in a land where the population even then exceeded four hundred million. China was a major news story in those days. An amiable book by an American commercial agent, Carl Crow, entitled *Four Hundred Million Customers*, was widely circulated in the last couple of years before the withdrawal on Chungking before the Japanese invaders— the same September morning as was the occasion for Father McCoy's address to Senior Second.

"You Canadian boys and girls would find it hard to imagine China and the lives of your Chinese sisters and brothers. Perhaps I can make it clearer and more interesting if I tell you that China is like Canada in one important respect. It is an enormous country. You know, I'm sure, that Russia is the largest country on earth (and we must all pray very hard to Our Lady of Fatima for the restoration of Russian Christianity) because Sister Matilda has told you all about the many beautiful Russian churches which have been closed, some even destroyed by the agents of godless communism.''

Sister Matilda and Father McCoy exchanged glances at this point, which seemed to recollect the priest to himself. He was silent for a moment, then went on with his talk. Something about the look in his eyes, a troubled shiver across his normally ruddy and agreeable countenance, made me stop ruminating over my father's ideas and my problems in art class. I began to listen to Father.

"Some people believe that Canada is the second largest country in the world, while others think that China is. All of us Canadians like to think ourselves the second biggest, but if the Chinese succeed in retaining Manchuria, or Manchukuo as it is now known, even though the League of Nations and the Japanese are trying to wrest the province from China, then China will remain the second biggest country and Canada will take third place, not a disgraceful place, I'm sure you'll all agree."

Sister Matilda gave a prompting grin, and we all smiled and chanted, "Yes, Father."

"In addition to being enormously large nations, China and Canada also have varied scenery, mountain ranges, huge plains, great rivers and ocean coastlines. There is nothing like our Great Lakes system in China, and we have nothing like their complicated, winding coast, and the seas and the small nations lying close to the Chinese mainland. Japan, actually, as you may know, is simply a chain of small islands along the Chinese and Korean coast.''

Father McCoy, all unawares, was giving me an introduction to the geography and geopolitics of the far east that has stuck with me till this day. I owe to him my awareness of the physical relationship of Japan, Korea, the kingdom of the Manchus and the central Chinese mainland. He went on, that distant day, to tell us of the Japanese invasion, which we could witness every Saturday in the newsreels and each Wednesday in the pages of *Life*. China was burning. Small Japanese soldiers in funny soft hats were bayoneting babies (maybe the very babies that our $5 had helped to feed) all the way from Shanghai and Nanking—the sack of Nanking was front-page stuff that year—almost to the gates of Chungking, the eventual capital and headquarters of Chiang's forces.

I couldn't assimilate all of this; it was too detailed, too politically complex. But I did know that my dad was solidly *au courant* with these matters. He often talked of André Malraux and Sun Yat Sen, about treaty ports and American gunboats. I suspect he would have liked at any time in his life to visit China. He talked lovingly and longingly of the Great Wall, fancying himself walking along its length into the infinite heartland of that far kingdom.

I took up the copy of *China* that lay on my desk and stared at the picture on the cover. Something strange about it, an altar and pillars quite like our church. I took another, closer look. By gollies, it *was* our church! The cover picture showed the ordination ceremonies of five young priests from the China Mission Seminary in Scarborough, one of them Father McCoy, a ceremony at which the new archbishop had presided in the most imposing way. You could see the high altar in the photo, the archbishop's throne, the five candidates for ordination kneeling before the altar, the familiar tubby pillars ringing the altar rotunda, even the statues of Our Lady and the Sacred Heart, which stood on pedestals halfway up the two pillars closest to the nave. It suddenly came to me: that's *my* church. I've been there. That picture was taken when Father was ordained. *I'm* in that picture; we were all there.

This administration of Holy Orders had taken place fourteen months before, say May 1937, and the picture appeared on the cover of the September 1938 issue of the magazine, not an unusual time-lag. It was executed in sepia, and you could readily identify Father Feeney McCoy from the shape of the back of his head. I squinted at the cover. I could see boys and girls from our school, strictly separate as to sex, in the front pews on the right side of the church, the Epistle side. The relatives—an exceeding great number—were on the Gospel side at the front. If I looked hard enough I might spot the back of my own head. I had been dying to go to the bathroom all through that interminable ceremony, and remembered vividly this embarrassing need, mixed with the scent of incense, and the special smell of melting, expensive candle-wax. It's hard for a child of today to realize what an extraordinary amount of time you spent in church if you went to a parish school in the nineteen-thirties. We were prepared for First Holy Communion almost the whole year in Senior First, learning the forms of penance, how to make an examination of conscience, whether Father Regan, the pastor, was terrifying in the confessional or as nice as his curates, who never prescribed a penance exceeding two Hail Marys. There was a large collection of folklore of an infantile sort on this subject, and a lot of jokes about it, and about priests and their eccentricities.

A motorcyclist offers a priest a ride on his machine and afterward somebody asks, "How long did it take you to get to the rectory, Father?"
"Two of the Sorrowful Mysteries, my child, and most of the Act of Contrition."

Not really irreverent anecdotes, telling much about the tellers as well as their subjects. There was nothing of the really biting satirical wish to crush out and kill of, say, the Encyclopedists, in our jokes about the Church. The boys my own age whom I knew at OLPH were remarkably free from indecency or gross irreverence in their discussions of sacred subjects. We used to compare family attitudes and jokes about religion, and Catholics and Protestants (almost never about Jews) in a very special mixture of legend and folktale and comic anecdote that reflected the complex subtlety of the religious and social forms behind them. We knew, for example, an awful lot about the various grades and circumstances of church appointments. We knew without anybody telling us that the Ladies of Loretto were more highly regarded socially than the Sisters of St. Joseph. The nuns at OLPH were Loretto nuns. We knew that St. Mike's had more prestige than Del, that curates never lasted long with the terrifying Father Regan, though it was whispered that Charlie O'Hagan had stood up to him pretty stoutly for a year or two.

My father elaborated a comic/satiric legend of Oka, according to which disobedient priests were shipped off to the monks at Oka on the Ottawa River 40 miles northwest of Montréal, a Trappist monastery of the sort later made well known by Father Merton's writing about the congregation at Gethsemane in Kentucky. I like to think of there being a Gethsemane, Kentucky, have for long relished this glinting irony.

Dad maintained vigorously, in the face of a total lack of supporting evidence, that misbehaving curates, sometimes even pastors whom the Archbishop desired to discipline, were shipped to this monastery, there required to maintain a strict observation of the rule of silence, and set to the making of the famous Oka cheese. So far as I know, there was no substance to the tale; it was a fantasy my father loved to embroider. When Mme. Archambault recounted stories of some admired clergyman or other, my father would murmur darkly "Oka" and she would grow irritated, then distinctly angry.

Heavens, but we kids knew a lot about religion and church affairs. The sisters began, from our first infant toddling mornings in Junior First, to educate us in the meaning and even (for the girls) the manufacture of the various altar linens and sacramentals: chalice, ciborium, monstrance, pyx, pall, paten, cruets, tabernacle cloths, chasuble, amice, alb, stole, cincture, burse, biretta. I could tell you the meaning, the Latin derivation of the terms, the kinds of metal or cloth used in the making of each of these articles, to the least detail. I could do this now, this morning, precisely as in 1936. The word "chasuble" comes from late vulgar Latin "casula," which means "little house," the chasuble being the priest's principal outer garment, something like a tent, the last vestment put on before celebrating Mass.

I can say at this instant what a dalmatic is, and how dalmatics differ as between members of the diaconate and subdiaconate, and I can recite the four minor grades of orders prior to the subdiaconate. I can tell the names of the corporal and spiritual works of mercy.

Years and years and long bloody years after these matters were instilled in my mind, I was to find myself standing in the Rijksmuseum studying a set of utterly superb panels by the Master of Alkmaar, with a loving companion at my side.

"What are those," she said, "what are they about?"

I can't explain how it was that the answer rose so fully and richly to my present mind out of the incalculable depths of recollection, but I can state exactly that it was a singular feeling, like being most mysteriously reborn. Of course I recognized the subjects of those panels, for I had heard them enumerated and had recited them back for Sister, when I was six. They represented in their space of 101 centimetres by 54 the corporal works of mercy. I don't know why the great masters of painting in the Low Countries in the fifteenth and sixteenth centuries are not better known to North Americans. I remember somebody saying about me, most disdainfully, not long ago, "Well! What can you expect from a person whose favourite painter is *Rogier van der Weyden*, I mean really!" This was meant to crush. Instead it exhilarated me. I accept the charge. He is my favourite, and the Master of Alkmaar is but a step behind.

To feed the hungry, to give drink to the thirsty, to clothe the naked, to bury the dead, to shelter pilgrims, to visit the sick, to ransom the captive. It is a noble list. And though I have not seen them, I am sure that somewhere there exists or once existed a companion set showing the spiritual works of mercy, superior in the natural and supernatural orders, seven further pictures by the same master.

Standing in the great museum, at that time quite ignorant of the power and mastery of these artists, but increasingly captivated by the beautiful sobriety of their technique and choice of subject, I hadn't the faintest notion, when my eyes first fell upon the series of seven, what they were, or were about. I didn't in the instant guess how well I knew the pictures, though I'd never seen them before. I didn't know or care that they were probably painted about the year 1504 by a Haarlem artist, a certain Pieter Gerritsz, for the church of St. Laurence at Alkmaar, though I knew who St. Laurence was and how he had been martyred. What I saw first was the extraordinary perspectival organization of the pictures, so deft, so wholly unlike Florentine or Venetian theories of perspective, yet so truthful and accurate a means of rendering the way a certain kind of intelligence apprehends spatial recession. Then I took in the purely illustrative aspect of the pictures, the clothes the women wore, the masonry of the buildings and their architecture. I saw what acts were being represented: how everyday they were, what holiness dwelt in them. I felt an extraordinary communion with the unknown painter who recorded this image of the holy in the daily, and with the woman who studied the pictures by my side. She too, I saw, had fed the hungry, cared for the sick. . . .

Master of Alkmaar, sober recorder, Rogier van der Weyden, unglamorous portraitist, with what precision do they affix their draughtsmanly edge around appearances, giving substance to things and faces, allowing their essences to transpire, as it were, through pigment. The meaning of the seven smallish panels swam up through patches of coloured surface, revealing itself to me without my having to make any effort of reflection. "They are the corporal works of mercy," I said, though I didn't know that I knew it.

152

Often pieces of art serve as ligatures to tie discrete experiences together through time and space; perhaps this is the soul of art, its form, function—to incite the projection of experience, and its publicization—the exteriorization of one's innermost reflections—so that your projection and mine can blend. Two people looking at the same devotional art, centuries apart, may arrive at the identical notion of the communion of saints, through the liberating agency of the pictures observed. This releasing action is notoriously the case of music, sometimes pretty banal music, to which we attach complexes of association of strange intensity. The popular songs of 1938, "Heigh-Ho," "Pocketful of Dreams," speak to the remembering man a generation after, as paintings do, and swarms of clustering images hang together like an infinity of bunched grapes suddenly glimpsed through the wind-lifted leaves of some extensive vine. Objects tie the interior worlds of multitudes together. Monty McNally and I used to play all through recess and lunch hour, and for extended late-afternoon sessions, with a select crowd of five or six other boys, most of them older even than Monty, down the hillside behind the schoolyard that sloped away into Reservoir Ravine. You could clamber down from the schoolyard right to the bottom of the ravine, or you could walk up Clifton Road a hundred feet or so, to the corner of Inglewood Drive, take a sharp left turn and descend from that corner behind and below the garden of a grey stone mini-mansion which once upon a time twenty years afterward was briefly the home of Dr. Miklos Skofic and his extraordinary wife, the lovely, great and famous Gina Lollobrigida. I love to fancy La Lollo, just about my favourite, looking down from her garden privacy in 1960 during her brief, comic Toronto sojourn, at what had been in my youth a sloping runway through trees, a bosky ravine retreat, in winter a sledded track, true, but in spring and summer soft and inviting as Gina herself.

Now that softly green track and sleigh run is over-paved with the asphalt of Mount Pleasant Road, has been since 1952. When Monty McNally and I, and Jim Barrow, and

the Phelan brothers, Morgan the eldest, Paul the middle
boy, and Harold, and certain other Dinky Toy enthusiasts
designed and built our extensive clay raceways down behind
the school there was only this muddy track curving down
behind Inglewood Drive, an access road for Parks Department trucks. Lying above and along this track and the
descending ravine, Rosedale and Moore Park comprised a
single region of north-central Toronto as it then was, in fact
the north end of Ward Two, with Mount Pleasant Cemetery
as the north boundary of the enclave and Bloor Street as the
outer limit on the south.

A significant element not found in this large district was a
high school. I've often wondered since why this should have
been so. I wonder if the departure of St. Andrew's College to
Aurora can have been an entirely free choice. Could it
possibly be that the residents of Rosedale and Moore Park
didn't want a high school and its discomforts—noise, high
spirits, rowdiness—planted in the middle of suburban calm?
The nearest public high school was Jarvis Collegiate, well
below Bloor. Northward, practically a Novaya Zemlya of
education was North Toronto Collegiate, where I found
myself a student in the troubled and fearful September of
1943, and nearby, well away from Moore Park, was Northern Vocational Institute. Beyond these again northeast
and northwest: Rolph Road Collegiate in Leaside, and
Lawrence Park Collegiate lying over toward Bathurst Street.

None of the private Catholic high schools were anywhere
near Rosedale or Moore Park, and after the departure of St.
Andrew's there was no boys' private academy of any kind.
There was, however, one unobtrusive campus whose nominal street address was No. 10 Elm Avenue. This was stately
Branksome Hall, one of the city's three premier girls'
private, Protestant, schools, the other being Havergal College up along Avenue Road, and Bishop Strachan on
Lonsdale.

Nine and twenty knights in all
Hung their shields in Branksome Hall.

Lines from the third stanza of the opening canto of the greatest best-seller in the history of poetry in English, Sir Walter Scott's *Lay of the Last Minstrel*. Branksome Hall was of course the seat of the Dukes of Buccleuch, that exalted line with whom Scott himself was proud to claim kinship. Older and more cynical at fifteen and sixteen, I used to take a certain satisfaction in the title of Scott's poem. I would ask myself, "What were those 29 knights doing with the girls in Branksome Hall?" As we have no access to futurity, I didn't know that my mother-in-law-to-be had attended Branksome Hall, liking the place not more than I did.

It stood there among the elms wrapped in decent obscurity, making no noise, throwing no snowballs, its quiet young ladies learning to be Christian home-makers. Thinking it over, I almost guess that a zoning ordinance had from the beginning reserved Rosedale and Moore Park for wholly residential activities. In the district there were no industrial installations, if we except the railway tracks. No cocktail lounges or theatres, or more than the tiniest of convenience stores: drugstore, dry-cleaners, beauty salon, small grocers and butchers, some of great excellence like the famous Quinn's Groceries in Moore Park.

There were churches, two small public primary schools and a private seminary for young ladies, two parks, besides the ravine walkways, and expensive private residences. And the residence of the Lieutenant-Governor until it was closed. The absence of large public secondary schools, like that of bars, theatres, stadiums and superhighways, was dictated by the influential people who lived there, churchgoers who liked it as quiet on weekdays as on Sundays. The lives of the grown-ups were not quite so centred on the church as were those of us kids in the parish school, but to speak justice of those adults, they were mighty church-minded.

A young woman journalist of the present day has bemoaned in one of the surviving Toronto dailies her incomplete understanding of big TO. She realized her ignorance, she said, because she didn't know what realtors meant when

they put the initials OLPH in their want ads. This shows a
really rather surprising ignorance (unless we are to become
completely cynical about journalists and journalism),
because what those initials mean in a want ad is that the
house for sale stands in the parish of Our Lady of Perpetual
Help, that is, in the district I've described, somewhere pretty
near to our church on the northwest corner of Clifton and St.
Clair. A house here was and remains a desirable property
whether located on Rose Park, Glenrose, Inglewood, Clifton, Heath Street, Moore Avenue (where I was to spend
many happy, impoverished days when later time came
round) or on Cornish Road, as was my second home, plainly
a desirable property though, as with my first home, only
rented. Glass doorknobs, yes! And four more very pretty
girls to add to my spreading acquaintance with females
around ten years old: Ginny Gorman, Jane Ledwidge, and
the Vrooman girls, Louise and Rose, all four living within
three doors of us, and all my age, or between my age and
Tony's.

At age seven, Tony had a dreadful attack of love for Jane
Ledwidge, possessor of beautiful, long shining red hair. It
might not have been her hair that caught Tony's eyes,
though it did mine. Big T was not the man to talk carelessly
of his infant affections, then or now. Jane Ledwidge took my
eye, though, with that flowing river of auburn tresses. She
also had a large red tricycle that we used to borrow for a
game of "busy street," which consisted of our assembling as
many wheel toys as possible, and driving them around and
around on the road in front of our four houses, narrowly
missing one another, the way you do in the Dodgem Cars at
an amusement park. We often engineered deliberate colli-
sions. Ginny Gorman, petite, extremely pretty, with a
predilection for blouses with dots on them, was a hell-for-
leather driver of her medium-sized green Eatonia trike,
didn't mind simulated, even achieved accident, and
wouldn't cry at a severely scraped knee. She was my
brother's first true girlfriend in adolescence, later marrying a

private detective who took her with him to the western seaboard of the US, a never-to-be-sufficiently-regretted departure, for Ginny grew up a beauty.

Those houses on Cornish Road were, some of them, semi-detached, but ours was separate, built sidewise on its lot such that the front door opened on the driveway, and a large, solidly built, stone and wooden-beam verandah faced the street. This verandah was unusual in that it had no steps, being enclosed on its three exposed sides, the front of the house forming the fourth side. There were attachments for full awnings, which indicated its possible use as an outdoors sleeping porch. Full screening was never installed during our brief term of residence, which from beginning to end lasted under a year. This seemed a long age to me at nine years but was in fact a month-to-month tenancy from September 1938 through mid-May 1939, surprising me now by its comparative brevity.

It was a very agreeable place to live, less drab than our house on Summerhill, very much more roomy, blessed with that spacious verandah, over whose roof hung a clutter of some species of vine. Some sort of small pink blossom appeared on these vines in the spring, as we prepared to leave the house. I remember with what poignancy I told myself that I would never know if the flowers were the product of a single freak year, or an annual Maytime visitant.

I had liked the house, hadn't wanted to move away so soon. I liked Jane Ledwidge, Ginny Gorman and both the Vrooman girls quite a lot. I had enjoyed living so close to Jim Barrow, whose house was on Moore Avenue, just at the end of our street. He was the first boy my own age with whom I formed a friendship not dictated by the fact of proximate residence. I had known him at OLPH since Junior First and had been overjoyed to find him at the end of the block, when we moved onto Cornish. We always walked to and from school together with Big T mutinously bringing up the rear. Jim slept overnight at our place several times, and I stayed with him on at least four occasions, which made me feel grown-up. Amanda Louise had often stayed with her girlfriends, and now that she had a room of her own was starting to ask her friends over for the night, something that had been out of the question when we all slept in a single room. Amanda was getting close to her teens now, an age when a young girl may reasonably claim a degree of privacy.

She got plenty of privacy on Cornish. These houses looked smallish and unassuming from the street, but were unexpectedly roomy for several reasons. We got an enormous amount of use from the verandah, eating many meals out there. There was a partially finished basement, one large gloomy panelled room. There was a third-floor attic, which enchanted us three kids. Nobody had thought to mention the existence of the third floor to us. When we moved in, and Tony, Amanda Louise and I went upstairs for the first time, we came upon the doorway and the staircase to the top floor and began to holler to the folks downstairs.

"Hey, hey, come and see what we found. Look, a secret passage, what is it, where does it go?"

"You're going to sleep up there," said my father, mounting the staircase from the ground floor.

"I'm not going to sleep up there," said Tony decisively, "am I?"

Now my mother appeared from downstairs. "Come and look," she said, leading the way to the attic, "and watch your heads here, where the stairs turn."

We followed her with traces of reluctance; there might be ghosts. None of us had lived in a three-storey house, and we were taken aback by finding further living space up where the roof ought to be. It was as if the attic existed in the fourth dimension; looking at the house from the street nobody would have guessed the existence of two large bedrooms, a bathroom, a storage room, which my mother insisted on calling "the boxroom," a term she found in cheap English novels, and several sizeable closets with sharply slanting roofs. We grew to love these remote and quasi-invisible quarters.

Amanda Louise had the front bedroom to herself; it had a little double window, which looked down onto that leafy byway, Cornish Road. It was a convenient street for children to play on, only one block; those motorists who appeared at either end were never moving at any speed, because they were returning to their homes and were therefore on the lookout for their own children and their neighbours'. No buses went up and down the street. No public transport penetrated these residential depths. The nearest TTC service was the St Clair streetcar line, just at that time being equipped with the then-new "Presidents' Model" cars, the same kind still in use on that line. The TTC was almost the first company to introduce these splended trams in the late summer of 1938, just when we were moving to Moore Park. We used to go for rides on the new cars, my mother and grandmother and us three children, along the extensive St. Clair line that September, admiring the delights of the new vehicles, their silence, smooth ride, the oddly clacking, sparking sound of the motor contacts as they opened or closed the drive-circuits, the gay paint and the tough, smooth, green leather covering the seats, the general air of modernity, of modernism, coming after generations of streetcars that retained the air, more or less, of horse-drawn vehicles, even when totally electrified.

The northeast terminus of that line was at Mount Pleasant just above Eglinton, where the cars looped round on the northeast corner just below Northern Vocational School. From thence we could catch a bus north on Mount Pleasant to Erskine Avenue. There we would alight and walk dolefully eastward to the entrance of the new Catholic cemetery, Mount Hope, where my father's mother lay buried, the first to be interred in the commodious Goderich family plot, now much more densely populated. At that epoch Mount Hope was still considered a new burial ground. Nowadays it ranges for miles eastward from the original entryway, and is just about spoken for, no further family plots for sale.

The other end of the St. Clair line was off in the exteme

west end of North Toronto, at Keele Street, past Bathurst, Christie, Lansdowne, past the St. Clair Theatre and St. Clare's parish church, not far from the theatre but spelling the patron saint's name in curiously Anglican fashion, though wholly Roman in affiliation. Afterward when I haunted the St. Clare's CYO, in pursuit of Rosemary Dunn, I spent hours in the back row of the St. Clair Theatre, first smooching, then necking, finally—it must be said—petting. The sub-deb column in the *Ladies Home Journal* was explicit in its distinctions among these terms. Smooching was plainly innocent fun; petting as plainly wasn't, was indeed, as "heavy petting," dramatically culpable. Necking was neutral.

In the definitive representation of the American teenager, the film of *Janie* which starred Edward Arnold as the father and Robert Hutton as the boyfriend, and the cutest imaginable little trick, Joyce Reynolds, in the title role, Miss Reynolds might have been thought from time to time to smooch, perhaps to neck. There was no petting in *Janie.*

Nor was there in Jane Ledwidge. Tony and I shared the attic back bedroom, facing east toward the parallel block of Clifton Road, whose gardens abutted on ours—extensive and irregular gardens, these were. Ours had been turned into a tiny golf course by Tony, who imitated my father not in his mildy satiric attention to golf, but in the more genuinely sportive aspect of the game. When we moved, Tony unearthed the set of golf clubs that Papa Archambault and my grandmother had given me on my fourth birthday. He used to call on Jane Ledwidge, with the greatest circumspection and *politesse*, clubs slung over shoulder. She would appear in a freshly laundered cotton frock in a blue or pink crisscrossed pattern; the two of them would sally into the garden to play a round of golf on a course that started at our back kitchen door, took in nine holes down to the back fence and around behind twin garages; the home nine came up to the Ledwidge's yard and returned to the starting point. Tony marked out the eighteen holes with appropriate little flags, though he was not permitted to dig actual holes in the lawn. They played course rules, such that the ball had to roll up to and tap the flagstaff on the final putt.

I often heard them quarrelling about these last strokes. Tony had only made three or four flags; they used to move on ahead of one another, advancing the flags as they played through the eighteen holes. They sounded like an old married couple. Tony was six at the time, and Jane was eight; she treated him with precocious maternal warmth.

"No Tony, you don't really mean that, no you don't. You know my ball hit the stick."

"I never saw it."

"You must have seen it; you were looking right at it. Don't be a poor sport. . . ."

This exhortation would always silence him; he was before everything else fair, and considerate of the demands of others. "No, you're right. I trust you, Jane."

I never understood how he managed to grow into such a decent person so young. I still don't. It has taken me 40 years to become as just and as easygoing about conduct as Tony was at six. What's to be gleaned from this, if not that conscience and virtue have little to do with either heredity or environment? We had the same parents, the same upbringing, but Tony was always more readily virtuous than I. It's a question of the roots of the person, too subtle to be unravelled without a lifetime's reflection.

Their voices would swim lazily to my ears. Light would glitter on young Jane's beautiful crown of red. I would stare over their heads at the abutting gardens of Clifton Road, wondering whether the streetcar stop at Moore and Mount Pleasant was really closer to the house than the one at Inglewood and St. Clair—this was a continual source of vexation to the inhabitants of our retired corner of Moore Park, the Ultima Thule of the district. Jim Barrow's house had a backyard bordering Mount Pleasant Cemetery; there was a dividing wall, quite high but not high enough to keep us from climbing on top of it and walking along, as one might on the Great Wall of China. It was made of rusticated concrete slabs, not an unimposing piece of construction, meant to mark off unambiguously the land of the living from that of those others.

There was no special need to deny entry to us boys. For whatever reason, Mount Pleasant Cemetery seemed a pastoral area, certainly calm enough and quiet, that we preferred to leave to itself, unranged by our wandering legs. We weren't superstitiously frightened; we just felt that there was little to be had out of the place. We had no mind to steal the flowers that from time to time appeared freshly coloured on graves near the Barrow backyard. Flowers meant less to me then than now. I used to kid Jim about the proximity of his darkened bedroom at night to the burial ground. It cut no ice with him.

"I don't believe in ghosts," he would state decisively.

I harboured certain doubts on the question, but said nothing about them. There was nothing at all alarming about the cemetery, or the Catholic one, Mount Hope, where I have spent a good deal of time in prayerful recollection. In the same way that I found myself in or around the splendid new romanesque parish church, recently completed under the aegis of energetic Father Regan, the creator of our enormous parish debt, I used to visit the graves of a succession of relatives, beginning with my father's mother, in a perfectly unassuming and natural way, without morbidity. It was just a thing you did, as natural as breathing.

This has always seemed to me like a sound approach to the fact of mortality; we just took it for granted, but we also took for granted the great religious truth of the communion of the living and the dead. Some sophisticated persons consider Wordsworth's poem "We are Seven" infantile babble, either the babble of the poet or of some half-mad child encountered in his peregrinations. Nothing could be more mistaken. That plain, small poem makes an emblem for the realization that our dead brothers and sisters and parents and grandparents and so on, are beside us, continuous with us, sharing our existence, not to be forgotten—in the communion of the living and the dead, easily learned in easy converse with those lying in Mount Pleasant or Mount Hope. We considered death the natural next step in the course of human action, beyond which another world rose free and illuminated. I do not think we were wrong. We weren't intimidated by cemeteries. Mount Pleasant, lying across mid-Toronto as it did, couldn't be missed or ignored if you wanted to pass from the older city down by the lakeshore toward the new suburbs that lie along the sloping ascent toward the height of land at Holland Landing, whence rivers flow either to Lake Ontario or to Lake Simcoe, depending on their source and course. To get to Hogg's Hollow and Thornhill and the towns above, Richmond Hill, Aurora, Newmarket, Maple, King, you had to pass the great cemetery of Yonge Street. In the same way the cemetery on top of Mount Royal in Montréal marks out the permanent conditions of life and death: useless to ignore them. Cemeteries and railways defined my comings and goings as a child; to these I might later add bus and streetcar lines and later on subways. Grown to manhood, I took my turn at airlines and ships, and have continued to bear in mind the relation between voyagers on wheels, on wings, on water, and those whose voyage has been temporarily stilled.

Wheels dominated our play as children. Behind and below the parish school lay the slope of a small bluff or ravine bank, which dropped down toward the bed of the ravine and the creek flowing along its length. Its soil was a loose brown clay of a very pleasant soft texture in the hands, which absorbed water readily and hardened to a near-brick. It was very plastic; you could mould and shape it. We used to wet it by peeing on it, rather than climb up to school to ask the choleric Mr. Finn for a bucket of water. Down this hillside we constructed, beginning anew each spring and fall while the vogue lasted, a complicated set of racing tracks, with banked turns of considerable ingenuity and solidly packed support for the track walls, clayey soil moulded and pounded by dozens of boys' hands, never mind the pee. Some of these tracks were 40 feet long. We made intersections and *chicanes* for them, though we didn't know that word yet, and we raced Tootsietoys and (infinitely superior in handling and balance) those model cars imported from England in the same line of goods as Meccano and Hornby trains and boats, under the brand name Dinky Toys.

Everybody knew what Dinky Toys were and strangely none of us felt embarrassed about using the word "dinky" though it suggested weird and perfect realms of silliness. "Dinky" was a girl's word, and an English schoolgirl's word at that. "How perfectly dinky," such a personage, called perhaps Charmian or Enid or Penelope, perhaps Mavis, April, Pam, might exclaim to a girl-chum during the action of a girls'-school story, replete with accounts of field hockey and other exotic pursuits, set in the purlieus of fictitious, ivied, grey-towered St. Edith's or St. Bride's. "Dinky," for heaven's sake. Dinky. Makes me snarl and curse to recall how we took those phoney Anglicisms for granted.

Nobody then thought to question the unwholesome prevalence of English or American children's toys in our play. No precursor of present-day cultural commissars, ready to impose import imposts on Meccano and Mattel, stood on guard for us and thee, O Canadian culture, warding off mass imports of Dinky Toys. We loved our model Maseratis and Ferraris, our ERA three-litres, our Auto-Union grand prix formula cars, so sweetly modelled after their full-sized prototypes as to take the most daring turns on our clayed pounded raceways in startling likeness to the originals. We modified their design. Monty McNally was the first to discover that if you filled the body of a racer with melted wax, then cooled it in your refrigerator till it was firm and hard, the car would hold the raceway in truly incredible style, making turns that were impossible without the added weight.

The tires—I ought to write the word as tyres—of these models were demountable. You could buy little cardboard boxes of replacement tires in case of split, crack, theft. Tony used to steal the tires from my two cherished model racers and chew them like gum. This drove me frantic. I'd be up in our attic bedroom strangling my brother and cursing at the top of my lungs during the lunch hour, having come home at noon to find all five tires from my blue Lancia sports *decapotable* missing, as if the little model had been put up on blocks for the winter. Tony's jaws would be working unobtrusively, suspiciously. A furious glare from me and he would start up the stairs on his escape-attempt. I often wondered why he did that; it cut off his line of retreat. He'd have done better to whip out the front door and off down the street, forgoing his dessert, but also avoiding near-throttling and many punches in the face.

He may have had some nutritional deficiency expressed in the form of a craving for Dinky Toy tires. He chewed mine at all times, and to do him justice they were chewy enough, rubbery and solid with a faint flavour of wintergreen. The tires on Tootsietoys would not come off so conveniently; they hadn't the enthusiastic hobbyist and collector in mind at the American company in the same way that the Dinky Toy people in England had. The English have that disturbed streak of infantilism which allows grown men to collect Dinky Toys and long for the complete set, a psychological phenomenon not found in the US. You couldn't tune up a Tootsietoy.

I was the one who found out that you could file the tread off Dinky Toy tires with a nail-file, so that they were completely smooth. This effected a distinct improvement in speed and a certain loss in road-holding qualities, which could be permitted in the interest of beating the clock on the final straightaway down the hillside into the ravine. We would have a timer crouched down there, without a real stopwatch of course, we couldn't have afforded that, but we did have access to a couple of old pocket watches with second hands, and we could time a descent pretty closely. Then we would note the timings carefully in old scribblers. There were different categories of racers. My blue Lancia was treated as what would now be called a 2000cc sports tourer, suitable for rallying or for use on tracks when modified to race. My other car was a superb toy version of Rudolf Caracciola's Auto-Union Grand Prix championship design, as raced in 1938 and 1939 at the Nürburgring. I got this car for my birthday in 1939, among other items, including two cardboard boxes full of tires. My parents were afraid I'd do Tony some violent injury if he didn't stop eating all the tires, and I didn't stop forcing him to spit them up by squeezing his throat while banging his head on the attic floor.

Nobody ever managed to get out of my brother what he found so tasty about these rubber morsels, or whether he swallowed them as a matter of fixed policy. I think he used to spit them in the toilet surreptitiously, after his teeth had rendered them unrecognizable in form. He was known to be a regular swallower of wads of bubblegum, which gave Mme. Archambault great offence, caused her to worry. She knew that Tony had been a favourite with her husband, and when she visited us now and then in the late thirties, when no longer in full residence, she would inquire with elaborate circumlocution about the more or less vulcanized condition of Tony's intestinal tract, as she imagined it, plainly sicklied o'er with gum arabic.

"Isabelle, that boy will have a blockage. He eats tires. Matt says so, and while Matt is troublesome he is not a liar. He is simply of a violent nature. He bangs the child's head on the floor, *boum, boum, comme ça. On aura une crise craniale, je te promets.*"

"Tony spits the tires out. I find them all over the house."

"For your sake, my child, I devoutly hope so."

My mother would say, "We'll have to face what comes. The tires are small."

"But physically indestructible, my dear. Have a care."

"Of course, Mamma."

"But did I tell you what the Archbishop said to Father Lamarche about the debt on Perpetual Help? He says that Father Regan has involved himself too deeply with the banks. . . ." Intimations of grave parochial disquiet would follow, and the state of Tony's colon would lapse from the foreground of the conversation.

"Easter collections, Pentecostal collections. And then there's always Peter's Pence."

"Peter's Pence are falling down," said my father, coming abruptly into the kitchen.

"Mais voyons, cher Andrew, je te comprends pas."

I would have been deeply disturbed if I had believed that he was poisoning himself with tires, having as most children do at nine or ten deeply divided feelings about my brother and sister. At some level of experience I might have wanted Tony to die, but his death would have broken up the structure of my personality so badly that I would not have arrived in early adolescence fit to traverse that awful stage of life. If this is love, I loved Amanda and Tony for the opportunities they provided for me to discipline my feelings. Rage at Tony wasn't the same as rage at Jakie Forbes or Eddie Reilly; it had a privileged character, being less criminal and less impersonal than the wish to stun some schoolfellow with a rock. Family love and hate: intense, privileged, unrelieved. I've never felt for another man what I've felt for Tony. When he ate the tires off my Lancia *decapotable*, I wished him dead at all levels of mental existence, conscious, subconscious, unconscious, and knew at the same time that he must not die, that if that were to happen I would have to punish myself by leaping into the grave hole.

We were unlike. We've never made an easy identification; the family recognized as soon as Tony arrived that I was the recollective one, and he the narrator. Thus when some person misbehaved at school, I was the one to ponder the sources of the ill-conduct, to comment that the bad boy was also a poor boy who wore patched clothes, whose father was unemployed. Tony would make the events of the broken window and later strapping into a vivid tale of crime and punishment.

"And then when Miss McHale gave him the slugs, you

should have heard him bawl. Paul Wickett told on him. Our class is out to get Paul Wickett."

"What, you bunch of squirts?"

"Gerry O'Shea is big."

"He's dumb though; that's why he's still in Junior First."

"Grade One."

"Oh, don't be a smart-alex. Junior First."

"Next year it'll be Grade One, and I'll be in Grade Three, and so will Gerry O'Shea."

"That's the only way he'll ever get to skip a grade, when they change the whole school around."

"He's bigger than anybody in your class. His hands stick out of his sleeves. He could beat up on you."

"On me?"

"Sure he could."

This remark would plunge me into deep waters of reflection, as Tony knew with perfect clarity. It was about this time that I began to see that my behaviour was as transparent to him as his to me. You can't really lie to your brother or sister.

"Matt loves Alanna. Matt kissed Alanna Begin. Hey Ginny, hey Jane, Matt kissed Alanna in the ravine."

Nasty cold stare from Ginny. Dirty damned kid brother.

I'd been sitting alone after school halfway down the largest of the clay raceways behind the school on the late afternoon of the third day of April 1939, pondering the seemly fact that Holy Week had come round again. Yesterday had been Palm Sunday and the weather promised a superb Easter season. At that time I was forming the strong chain of associations that united the weather of early spring with the hope of resurrection, in the recesses of my imagination. A year had passed since the day I had ruined Alanna Begin's dress and been strapped for it, seen Mr. McCoy dressed in white tie and tails near the Eucharistic repository, collected blotters from the representatives of the Beverly. Now I wore new Sisman's Scampers. There was sand in my stockings collected from roadways recently cleared of winter ice. Those first two weeks of April in Toronto, what pure bliss they were, warm but never hazy, windy, permitting one to open his windbreaker and feel the air rushing through the woollen sweater.

I wondered where the other guys were, then realized that I could hear loud voices coming from the softball diamond on the school playground. I picked up my Auto-Union racer and quietly spun the wheels; might have been miles out of town.

For some reason an immense sadness invaded my feelings. A year since last Easter. I'd be nine years old soon. I was starting to have a history.

"What are you doing down there?"

I looked up at the edge of the playground 25 feet above me. Framed in a bright sky a girl was standing there, her face and the colours of her dress and cardigan hard to distinguish.

"Who's that?" I said with some surliness.

"It's me," she said scrambling down the hill.

It was Alanna Begin.

"Don't kick in the side of the track," I said commandingly. "It took us ages to pack it down."

"Poor Matt. Won't the other boys race with you any more?"

"Certainly they will. It's only that there's baseball now. Everybody wants to play softball the first while; they'll be back racing next week . . . or no they won't . . . we have holidays next week. But the guys will want to race again after the holidays."

"Don't you like baseball, Matt?"

I affected a manly incapacity. "I trun me arm out," I said. It was a conventional explanation; nobody ever paused to think what it meant. You went out to a park that first bright, dry day of spring, and galloped joyfully across the wide outfield in pursuit of fly balls. After the catch, or more usually after the ball had rolled to a stop, the flychaser would relay it to the infield with a mighty and inexpert heave, then clutch his shoulder in real or simulated discomfort. "Trun me arm out." I said that because I wasn't much of a ballplayer, and preferred activities more suited to my temperament, like clocking cars and tabulating times.

"I'll race with you," said Alanna.

I took a long look at her, wondering what her motives could be. We had no special link that I knew of. She looked just the same as always, very slightly overweight, big brown eyes, plenty of taffy-coloured hair. Fair. Fair. The same age as me almost to the day. Her family lived on Rose Park Drive halfway between Inglewood and Clifton, a block much used for skating by neighbourhood kids because it was long, free of traffic and a fairly steep slope. Saturday morning was roller-skating time; we might put in four to five hours of it. I remember that Alanna's father ran a translating service out of which he must have done pretty well. Their place in Rose Park must even then have been well up in the five-figure class, with large gardens front and back, and plentiful shrubbery.

"You don't have a car to race," I said positively.

"I could get one from my brother."

This was undeniably correct. She had a brother a couple of years older than we were, a slow learner only a grade ahead of us, Tommy Begin, the first boy I ever knew to have a greenstick fracture, which he toted around in a sling all that spring. He broke his arm falling out of bed, which suggests the quality of his ill-coordinated physical movements. He was an engaging-looking fellow, Tommy, and had sometimes raced his inferior Tootsietoys against us, with the predictable results. It was his slight lack of physical coordination, endemic in the Begin children, that had caused me to eye Alanna with misgiving as she picked her way hesitantly down the hill. She was not as clumsy as her brothers, but *much* clumsier than her big sister Claire, who had reached early adolescence and lost all of the traditional Begin clodhopper's stance, exchanging it in some wonderful way for a supremely female grace. The parish should have

been prepared for the sensation created by the sudden alteration in Claire Begin's appearance as she matured. Her
mother had been sweetly pretty, and Mr. Begin, not in any
sense a handsome man, was nonetheless powerfully, even
ruggedly constructed. He had the conformation of a totem
pole and qualities that in the US are called Lincolnesque.

This combination had issued, in Claire Begin, in an extraordinary kind of looks, what I would call rugged
sweetness, if that didn't sound like utter nonsense. She had
her father's strong and slightly off-centre frame, and her
mother's girlish delicacy; the combination proved devastating for more than 40 years. More. More.

Alanna wasn't yet nine, but as I squinted at her carefully
in the late afternoon sun, of which we got a full measure sitting on the west face of that low hill, I could see certain hints
and fast flying tones suggestive of her glorious sister. I didn't
then grasp what these were suggestions of. I matured very
late in this direction and at that period had no formed notion
of the sexual aspect of woman's beauty. I used to stare at
Alanna and her sister from a distance of three pews in church
on many occasions during Holy Week, expecially on Easter
Sunday, wondering what caused my gaze to fix itself again
and again on the back of Claire Begin's skirt. There seemed
to be something about the shape of that part of her clothes
that drew the eye, some breath-stopping fragility of line, that
arrested sight. I didn't think of this as in any way related to
the live girl's body under the cloth. I just wanted to stare at
her skirt for an obscure reason that made me feel like crying.

Who knows, I thought, sitting there in the late sun, maybe
Alanna has the same shape, or will have when we're older. I
ought to be nice to her. This suspicion smacked of disloyalty
to my male companions. I couldn't have justified it to
Morgan Phelan, certainly would have been deeply ashamed
to reveal it to Mostyn McNally, who was about to graduate
from Jarvis Collegiate with highest honours. Mostyn would
recognize nothing, I sensed, wrongly, of what I was feeling,
would probably think shameful abasement of this kind before

woman or girl. I wished Alanna would go away somewhere.

"Tommy wouldn't let you have one. And anyway he's only got that one fire-engine that can race with us."

With the sorcerer's cunning sleight-of-hand she produced the very vehicle. "I've got it right here." I saw that she had been planning this meeting, and the awareness distressed, pained and oddly pleased me. "Oh all right, let's see it, and I'll tell you if it'll go at all. The wheels might be clogged."

She got up from where she was sitting, handed me the fire engine and twisted round, looking for marks of dirt and trickling water, bits of twigs and grass. I looked involuntarily at the back of her skirt as it passed my eyes. It did look a bit like her sister's.

She came and sat right beside me. I could feel her side pressed against mine. I turned the little red toy around in my hands. The imprinted trade mark *Tootsietoy* registered itself sharply in my sight. Somehow or other a lot of Alanna's hair had blown across my ear and face. It tickled.

Until now I'd always adopted the posture of a child before its mother, where women were concerned, or else that of the ham-fisted and fumbling servitor. I'd half-consciously cast myself in a submissive role. My real-life mother paid no attention to this; she ignored it and insisted on my behaving toward her like any other adult male. Mrs. Bannon, however, relished my supplications and seemed ready to baby me as much as I'd stand for it. Poor woman, she must have missed her husband, so early and unexpectedly dead. She couldn't baby Georgie-Balls, who was always out playing some sport. She would sit me on her lap, when I was three or four, and croon to me in half-formed words—an action never performed by my own mother. When I began to attach my interests to girls my own age, or close to it, I either picked those who in the natural course of events would pay no attention to me, barely even see me, like Letty Millen, or others who stood to me in the classical pose of distant princess, like Bea Skaithe.

When Alanna Begin sat down beside me, pressed her flank

against mine and allowed her scented hair (cocoanut-oil shampoo) to flow across my field of vision, I was alarmed in an unprecedented way. It almost seemed as if she were after *me*, begging me to take command of the situation and dominate her, the way my father very occasionally did with Amanda Louise, never with my mother, never with Mme. Archambault.

I turned and looked straight into her face, then I exhaled explosively and blew her hair off my face. "You're making me sneeze," I complained, and she leaned forward and kissed me. I suddenly realized, without in the least being able to express the conception in words, why she was so bad in art class. There were elements brimming in her person that wouldn't go into watercolour on cheap art paper, couldn't be figured in cutouts of Christmas trees or bunnies. A larger, more capacious art form would have had to be put before Alanna in order to confine the intensity of her almost-nine-year-old passions.

Her lips on mine felt unbelievably soft and delicately grained, exactly like rose petals, a comparison that troubled me then because I suspected that it was a cliché. Now I just accept the fact; her lips were really as soft and dry and exciting to taste and touch with my own lips as rose petals would have been if I'd been in the habit of tasting them.

I could hear Tommy's red Tootsietoy rolling away behind us to the end of the track. I hoped it wouldn't get lost and was amazed at how clearly I could hear the squeaking of its wheels, a tiny sound to pick up at 30 feet and receding . . . we kissed again . . . a third time . . . and clung to each other happily, enjoying very fully this fleet of new sensations.

"You're the nicest boy in the parish," said Alanna softly. I knew this wasn't so, but was glad to have it said. "You look so nice in your soutane on Sundays. My mother says you might have a vocation, do you think so?"

I thought not. "No, Alanna," I said, squeezing her in my arms, excited by how soft and, as it were, compressible, she was; "no, I don't have a vocation." That was something all

the boys in the parish watched for anxiously, like an out-
break of spots. This sounds flippant, but I don't mean it to
be so. A vocation was deemed by us to have the fixed,
unalterable and irrevocable course of one of the diseases of
childhood or early adolescence. You knew when you had it,
and what would happen to you because of it. Sometimes during the more perfervid penitential seasons of the liturgical
year, at Lent or during Advent, we might pray for vocations,
our own or others'.

I used to hope secretly, whilst public prayer for vocations
was going on, that God's choice would fall on somebody else,
anybody but me. I didn't want to become a priest because,
as I saw it, priests weren't interested in trains or cars or
planes, and never got out much, and lived in gloomy rec-
tories with uninteresting steel engravings of Renaissance
masters on the walls, and a lot of brown fabric glued to those
walls in lieu of gay wallpaper.

"I'm only on the altar because of my family," I said, giggling, "and besides priests don't get to kiss girls as nice as
you." This sally, which rose unbidden to my lips, made me
feel more sure of myself, and bolder. I raised my right hand,
lifted the forefinger and stroked Alanna's cheek with it, on
the downy soft place beside and below her left ear. Much was
certainly implied in the difference between boys and girls. I
felt much older and bigger while I stroked her cheek. I found
myself saying over and over, "Baby darling, baby darling,"
with no wish to convey a clear meaning. We rocked back and
forth and were happy and calm and quiet.

I was looking up at Alanna, being seated slightly below her
on the hillside. Squinting through clouds of baby-fine hair I
suddenly saw somebody standing at the top of the hill spying
on us. A boy, but which boy? I couldn't tell because he had
the sky at his back and was nothing but a purple shadow. A
horrible yell fell upon us from above.

"Haw haw haw haw, Matt's kissing Alanna. Matt loves
Alanna. Matt loves bad Begin. Goody goody Goderich loves
Bad Begin. Haw haw."

These nasty cries died away as our observer fled to spread his news.

"I'll walk home with you, Alanna."

She got up and shook out her skirt and I helped her brush it off. "Where did I put my books? Oh gosh, they're in the lunchroom I wonder if it's still open? I'll bet Mr. Finn has locked up."

"Come on, I'll race you." We scrambled up the hillside. I suddenly thought of Tommy's fire-engine and had to go back for it, and when I started to climb again Alanna was already disappearing over the top of the slope. I climbed fast, puffing, and chased after her across the playground toward the girl's door, where a small mob of teasing softball players already surrounded Alanna.

"Let me through, I've got to get my books. I've got to get into the lunchroom, oh, I'm late, my mother will kill me." I saw that Eddie Reilly and his brother Maurice were holding her back and without thinking about what I was doing I grabbed Eddie by the shoulder and pulled him backward away from her side, at the same time giving him a sharp elbow in the chest.

Maurice Reilly, a round-faced peaceable fair-haired child, stared at me in horror. His brother was notoriously the toughest kid in the parish, and would now simply eat me alive. I guess poor Maurice had now and then been the object of his brother's pummelings, and knew their painful directness too well. His eyes were like saucers.

Alanna darted through the girls' entrance.

Eddie Reilly squinted at me with horrible menace. His squint was caused by severe near-sightedness, but nobody knew anything about that in those days. I don't suppose Eddie Reilly had an optically correct pair of glasses till he was grown up. This did not inhibit his punching power, however. He squared his feet professionally and hit me on the nose with great force. It hurt like hell. Then he hit me in the pit of the stomach with the other hand, knocking my wind out and causing me to double up. Then he hit me on the back of the head with his loaded schoolbag, flattening me on the gravel, into which my face was pressed by the impetus of the fall. My cheeks were mightily scratched. Eddie kicked me in the side once or twice over the protests of the small crowd, mostly girls, then walked off bound for home.

My head was making that noise that crickets make in trees in May, a ringing, trilling, electrical buzz. My eyes were smarting from the cuts on my face but thank the Lord I wasn't crying. Two big girls who were friends of Amanda helped me to my feet; one of them wiped my face with her sleeve.

"That Eddie is going to get it one of these fine days. You should get your father to report him."

At that moment a maxim took clear shape in my mind, continuing to illuminate my behaviour thereafter, apparently in perpetuity: if you've lost a fair open fight, write it off. Don't complain; don't try to get the decision reversed. People will respect you for this.

This maxim is doubtless neither right nor wrong, but is simply a guide to feeling and to conduct. I sensed obscurely while I was wiping my face and feeling like a hero, waiting for Alanna, that by risking combat with Eddie, who notoriously had me out-gunned, I had in some sort established myself as a person willing to take various kinds of risks in the interests of higher motives, such as protecting fair young womanhood. I haven't the least idea where I got this chivalrous, possibly incorrect motive. It might have been from reading. That year I read several books by Joseph Conrad including *Lord Jim, Chance*, which I couldn't make head or tail of, and a very agreeable work called *Victory*, in which a supremely detached hero gave his life to protect an innocent and defenceless young woman. Their first embrace had been rendered, in Conrad's subtly nuanced prose, in much the same terms as my first delightful coming-together with Alanna—the first kiss, especially, in *Victory* had been like our kiss, tentative, only half-intended, marvellously sweet because surprisingly dry. I now saw myself, I suspect, as Conrad's

Heyst, though we had little in common. I was just not quite nine years old, and I hadn't understood that novel.

A flock of big girls and two little boys stood staring at my dripping cheeks. "That's a lot of blood," said a small boy admiringly.

"It's nothing," I said. I was learning.

Then she reappeared in the entryway, schoolbag in hand. Holding onto each other, we walked out of the schoolyard and up Clifton to the corner of Rose Park where we parted, not quite swearing eternal ties. "Go straight home," said Alanna in strongly and vitally maternal tones, which made me suspect that active lovemaking might end in passive cuddling; she was taking a high, possessive line. "Come and roller-skate on Saturday. It'll be Easter Saturday. No church, or not much."

There was only the lighting of the Paschal Candle and some few other oddments of the liturgy of Holy Week remaining on Holy Saturday, the liturgical explosion, so to speak, having eventuated on the preceding Wednesday and Thursday, and on Good Friday—the Mass of the Pre-Sanctified—the single day in the year, at that epoch, on which you couldn't receive Holy Communion. No consecration of the Host took place on Good Friday. At the Mass of the Pre-Sanctified the priest consumed a consecrated Host of the day before, taken from the side-altar repository. That Mass wasn't therefore a true Mass, but an enactment of the sacred service without the mystery at its heart that animated it and made it sacred. I was always powerfully impressed by the vacant and ghostly feeling of that unique Friday rehearsal.

Alanna was right to surmise that the Saturday which followed our falling in love, as she called it, greatly to my embarrassment, would be relatively free from ritual observance. When I got home that Monday night, after promising stoutly to come and play with her on Saturday, not much minding the prospect because her street was the best in the whole of Moore Park for coasting on roller-skates, my mother was obliged to retract her promise to allow me to attend Tenebrae during the ensuing Holy Week. She thought my face too bruised and contused and scratched, altogether too warlike and comic in aspect, for those solemn evenings. The word "Tenebrae" was another of the deeply resonant, poetic words that cluttered my verbal imagination as a boy. I knew it wasn't a Scotch word, but its final syllable got foolishly linked in my ears with the banks and braes of Bonnie Doon, and those other braes, Maxwellton's, sacred to Annie Laurie. There were Maxwellton's braes, and those of Bonnie Doon, and then there were Tenebraes, all mixed up.

Sometime later, Amanda Louise, then beginning the study of Latin, informed me that the word was the plural of "tenebra" which she construed as "shadow." And years later, when a literary critic spoke in my hearing of Virgil's "cool tenebrous excellence," the anglicized adjectival form resonated loud and clear in my thrilled ears. The word was so pleasingly evocative, running together Virgil, Our Lady of Perpetual Help Church, Maxwellton's braes, the colour green, which had somehow or other got mixed in—because I had concluded that anything tenebrous would have to be green. A tenuous but far-flung net of implication.

This sort of cross-referencing was always happening to me and even more, I guess, to Tony, to whom a new word that put him in mind of other, older, words was sometimes an incitement to pleasure so keen that it could actually give him an itch. I've seen Tony, upon hearing some delightful new polysyllable, actually put his hand up between his shoulderblades to scratch the major nervous ganglion located there.

Tenebrae. Mme. Archambault and my mother and now Amanda Louise as well, together with multitudes of McCoys and Begins and other members of the Altar Society, Rosars, Holdships, O'Connors, many ladies in flowered Sunday dresses, would be over in the parish hall in the church basement, where the Holy Name Communion Breakfasts and the Altar Boys' Banquet were held, arranging masses of spring flowers against the decking forth of the high altar on Easter

178

Sunday. The smell of pollen and of incense would be thick in the vestry, where Bob White strove to ignite the compressed block of fragrant solid staff at the bottom of his censor, while Father Regan eyed the lad with authoritative misgiving in his glance.

They wouldn't let me go that year, not unless my face healed unnaturally fast. I considered it heartless of my father to laugh as he did, while contemplating the nine scratches striped by the gravel across my cheeks and the badly skinned bridge and nostrils of my poor nose.

"He did all this for love?" said my father in tones that I didn't understand then, though I do now. They were admiring tones; he was pleased with me, but I didn't feel this then. I thought he was teasing. He turned to me. "Never mind about Tenebrae, Matt. I agree with your mother, I don't think you should go because by Wednesday those bruises will be purple and yellow—Easterish enough in all conscience— and you'll create a distraction."

"It must have hurt," said Amanda lovingly. I saw suddenly that the family weren't angry at me or making fun of me. They seemed strangely to approve of my having attempted combat with Eddie.

"It's remarkable," said my father, more or less at large, "how often you can win by losing." He smiled at my mother. "There's a Scriptural application . . . whether I should draw it out is questionable."

Amanda caught it quickly. She said, "Whosoever shall lose his life shall find it. Isn't that what you mean, Dad?"

She was always an ardent student of the Catechism, leading an imaginative life if possible more deeply immersed in the dramatic properties of Catholic ritual than anybody in the family, Mme. Archambault alone excepted. People sometimes used to wonder whether Amanda had a vocation to the sisterhood, but she didn't.

My father didn't answer her directly. "The sayings of Our Lord are inexhaustible," he said quietly. I wouldn't care to give the impression that his professional interests had left him a mocker or an anti-Christian thinker. He was a reverent man, slow to speak questioningly of received religious institutions. Mind you, his tone varied from very light to very dark. He was rarely solemn, sometimes might have sounded frivolous, even mocking, to those who knew him only slightly. He never did anything to undermine right thinking and right feeling among us kids, or anything that might unsettle our minds. His legacy to the world includes three of the most secure persons imaginable. My sister Amanda Louise is so secure that her family and friends often complain about it.

She was really quite sweet to me about the fight with Eddie, glad that I'd undertaken this possibly misguided chivalrous action, attributing to me a more definitely planned inclination to fight than I'd actually had. When I'd bumped Eddie in the ribs with my elbow, it had been almost a reflex action, which surprised me as much as him. Those few seconds during which he'd stood squinting and deciding where to strike first were among the most existentially weird of my life, moments without fear or apprehension but replete with grave certitude. The die had been cast.

I saw during this Monday night debate over my going to Tenebrae with bruised and battered mug that one's family isn't at all a snake pit, a dreadful teeming writhing tangle of hatreds and conflicts. Quite the contrary. My family supported me strongly over the Eddie Reilly fight and Alanna's crush on me—for that was what it was.

They were disagreeably familiar at that epoch with the disguises and ramifications of love in its passionate aspect, with tinges of sexuality, infantine or senescent. In my father's thinking, and in his calculations about a means of livelihood for us and for himself, physical and romantic love just then played a paramount role. He had left the university in the previous June, received a small capital sum in settlement of his claim against the faculty's primitive pension system, and had selected that moment to move from Summerhill Avenue because Mr. Faucett proposed to raise the rent ten dollars a month. Feeling it necessary to hold the rent line in face of impending joblessness, he'd scouted around energetically and located our Cornish Road house at the same monthly figure he'd been paying through the thirties, $40, but only on a month-to-month tenancy. He got the place, I learned later, because its owner, a retired bank inspector, had died very suddenly just at this time, and the house was unoccupied pending its disposition as part of his estate.

Through the winter of 1938–39, various individuals of a legal cast of countenance would come around in the evenings to have a look at this valuable property. They would have copies of the Ward Two assessment rolls in their hands, and duplicates of the formal title to the house, vested in the estate of the late Mr. McCabe. My parents would look uneasy during these visitations, and we children found them distinctly unsettling. We never felt absolutely at home on Cornish Road because of this pall of impermanence which drooped over our tenancy. We all knew that we would shortly be moving on, when once my father had roused himself from the spell of inaction that plagued him, another very Conradian motif strongly streaked through the wash of family feeling at this period. I think of that winter, and the spring that ensued, as somewhat inane time, when many decisions and resolutions were gathering to their head, though not yet ready to declare their tendency. An analyst of our mode of living in the spring of 1939, observing my father's repeated attempts to begin a new course of life at almost 40—he never forgot that he was coeval with the century and wouldn't likely survive it—might well have treated our private agonies in appropriately Conradian diction: dim retired indecisions eddying below the keels of sheltered schooners moored up elbows of nameless creeks, paralyses of will induced by the failure of self-image and overt behaviour to coincide. I never understood at that time how my dad could have left the university as a socialist, then gone into business for himself.

Yet that is what he did. He marked time, as the whole of modern history marked time that evil winter—there may even have been a real connection, the individual man's paralysis of will a feeble reflection of the general political situation, as the socialist impulses and the reactionary politics generated by the depression seemed locked in a struggle whose end was hidden from view. Where 1936, 1937, 1938, had been starred by successive decisive strokes from the dictators, this year, in which we now found ourselves collecting our wits and preparing for new modifications of personal or political power balances, began in relative serenity. Dad sat at home, pondering the possibility of writing a third book, which would earn him nothing whatsoever, as had been the case with his earlier works. He decided to forsake authorship in favour of more obviously gainful work, counted up his diminishing capital and began to think of launching himself in a small independent service business of the kind he had described in *Property and Value* and even earlier in *The Place of Conceptual Thought in Ethical Judgments.*

I want to indicate the terrain of his choices, so to speak, quite clearly. My father thought at that time—in contradistinction to views he came to hold later on in public life—that a fully socialized economy wasn't so much philosophically as practically undesirable. He would not defend the institution of private property where it swelled to institutional size—as in slum landlordships or the ownership of private investment banks, department stores, industrial powers or the great natural resources like water power, petroleum or the airwaves. These major sources of wealth and production he saw as necessarily common, and fully socializable in ownership. He did not believe that small farmers, home owners, certain small-scale services like restaurants or dressmakers, could be sensibly organized in common. Nor could the arts; he criticized very harshly the idea of artists' soviets.

He would say, "I don't see how a piece of art could be produced in common; that would be contradictory to its nature."

But all the same he would strictly maintain that although a

painter or a story-teller could legitimately offer his work for sale to maintain himself and his independence—in the primary sense of getting his living from it—all valuable work in the arts derived from our common humanity, was ethically vested in it and should revert to public ownership at some decent time after the death of the artist.

In *Property and Value* he devoted an entire chapter to the paradoxical case, as he considered it, of the artist's property right in his work.

> Proprietorship in the fine arts [he wrote] constitutes the limiting case in analysis of the notion of private property, unless we are to consider our bodies as our property, for only our bodies are more intimately held by us than the products of our most disciplined reflection upon, and expression of, our experience. For when we speak of "our" experience, we use the possessive adjective naturally and correctly. One's experience is non-transferable; nobody can take a bath for you. But nobody will treat his direct experience as his possession, any more than his person or his body, for it is our persons, our self-embodiments, that act as the subjects of our instinct to possess. All this is undeniable. We don't possess our bodies, our experience, our lives. We act them. We do them. We are them. Now action in the arts, especially when powerful, intense, meritorious, seems in some way to partake of our self-embodiment, and equally we do not possess our works. They are an extension of our agency; the brush is a longer, more finely tipped finger. . . .

He went on after this idealistic beginning to divide the question of the various kinds of ownership that might be thought to hold sway over a painting, a story, a piece of sculpture by an unknown artist of the eleventh century, and so on, and wrote more effectively on the question than anyone in North America, at least, had done up till that time. Of course I'm somewhat biased in his favour, but I think that the question, "Who owns art?" is still best approached in my father's way. In effect he held that it was a special case of ownership, wholly psychologized, and unlike the so-called ownership of investment capital.

He was better equipped to think such a matter through than I am. But he couldn't feed his family by sitting on our verandah and thinking about a third book on the question of the title to the arts. We all kept getting hungry and bringing our large appetites home for him to assuage, while his small stock of money shrank over the winter, and the estate of the late Inspector McCabe came closer to final settlement, at which time we would either have to vacate our house or buy it, and the second alternative was out of the question.

By about February of 1939, he'd decided to liquidate his possessions, borrow money from his father, and open a small restaurant in a summer resort 50 miles north of Toronto on the genial shore of Lake Simcoe. From the perspective of a later generation, the decision seems ludicrous, almost impossible to understand. No university professor of today would undertake such a course. Food service? Restaurant operation? And him an author? Impossible!

The extreme unlikelihood of such an action, as it seems to us now, clarifies the distance between ourselves now and ourselves then, because it seemed a very reasonable thing to do at the time. Dad was interested in the nature of small businesses; he had had quite enough of teaching for the time being; there was no place for him in government as there might be today, and no opportunity to appear on the CBC and lay down the law on public affairs, as is all too often the career choice of the disillusioned professor of our own time.

He went downtown and wandered around on Wellington Street and Front Street, looking up at the captivating display windows of the great warehouses and wholesale emporia. He knew little about the restaurant business, and didn't have sufficient capital to provide underpinning for the operation he had in mind, but he started to visit the showrooms and offices of firms that rented cutlery, glassware, tables and chairs, coffee urns . . . and he began to have an entrancing experience of a kind seldom vouchsafed to those who pass their lives in the academy, the inside knowledge of an intensely experimental, pragmatic business.

He found his way into Cassowarys' Limited, on Front Street, and from the moment he paused at the entrance to the display rooms he was lost. He discovered that this firm supplied every conceivable kind of china dinnerware, glassware, cutlery, table linen, salt and pepper shakers, everything required for restaurant or guest-home operation, for hotel work, tourist cabins, an entire industry. There were illustrated catalogues showing all ranges and sizes of objects to drink from: tumblers, cocktail glasses, Coca-Cola glasses, sundae dishes, snifters. There was no turning back.

Like many men whose learning and discipline are mainly seated in the intelligence, he had a rooted respect—amounting almost to awe—for men who know how to manage practical affairs: carpenters, construction workers, cooks, plumbers, restaurateurs, automobile mechanics. This admiration has descended to his children; nobody has more respect for *métier*, and command of one's *métier*, than Tony, unless it be me. This is why I've been so interested all my life in the way things in fact get done, what a drypoint is, what gouache is made of.

The helpful staff of Cassowarys' Limited gave my father an immense amount of information about restaurant management, to the point where he began to feel that he had effective command of the subject, a fatal error. I have a hatred of amateurism, in the arts, in cookery, in food service, and I remember vividly various resort hotels operated by husband-and-wife teams with a small capital, who proposed to make up for their incompetence and lack of understanding of the meduim by "personal service," which invariably meant chattiness, slow service, lukewarm food, damp beds.

My parents weren't guilty of quite this blunder; they were too sensitive to nuance and to their customers' reactions.

While he was running a restaurant, my father made a point of leaving the customers alone to enjoy solitude or private conversation, or simply the taste of what they were eating. He preferred to remain invisible unless called for, shielded by an enormous, baroque cash-register, which he rented for the summer, bronzed, gilt, mirrored and capacious, plenty large enough to hide behind.

Now for finance, he thought, during that becalmed spring while the rest of Toronto decked itself with bunting, and shaky bleachers were erected in unlikely and unhandy locations throughout the city in anticipation of the Royal Visit, timed to take place in mid-spring, so that the royal pair might enjoy the running of the King's Plate and present the royal 50 guineas personally in a handsome purse to the owner of the winner.

Dad paid no heed to bunting or bleachers. He meant to have us out of town and well launched on his summer enterprise by the first great holiday weekend, which would be close to the twenty-fourth of May, Victoria Day, Fireworks Day, which occurred, as it happened, in the middle of the week, in 1939. It was a Wednesday, an omen which I'd have meditated most carefully if I'd been thinking of opening a restaurant. It appears that the success or failure of such an undertaking, at a summer resort, depends almost wholly on your takings through fifteen weekends from Victoria Day, as it used to be known, to Labour Day. It's in effect a throw of the dice against the weather probabilities. I suppose Dad had thought of this; perhaps he felt private qualms when it came home to him that Victoria Day was a Wednesday, and that therefore few people would travel to Lake Simcoe to open their cottages on that one-day holiday.

He had determined, however, at some point in the late winter, that he would conclude a lease with the owners of a restaurant property located on the main street of Jackson's Point.

"A beautiful location, look at it," he would exclaim, indicating the property in photographs the lessors had mailed to him. "You can easily park on that sort of boulevard there, see? Right in front of the door."

A very large electric sign over the entrance said LAZY BAY GRILL.

. "What about that sign, Dad? Will they re-paint it?"

"No, no, no, we'll leave the name the same. You see, there's an element called goodwill—the reputation of the place from before, the way people think about it. Who knows, there might be people from Toronto or Hamilton or London, Ontario, with cottages on the lake, all just dying to get to the Lazy Bay Grill for a soda. We don't want to confuse them by changing the name, for this year anyway."

This remark made me see that he meant to stay in the restaurant business permanently, and I wonder what plans he had for the ensuing winter. Whatever they were, they cannot have included its peculiar reality. He had no idea—cannot in the nature of intelligence and history have formed any conception—that late 1939 would bring the terrible changes in all our lives that it finally did. It's a very good thing that our future is a closed book to us. Dad fully expected to mount a successful restaurant operation that summer, then spend the next winter planning the development and expansion of his business. I don't see what else he could have had in mind. Meanwhile, Victoria Day would be on Wednesday, 24 May, and he had to get busy and borrow additional capital, most likely from his father, to underwrite the purchase of inventory: coffee, tea, ice cream, candy, sugar, fresh vegetables, meat, salt and pepper and spices, Alka-Seltzer. He had a thousand things to learn, more than a thousand, in the ten weeks before his decision to go in business for himself, and the proposed GRAND OPENING: FREE MILKSHAKES.

He had to make connections and establish credit with Hayhoes, Ltd., with Higgins and Burke, with Rose and LaFlamme, all suppliers of the various needs of restaurateurs. He had to find an experienced chef. He and my mother had to learn to plan menus. He didn't know how to do any of these things.

My mother had taken two or three courses in "Domestic Science" during her time at University College. For twenty years thereafter her textbook in one of these courses, *The Source Chemistry of Food Products*, was prominently displayed on her personal bookshelf in the parental bedroom. I would beg her to let me read it as a treat, when I was home from school with a cold and bored and whiny. It was full of captivating material. I learned here that peanut-butter was 28% protein, higher in substance than anything else including beef, a fact I've never forgotten, which has even been of use on occasion. There were charts and graphs in this book, and photographs of exotic aspects of food preparation. Chicken-plucking, butchery and less murderous occupations, like those of the pastry-cook. Some of the photos of the butcher at his block gave me a brief enthusiasm for vegetarianism, which I found fairly easy to suppress when the Sunday roast hove into view.

On the strength of her three courses in what she insisted on calling "dietetics" my mother set herself up as the official menu-planner of the Lazy Bay Grill, and a note to that effect appeared at the bottom of a showcard announcing the proposed opening:

Andy and Isabelle Goderich
announce
the Grand Opening
of
THE LAZY BAY GRILL
under their exclusive management
Jackson's Point, Ontario, Saturday,
20 Máy, 1939, at 12:00 noon.
Available for weddings, banquets, bar-mitzvahs.
FREE MILKSHAKES OPENING DAY FOR KIDS
Isabelle Goderich graduate dietitian
in charge of cuisine

This showcard had been printed up in an attractive green ink; it was the first time in my life I'd ever had any connec-

tion with the publication of messages in print. It had a
strangely *crystallized* air. And it created two hitherto non-
existent personalities, by the mere act of enshrining them in
spidery typography. Andy and Isabelle Goderich.

Faced with this formal announcement, asked to give a
reaction, a month before my ninth birthday, I felt flustered
and foolish when I asked, "Who's Andy Goderich?"

My father said, "Me, naturally. I thought that was a nice
touch, relaxed and informal."

I said, "I think it's silly."

"Why?"

"It doesn't sound like you."

My mother said, "He's right, you know, Andy," gurg-
ling with partly suppressed laughter.

"Oh hell, don't you think they'll fool anybody?"

Amanda said, "You don't really want to fool anybody, do
you, Daddy?"

"No, no, I never fool people; that would be lying. I was
just trying to seem friendly . . . and so you don't think 'Andy
Goderich' sounds sincere?"

Amanda said, "You might get like an Andy after a bit."

"Oh I'm sure I will."

Tony said, "Do you want to do that?"

"Well, I might. I can't tell. Anyway we've gone and had
the cards printed; your grandfather paid for them. I think
you should know that." All at once he began to laugh and
my mother stopped holding herself in, and all five of us filled
the living-room of Cornish Road with the laughter of the
Goderichs as we crumpled newspaper and wrapped china in
a room filled with barrels, in which our furniture was going
to be stored for longer than any of us guessed. Straw and
crumpled paper and half-wrapped bits of treasured china lay
on bookshelves and side tables. My mother wasn't entirely
sorry to see these articles disappear into the storage
warehouse; it meant less dusting. They had been wedding
presents, mostly from college classmates and relatives, and
were rarely used. She picked up one of my favourite teacups

as we sat there talking, and began to wrap it in sheets of the
Catholic Register. The cup had a picture of a red-coated hunts-
man on a black-and-white horse on its side. There was a
matching saucer with a fox running round the rim.

Her shoulders jerked convulsively. "I don't know why
that's so funny, your poor father. It wasn't as if he hadn't
any other ways to spend it." She suddenly dropped the
teacup on the glazed tiles set into the floor before the
fireplace. It broke in bits. I felt a terrible wave of apprehension.

My mother stared at the shards with relief. "I never liked
that cup," she said.

"Can I have the saucer?" I asked.

"Yes, Matt, of course. I'm sorry dearest, that was one
you liked, wasn't it?"

"It doesn't matter."

"We'll buy another," said my father, but we never did.

The showcard carried a cheerful line-drawing of the
restaurant building in light green ink, traced out as the
background of the lettering, on the whole professional and
assured. We had ruddy thousands of them. I think Dad must
somehow have negotiated a capital loan—one he'd been
seeking for some time—from Grandpa Goderich, to finance
the outlay for these advertisements, and for the many articles
of restaurant equipment, bills for which now began to arrive
in the mail, as we packed our furniture to put it into storage,
with some persistence. For years thereafter copies of the
showcard used to come to light in unlikely places, old
steamer trunks, under the seats of our antiquated Durant, in
Ward-Price tea chests, as backing for framed photos. I
wonder how many were produced, and at what cost. Isabelle
and Andy!

"Your father phoned at lunch," said my mother, kicking
shards of teacup into the fireplace. "He wants to come for
dinner on Sunday."

"I won't be here for Sunday dinner," said Dad. "I'll be
on the road. I'll probably be in Pefferlaw."

I believe this was the first time any of us kids ever heard that unusual place-name, which made us giggle. Pefferlaw, Pefferlaw, Indian perhaps? Pennsylvania Dutch?

None of us ever ascertained the derivation.

"I'll take Matt with me on Saturday," said Dad. "I'll tell you what, if Dad calls again, tell him I'll be back in time for dinner Sunday night. We'll have the roast at night for a change. Yes? No?"

"That would be fine," said my mother, a touch grimly.

"We'll complete the arrangements, and I'll be able to tell him how I did with the advertising. I'll take Matt with me, and we'll put them in every store window from Richmond Hill to Sutton."

"Will you have to pay for display space?"

"I don't believe so; there's a kind of reciprocity about these matters. I'll invite them to drop in for a meal, and a high proportion won't ever appear."

In this prediction, as in many others connected with retail storekeeping, my father was mistaken. As long as he ran the Lazy Bay Grill, storekeepers "from Richmond Hill to Sutton" kept on showing up at the restaurant at dinnertime with their hungry families, just dropping through on their way to the lake, taking him up on his offer of a free meal in return for display of his advertising card.

"I fed a family of five at least once for every card displayed," he would say peevishly, "say ten dollars a time not including the tip."

He always tipped the waitress after these guests had left, so the girls wouldn't lose anything on the service, though nothing went into the cash register.

"I want to come too," said Tony, naturally enough.

"No, you're too small; you'd be too tired by late Sunday afternoon. Another time, Tony."

"There won't be another time."

"What about me?" said Amanda, *pro forma* more than anything else.

"You've got tap-dancing Saturday."

"Yes."

"You don't want to miss that."

"No."

"All right then."

The next Saturday, late in March, Yonge Street then as now a terrifying traffic trap north of, say, Willowdale, my father and I sallied northward in that rickety auto, that vile Durant, which I recall (as most of us do the first cars we were associated with) with complex feelings of love, nostalgia, resentment, downright frustrated hostility. It would not then go over 38 miles per hour. I doubt if there had at any given time been any question of exceeding the speed limit in the vehicle. An old car. Treated as such with attitudes at once essentially North American, comic and fearful, by my parents as early as I can remember. It ran and ran, groaning, rattling, squeaking, persisting in inconvenience: the Durant.

The historian of the auto in North America will feel his pulse race and his eyes light up at the name *Durant*, for of course it stood for the illustrious William Crapo Durant, the man who thought up the idea for General Motors, among other inventions, the most creative company promoter in North American automotive history, a real old genuine industrial pirate of the authentic nineteenth-century stripe, whom my father would reminisce about fondly whenever he thought of that car.

"A criminal, Durant," he would assert laughing. "Ought to have been jailed as soon as he appeared on the scene. But a great man."

People like W.C. Durant never failed to make their specific impression on my father, who would have been enchantingly attractive to con-artists of every persuasion if his university appointment and then his poverty hadn't shielded him. Our Durant was a 1927 model, acquired new from the Toronto factory by my grandfather Goderich as a belated wedding present for my parents. The marque, which flourished briefly in the mid-to-late twenties, then went under at the onset of the depression, had been created by Durant himself after he was squeezed out of the management of General Motors. God alone knows whose money financed the manufacture of these cars, but it was Durant's name that went on them, somewhat as Walter Chrysler made use of his own industrial reputation in the mid-twenties to advertise his new marque. The Chrysler corporation prospered, probably because its founder's automotive credentials were in the area of design and plant layout, while Durant's were to be found in the mysterious web of corporate finance and share issue.

Anyway our Durant was an old car when I first laid eyes on it, painted a most peculiar black, which varied in tone and depth and never took a polish. The car seemed to have been finished in stove-blacking that had subsequently streaked, leaving untreated metal exposed here and there. Even in heavy rainfall its surface would neither shine itself nor reflect the light of oncoming headlamps. The fittings, the door handles (it was a four-door sedan) and the shaky trunk rack, on the other hand, were unexpectedly handsome, trimmed in some light metal that antedated chrome. It might perhaps have been a cheap nickel alloy; anyway it was rich-looking, resembling silver in a touchingly spurious way. This spurious tone is what I recollect with most affection about the Durant. There was an engaging phoniness about it, recalling certain postures of W.C. Fields. It was in fact such a car as Fields himself would have cherished.

In our non-confidence-inspiring automobile, my father and I trundled north along Yonge Street at 30 miles an hour, through villages and towns that were strung out along the highway and actually separated by bits of green belt. Nowadays there are no breaks in the built-up areas; it is uninterrupted cheap rapid construction as far up as Holland Landing. In 1939, Richmond Hill, Aurora, Newmarket, were separate places with distinct inclinations and popula-tions. In each we stopped at druggists, hardware stores, garages, grocers, butchers. Not at restaurants. Everywhere my father made the same speech, got the same moderate reception, with trifling modifications depending on locale.

"I'll take a two-and-a-half flat bastard," he would holler out in the Richmond Hill hardware store, having rehearsed the line mentally on the way from the car to the store, "and oh, say, if you don't mind, could I stick up one of these?"

"One of what?" the hardware store man would say.

"My display card."

"Let me see that." Slow scrutinizing pause, the search for possible concealed indecencies. "No. Yes. That's all right. Pin it up next to the door there, while I go get your file."

· In every other matter scrupulous about his conduct, Dad took a great delight in putting up two, or even three, of the green cards while the storekeeper was out in the stockroom looking for some obscure item that would take five minutes to find. In butcher shops he asked for brains or expensive steaks, in pharmacies horse liniment perhaps. My father had a convoluted mind; he greatly enjoyed this expedition. I believe that he was seeing himself dramatically, as man of affairs, the practical hard-headed entrepreneur who could get things done.

"Got four of them up in there, Matt. Neat work, eh?"

He grew very adept with the enormous thumbtacks he'd found somewhere in Toronto. White, they looked attractive over the white and green treatment of the showcard. In the end we managed to affix perhaps 180 of these cards to wall spaces in stores from Willowdale to Sharon, a village of hardly more than a cluster of houses on either side of the road, with a single store selling variety goods and serving as post office. The distinction of this community is the remarkable Sharon Temple, visible briefly as one passes through town northward.

"No nails in that building," my father said, as we passed in the late afternoon; it was about four o'clock and his enthusiasm for placarded advertisement had somewhat sapped his energy and mine. He seemed content to continue toward the north, up a ridge or roll of hill from the top of which, about 4:30, I had my first glimpse of the lake, or more correctly of Cook's Bay, the southernmost arm of Lake Simcoe. I felt like Champlain. I remember how for years our hearts would lift, when my father brought us north from the city for a spell in a cottage by some Ontarian lakeside.

That first afternoon he paid no further attention to the stack of signs as they jounced about and slid sidewise on the back seat. We drove slowly through Elmhurst Beach, Indianola Beach, then through Keswick, which was the first fairsized village along that stretch of shore where the lake widened out. Keswick gave a true picture of the small summer resort of the thirties, with abandoned Model T Fords lying desiccated in fields, Gurds Ginger Ale signs tightly screwed to the weathered siding of dancehalls and hot-dog booths whose shuttered counter-windows had not yet been opened for Victoria Day. Dogs lounged at their ease in the middle of the street. Once in a while one of the elongated puffing old Leyland buses, spare tires hanging from the rear, operated by Gray Coach Lines, would struggle noisily along the imperfectly paved street, stopping at each small red-and-yellow crest indicative of a ticket office.

We pressed on around the pleasant waterside through Orchard Beach, Roche's Point, Island Grove, everywhere the faint intimations of summer stirring behind closed windows. Smell of motor oil hanging in the air. Past the site of Fanny Breen's Blue Water Camp, whose denizens used to chant:

Ta ra ra boom de ay,
Ta ra ra boom de ay,
We have no beans today
Cause Fanny Breen's away.

The boat rentals of Willow Beach. Then the site of De La Salle Camp, swimming raft securely chained to rocks by the shore, wreck of an old power cruiser balanced on rocks in fairly deep water just past the camp. And on past the Lakeview Hotel and the large yellow frame hotel operated in strict conformity with the dietary laws of the Jewish faith, a kind of low-key Grossinger's, which was full, every summer, of quiet, unobtrusive people who came and went very mysteriously and seemed to have slight connection with anything that went on in the village. Past Bustin's Drugs to the centre of town and first sight of the Lazy Bay Grill on the right side of the street as you drove north, plainly the advantageous side. First sight of two competing restaurants across the way.

"Hmmmmn," said my father, catching sight of them. "Competition."

He had never had first-hand experience of economic competition, barring the two salary cuts from the university and the ensuing tales told him by his colleagues, one of whom, for example, used to insist that his wife's recent miscarriage was a direct consequence of the university's parsimony. His poor wife had had to continue to work during three disastrous months, long after she ought to have stopped, and finally lost the baby. This particular colleague had been permanently enbittered by the accident, never forgot it, complained about it a generation afterward. "They cut my salary almost without notice; we had to have the extra money. Irene just had to hold onto her job three months too long, that's the rub of it."

During this sadly moving recital my father used to catch his breath, then wish that there were something he could do to console his friend. It was a hard thing to bear. Times were tight, calling perhaps for corresponding tightening of belts, but surely not for the deprivation of those yet unborn. Apart from such sorrowful personal instances, he knew nothing of the behaviour of money in circulation, of the world capital markets, of investment and the laws of competition. But he did know that he needed to borrow money from my grandfather, and that sometimes passionate love intervened to disturb economic calculation, as it might be said to have done during my liaison with Alanna Begin. I would never have fought Eddie if it hadn't been for Alanna. My father would have had no trouble in raising an extra few thousand from Grandfather Goderich, if it hadn't been for the sudden appearance in their lives of Nancy Carroll.

Not, of course, the movie actress Nancy Carroll, whose career was just then drawing to a close. My grandfather's Nancy Carroll was a legal secretary in her comfortable early forties. She possessed a dark leaf-green velvet afternoon dress, which she wore more than once to Sunday dinner on Cornish Road. I recall her as creamy-skinned and deftly rouged, with a full, round face and masses of dark brown hair, and this soberly feminine dark green velvet, whose muted, rich tone suited Nancy Carroll between whom and my grandfather, as everyone used regularly to assert, "nothing in the least improper was going on." She was a modest, coy legal secretary, stately of movement, not slender.

This lady came often to meals and evening discussions through the opening months of the year; she took a proprietary interest in the subject of certain talks that went forward between my father and grandfather concerning investment in the restaurant business. Dad wanted to lay his hands on sufficient capital to make physical improvements to both interior and exterior of the building, a paint job on the stuccoed exterior to freshen up its dingy grey. Repainting for the electric sign and some new neon tubing. Complete renovation of the customers' washrooms, very unprepossessing as they stood. Special cookery equipment to meet specifications outlined to him by the Chinese chef he planned to engage for the first season, a Mr. Charlie Lee. Cash payment on the first big statements from wholesalers, to establish his credit on a sound basis. Some sort of operating-capital guarantee against the chance of poor weather during one or more of the fifteen important holiday weekends.

Grandfather Goderich and Nancy Carroll went into my father's estimates carefully, she drawing long lines on the dining-room table-cloth with a fork, a nervous habit she retained all the time I knew her, perhaps an outlet for overflowing endowments of nervous energy that found no other expression in her sad and majestic demeanour. I've often wondered about her, where she came from, how she drew my grandfather's attention, what they felt for one another. He was then just on the verge of 70, of apparently almost unimpaired vitality, still abundantly able to treasure up disappointment. He'd met her at some lawyer's luncheon where she came as a kind of coadjutorial right-hand woman to a lawyer imperfectly in command of his memory. She'd sat beside her principal, guarding a bulging briefcase and a notebook with crackling documents interleaved through it.

My grandfather never did well in the Toronto firm he joined upon arrival from Nova Scotia. He never became a partner, for example, and never enjoyed anything like the ascendancy he'd established in his native corner of the world, never came near a judgeship. He did have his KC, however, and his commanding personal exterior; failure and embitterment late in life hadn't sapped the physical springs of his authority. Though a relatively short man, not by any means obese or even stout, he managed to diffuse around himself an air of bulky authority. He had a very keen eye and a penetrating voice. I wasn't afraid of him—he was always kind and generous to me—but I see that others were. My mother entertained highly ambiguous feelings for "the Squire," as she sometimes called him, not entirely satirically.

At this time he took it into his head to move from his comfortable flat on Beaumont Road, which I had so often visited as a *Saturday Evening Post* boy. His interest in—almost his pursuit of—Miss Carroll had caused serious dislocation in his relations with Uncle Philip, who now quitted the city semi-permanently, bound north for seasonal employment with an Ontario government civil-engineering crew engaged in some sort of topographical survey in the area of Groundhog River. This began my uncle's intermittent connection with the northland, never definitively established, really fictional in character, which haunted our association for three decades. He served as geologist to this survey party, having taken a number of undergraduate courses in the field, much as my mother had qualified as "dietitian" of our restaurant venture.

Uncle Philip understood the fundamentals of geology from what he retained of his university work, and he bought some lavishly illustrated volumes on rocks and crystalline formations of the Canadian Shield. These, and the handsomely printed official publications of the responsible department—was it Lands and Forests?—gave him the minimal necessary background, and he did, in fact, spend several summers in the mid-northern parts of Ontario. Sioux Lookout, Pickle Crow, Moose Factory. He never visited the far north.

Between the father and the excitable, unsettled younger son, grave antagonism now arose over the question of loyalty to the memory of my grandmother, dead eight years. Uncle Philip took on this job and left town, his employment a sign of certain faint stirrings in the economic life of the province, which might have been held to imply the parting of the dark overcast of economic depression. Grandfather Goderich moved away from Beaumont Road. When I heard about it, I saw that a definite period had been achieved in my own life. The days of magazine salesmanship and yearning over Bea Skaithe were banished to the past. There was the Alanna Begin matter to contend with, as there was for my grandfather the Nancy Carroll involvement.

He took a larger flat, almost an apartment, in a large, recently remodelled private house on St. George Street near Bernard Avenue, an expenditure on shelter which, now that he was theoretically living alone, seemed to my parents unjustifiable. He paid more in rent, they told each other more in sorrow than anger, than they did for Cornish Road. Did he really need two bedrooms? A large kitchen? He claimed that Uncle Philip might require the second bedchamber from one moment to the next, but my uncle didn't appear.

There wasn't the faintest hint of salaciousness or undignified curiosity in my parents' thoughts on this subject. They trusted my grandfather's ethical and moral capacity in all respects; my father often remarked that his dad was the soul of personal dignity. At the same time, my grandfather had started to spend his money pretty lavishly on the furnishing of his new quarters, on his clothes, on little dinners and evening entertainments for Miss Carroll. She was said to have a low opinion of the food-service industry as an investment opportunity.

Often bemused by these unfocused family feelings, I took to sitting on the hillside above our raceway of clay, musing about love, about food, about Groundhog River and my uncle, for an hour or so after school, sometimes with Alanna, sometimes alone. Once, just before my father removed me from school a month before it ended officially, so I could accompany the family to Jackson's Point, I was idly patting clay walls back into place after a flooding spring rain. I heard somebody coming down the hillside and looked up, It was Monty McNally, with a couple of new Dinky Toys from his collection that he wanted to show me, little airplanes of a kind I'd never seen before, monoplanes, one silver, one coloured yellow and green and brown.

"It tells what they are under the wings," said Monty, squinting at very fine lettering. He handed me the silver one and looked again at the one he was holding. "I can't make it out," he said. "Can you read the other? I just bought them."

"I'm not sure," I said. "I think it says 'Spitfire.'"

4

"There aren't any nails in it, only wooden pegs, something
to do with the Wilsonites and their convictions, something to
do with the Crucifixion."

My mother would say, "Are you certain you don't mean
Shirley Temple?" It was her customary pleasantry as we left
Newmarket behind, turned northward and closed on the
lake. The curly-headed moppet, mainstay of Twentieth-
Century Fox Studios and chief of production Darryl F.
Zanuck, was at this epoch just past the peak of her immense
popularity, as the resourceful Zanuck cast her opposite progressively taller leading men: George Murphy, Victor
McLaglen, in order to preserve the illusion that she remained "La Belle Diaperina"—title of her earliest short
subject, then some years behind her. Ascendancy among
teen-aged stars this year passed to lovely Deanna Durbin,
ex-Winnipegger, identified many decades later in late-late-
show previews as Dina Durbum.

We didn't mean Shirley. We meant *Sharon* Temple, the
exquisitely proportioned wooden building standing in its
tiny grove of scattered trees on the left of the back highway,
which we passed and repassed for several years on our way to
and from Lake Simcoe, though we only spent a single summer in the local restaurant trade. Shirley Temple dolls,
Deanna Durbin dolls, for that matter. Shirley Temple signed
coloured photographs in Woolworth's. Shirley Temple
dresses. Amanda Louise refused to wear the Shirley Temple

dresses given her at birthdays in the late nineteen-thirties by loving, fairly distant relatives. No close relative would have risked the gesture, for Amanda Louise could be fiery when roused, and the image of the tap-dancing child star was one she would not permit in any way to be associated with herself. She repudiated organdy and sweetheart roses, the moppet-style, as it might be named.

Calendar time. Chronological time. Psychological and emotional and instinctual time, physiological growth time. I used to imagine all the varieties of duration as proceeding at the same measurable pace, shown best perhaps by the movements of the chronometers at Greenwich Observatory. I had a naïve and uncritical view of chronology, duration and history. My father wrote virtually nothing on the subject: he couldn't fix its connections to moral science, choosing to treat the theory of time as a problem in the philosophy of science or possibly in epistemology, and he was not a specialist in either field. Later in life he came pretty close to the view that if ethics, psychology and axiology belong to philosophy proper, then logic, the postulational basis of science, mathematical theory and epistemology could not and did not. It is a persuasive position for some philosophers; the reverse view is for some others equally pressing. Each group regards itself as the tough-minded, the other as the tender.

It struck me then, naïvely, as I have admitted, that an hour was an hour, a minute a minute, and no unit of time took longer or less long to elapse than it took the second hand that swept round the dial of my new wristwatch to mark off the unit in question. I never tried the experiment of, say, keeping my eye on the second hand while I was kissing Alanna. I might have had my first experience of the elasticity of time earlier than was the case.

All the same, residence on Cornish Road was deeply tinted with multiple feelings of temporal awareness. The nine months we dwelt there seemed both immensely protracted and immensely compact. When we left, I felt as if we had always lived there, or certainly at least as long as on Summerhill. I remember thinking that there was a certain illogic to this feeling. Why should time passed on Cornish Road seem to have from three to four times the value, so to speak, of Summerhill time? Was it simply that earlier time seemed truncated or somehow foreshortened, telescoped as it receded into memory? It is impossible to say. Looking back, I can judge that certain epochs of my life seemed immensely drawn-out as they occurred, then later shrank alarmingly into brief incidents. But the Cornish Road period wasn't like that. It was relatively short, in terms of the number of calendar pages ripped off, but seemed very long and fraught with incident and has continued to seem so. Time is involved with value in some way, a point I ought to have made to my father. That period is an instance of double-chronology, psychological "felt" time and that of the calendar.

Why did I think that the months from September 1938 through May 1939 were so much longer than any similar span of time in my infancy and early childhood? Was this just because I was maturing, becoming more aware of the fecundity and multiform qualities of historical incident? Was it perhaps because these were crucial months in modern history, or because a sharp break took place in my family's living habits, or because my uncle Philip departed for the north, or because Miss Carroll was dating Grandpa Goderich, then almost at the scripturally determined limit of normal life-span? I don't think it reasonable to conclude from this one instance that it is simply the number of things that happen in a given span that determines how long it is, or seems to you. That would be too easy, because it would ignore two of the most pressing questions that puzzle historians. Firstly: how is any given happening, or event in time, to be marked off distinctly from all others, inasmuch as events seem to run into one another continuously? There is some sense, clearly, in which everything that happens in time is connected to everything else as if time were some enormous sea, in which events are like bits of water. They can be lifted out in cups, but the cups drip, and once poured back into the sea, the drips merge with the rest.

Secondly: supposing that events can be definitely distinguished from each other, how are we to evalute them, giving to this one eternal and immutable value to save, to heal, while to that we assign ephemeral unimportance? How do I form the opinion that what happened in the winter of 1938/39 was so intense, so richly felt by me, or by other persons, that it seemed longer than, say, the summer of 1933? The two radical difficulties of the historian, or the philosopher of time, or the student of style in human life, the art historian, come down to the simple formulas: what separates one happening from another, and how can you tell that one happening is worth more, and causes more valuable feelings in you, than another?

And yet, you know, some do, and we see that they do. When I started to puzzle over these matters, at Jackson's Point in 1939, I first thought of myself as like a young tree, adding a ring, a year's growth, as each cycle of the seasons drew to completion. I could almost feel myself forming a new ring around my middle, the older wood deep in my guts compressing, turning a darker colour, while fresh, sapoozing white fibre formed under the skin. When I thought of summer coming along, I felt like a tree. I had a new ring. I never felt as I'd become a different person. Meditation convinces us of this: we can't imagine ourselves as you or him, only as "I." There is a good deal of loose gabble about schizophrenia traded back and forth amongst members of the para-medical professions, about loss of identity, identity-crisis and divided personality. Yet many human beings who have suffered grave distress from mental disturbance for years, decades, find their persons again when distress recedes, strong and unbroken, built like iron, substantial. Schizophrenia is illusory: you can't break a person.

But the person grows and changes somehow: learning, experience, the new ring. I grew no bigger in 1939. I was a small child, at nine years was barely four feet tall, and I was never very fat. All the same I was mysteriously expanding. I knew more. I had the beginnings of a past and could compare three dwelling places, had already lived during the reigns of three English kings, two popes. I had the start of a sense of style, could readily understand why Amanda would have nothing to do with Shirley Temple, a poor artist. History was beginning to pull into shape around and behind me, the way the scales on the piano pull into shape when played to the clacking pulse of the metronome. For the individual consciousness, history is what is available in his memory plus what he knows how to find in a library. This is an interesting point: are society's archives part of an individual's memory? If so, how?

The personal memory is, as it were, embodied by, rounded off and made public by, the forms of behaviour known as "manners." Our group and individual awarenesses that there are regular ways of doing things. I don't, mind you, mean "good manners." The manners of the bomb-thrower, the holdup man, the nursemaid and the member of Parliament all qualify as manners pure and simple. They aren't simply a matter of which fork you use to eat fish with, but how one decides on his personal style, what clothes are available, what girls can reasonably be asked for a date. They include the various signals that indicate one's earning power and/or sexual capacity. Manners.

They are most pressing, most high-powered, in our deeply felt, carefully chosen personal decisions, where our personal styles are most intensely expressed—at the point where style is interiorized by us so that we are no longer acting our social role, but really being ourselves, in the sense that we *are* our style. Where we see ourselves as if we were in some brilliantly directed film, objectified on the big screen of our imagination, where we study the game films, look over the rushes, examine the tape of the interview. Or watch one of our old movies that we made in the thirties. The Deanna Durbin style. The Matt Goderich style. Personal life.

There was a crowd, as large as any gathered in Toronto up

till that date, around the dark-red City Hall on that May morning. I wasn't there. I missed it by a week, having departed for the north, for Lake Simcoe and the oncoming bliss of vacation time. May morning, the occasion of how many thousands of poems about the visions of a gracious and heavenly queen, advancing toward us across a field of green dotted with daisies, the day's-eye, the marguerite. In Toronto that May, on Queen Street at Bay at the steps of the foolish 40-year-old building, not yet sufficiently historical to be redeemed from mere ugliness by the pleas of Save our Historical Monuments societies, stood a frail stammering youngish man in the uniform of an English Admiral of the Fleet, beside him his gracious and forthcoming consort, the Queen Mum, dressed, or so I'm told, in a day gown of palest blue pastel like chilly angels' wings, with a kind of boa or wrap of impalpable marabou around her neck and shoulders against the cruel frost. Mid-May can be cruel in that city, even to the most forthcoming of royalty.

What they were doing there remains an indecipherable mystery to the historian, at least to the political or constitutional historian. They came to us, we are told in official histories, as King and Queen of Canada. Sure they did. *But why were they there?* Quite a different matter, the constitutional headship of our state being then as now an anomaly. Who sent them? Why were they there? Who needed their presence, set the wheels in motion, mailed the invitation? What is the use of these pageants, if not to keep the populace in an acquiescent state of mind?

The government of the day, that is, Mr. King, invited the King, the sort of confusion of names and of levels of existence that can tease the mind for generations. King inviting King pleases me endlessly.

The Conservative Party in Britain, then seated in power with modest security, must have seen that the time was ripe, or ripeish, for some door-to-door imperial salesmanship. Never wildly popular at home or abroad under the aegis of Baldwin. and later Chamberlain, more especially since the embarrassment of Eden over Abyssinia, and the reduction of the League of Nations to impotence, the party must have wished to ensure a measure of compliance from Ottawa in its political adventures in Europe vis-à-vis Mackenzie King's sometime correspondent, Herr Hitler.

There they were then, this poor pair, confronted on the steps of the peculiar municipal building by the mayor of that year, a dignified, energetic, prosperous gentleman with a long record of quite genuine service to the citizenry. There was a dais, from contemporary photographs seen to be an imposing one, though temporary. A deep-piled red carpet led up to it, not one of your sleazy, worn red carpets such as are seen at the openings of movie palaces, or in our degenerate age of shopping plazas, but a rich, springy, wine-red, royal-looking runner over which trod with dignity the former Duke of York and the daughter of the house of Glamis, the former Lady Elizabeth Bowes-Lyon, quite an agreeable young married couple, according to their friends.

Flowers were being presented before rings and roundels of Brownies and Guides, not however by one of them, but by the mayor's daughter, then aged ten, wearing pantalettes—or so she claims—under pink silk, puffed sleeves, tiny satin-covered buttons, and the dearest pleated skirt in a smart length, just reaching the knee, with a swinging girlish swish to the material, the laboriously-ironed pleats. And sweetheart roses, yes indeed, at bodice and waist. She has the dress still, the mayor's daughter, pressed away in tissue paper in a large wardrobe trunk, her dress for meeting royalty, although like the rest of us she has been altered since the great day.

She stared forward and up at the figure of King George as he approached over the red runner, entranced by the vast extent of his gold lace. None of us had seen so much gold lace deployed on a single sleeve; an Admiral of the Fleet's insignia of rank consists of one very wide band of gold, with four thinner bands rising above it. The lace ascends to the elbow; in short-armed admirals possibly above the joint. Looking at pictures of senior officers during the following years, I often wondered whether the naval men found it easy to bend their arms with the stiff, metallic, expensive gold ribboning encrusting the point of flexion.

King George was the same age as my dad; his older girl was Amanda Louise's age and Princess Margaret Rose was within months of my own age. I point out in haste that I haven't confused my father's history with any kingly myth, and have never mixed myself up in imaginings of a royal station. I never thought I was a prince, or the Princess Margaret Rose, come to that. Still, we all belonged to the same epoch and had, I expect, pretty similar feelings about it. I suppose King George, catapulted onto the centre of the European stage from minor and inconsequential bit-part as younger brother of regnant monarch, was still in May 1939 recovering from the shock of sudden accession and coronation after his brother's remarkable departure for Paris, later Jamaica. King George had been known chiefly as the tennis-playing Duke of York, not that bad a tennis-player either, having played at Wimbledon, always on courts very far removed from the centre. We used to see photos of him clad in V-necked sweater with racquets in presses under his arm, arriving at Wimbledon for his match accompanied by the then Lady Elizabeth Bowes-Lyon. Those sporting afternoons were not that far in the past.

Active in the Boy Scout movement; on easy terms with dignitaries in the Church; going about doing good and afflicted by a minor but perceptible speech impediment, this harmless young man seemed likely to live out his life in comfortable obscurity like his immediately younger brother, the Duke of Gloucester, alive almost to this day in that happy state. I can't remember the Duke of Gloucester's first name. Was it perhaps Fred, or Bert? The most Teutonic in appearance of the family, clearly overweight, with the loose-lidded pop-eyes of his grandfather, the estimable Edward VII, he was now and then glimpsed passing through Reading or Newbury on his way to open a dog-show or sale of work.

While growing up I used to muse about the eerie disparity

between this mildly-peculiar-looking royal Duke and the character of the same name who flits through the history plays of Shakespeare. Gloucester, Worcester, Northumberland, Scroop, an adventurous and mettlesome gang they must have been, those quarreling feudal politicians, unlike the Duke of Gloucester of our own age.

The fourth son of that family, our most noble brother Kent, handsome, married to glamorous Marina (another Shakespearian reminiscence) of Greece, perished somewhat later on in an air crash, if not actually in battle at least not far from it. This romantic end to the second-string idol of a generation seemed more in touch with the tough strength of these same names as attached to Shakespeare's invention, the best known Kent in Shakespeare being the faithful follower of poor mad Lear. I wonder if the modern Kent ever in his life thought of Lear's retainer, ever pondered the connections between the historical holders of his title.

No such meditation could have troubled the fantasies of the newly created Duke of Windsor, that title being nowhere to be found in the plays of the Bard. Excess of national feeling in war, I thought, might sooner or later issue in a rewrite of certain passages in the minor history plays such as *Henry IV Part 2*, admittedly not a stageworthy piece. Here a spot might be found for the insertion of admonitions of a character designed to unite in imperial purpose the reigning king and his errant brother:

But who comes here in use of war's accompt
If not our elder brother and most royal coz,
The warlike David Albert Edward Christian George,
Sometime of Wales, now of Windsor hight,
Who erst did'st occupy this royal seat. . . .

And so forward. Propaganda really, like all of Shakespeare's chronicle plays, and why not? If political rhetoric is to be excluded from the great books, the imaginative clothing of mankind, where will we all be?

The mayor of Toronto's daughter felt mighty put-upon as she watched this tall admiral advancing with his sweet, radiantly beaming consort who had, as she at once announced, two little girls just like the mayor's child, back home at Sandringham.

"My younger child is just your age, sweet, and she has a perfectly beautiful doll house that my two girls can walk inside to play in. Are these for me? Aren't they lovely! Are they from your garden?"

"Oh no, Ma'am," said the mayoral offspring. "You'd never get any flowers from our garden this time of year."

The King now replied to the Mayor. Hoofs clop-clopped on brick paving, rang out over streetcar tracks, a barouche-landau mysteriously conjured from the past, brass lamps polished to blinding light, seat cushions cajoled to flexible comfort, now appeared below the dais. Tens of thousands cheered, as many flashbulbs popped. Later the scene would be depicted on many, many editions of calendars for the year 1940. The royal party made its way to the carriage, King and Queen, Mayor and Mayoress, aides-de-camp. The little girl was handed over to the care of a solicitous alderman, then taken to a lavatory to throw up—such a strain.

And the barouche-landau, formerly in the stables of the Lieutenant-Governor of the province and lately recon-structed for this great occasion, rolled insecurely away along Queen Street, between Eaton's and Simpson's, encompass-ed by cheering, toward the Woodbine and the King's Plate, Canada'a premier horse race, for three-year-olds, the purse to consist of a sum of ordinary money, plus 50 guineas in metal coin, plate, the gift of His Majesty. Until that time, no member of the Royal Family had ever been present at the running of the King's Plate to present the guineas in his proper person. Today he would be there. Horsemen across the Dominion had planned and schemed and trained, cajoled, coaxed their animals towards the winner's enclosure at the Woodbine on this May afternoon. Almost a unique historical occasion. Perhaps the monarchy would founder in a

210

generation, no horseman ever have this chance again. Perhaps, perhaps. The breeding of thoroughbreds is a notoriously dicey business from stud-fee to trial gallop to maiden outing to stakes racing as three-year-old.

"It was the nervous strain," said the Mayor's child. "They promised me a great big strawberry sundae if I got through it all right. They even showed me the refreshments all set out on a sideboard, on solid silver plates. Some plates were gold, the only time in my life I've ever seen gold plates. And I'm rich! Oh, how sick I was. Alderman Wilson from Ward Two was looking after me, and I think he was afraid I was going to die. He was a nice man; he owned a tavern."

"Then what did you do?"

"My old Dad and Mum went off in the coach with their Majesties. Doesn't that sound ridiculous? Like Ionesco?"

"It's part of history though, can't be altered or denied."

"I suppose not . . . well, after the royal party rode off in their pissy old coach . . ."

"Actually Marie, it can't have been that pissy."

"Possibly not. That's how I felt about it. Alderman Wilson sent me home in a car. As you know, I lived up in Rosedale, and the royal train was sitting on a siding at North Toronto station, waiting to accommodate their Majesties."

"Those tracks? I used to live by those tracks."

"I know you did, my sweet, but this is my story."

"Sorry."

"All the children along the street were going up to the CPR tracks with new copper cents, to place them on the rails so that when the royal train left the station it would press the coins flat, and they would have them forever as souvenirs. They begged me to come but I'd had enough royalty for the day. I lay on my bed and felt my stomach heaving."

Sidelights on the folklore of empire.

At the old racetrack out along Queen Street, the royal vehicle rolled in off the street and onto the loamy, turdy, earthy surface of the track and on around a half circuit toward the Royal Enclosure. Ascot it wasn't, God knows, but at a distance it resembled that distinguished meeting. The lesser races of the day were run off. Grey top hats on the heads of bond salesmen and share brokers, brewers, storekeepers, newspaper proprietors, the customary associates of the Crown, came and went in the Enclosure. At last the feature race was announced, the premier Canadian stakes event for three-year-olds, the oldest consecutively run stakes race in North America. All that.

Archworth an easy winner. The genuine thing about that storied afternoon was the elegant excellence of the horse. It would have had to be that way, to point the moral of the tale: a real horse in an unreal place. Archworth romped home, the field nowhere, the favourite of the small bettor, the pride of Mr. C. George McCullagh, publisher of the Toronto *Globe & Mail*, a young man, darkly handsome, who received his purse of plate from royal hand direct, dressed (if memory serves) in grey top hat and claw hammer coat. Where are those guineas now? The day is over, the racetrack demolished and rebuilt, the newspaper publisher in his grave, the King too, the horse simply legendary. The guineas, hard, cold, indissoluble by ordinary time, remain somewhere. Where? In the vaults of the executors of the estate of C. George McCullagh perhaps; perhaps in the museum of the *Globe & Mail*. 50 pieces. Were they donated by the McCullagh heirs to the Jockey Club, for display in their clubrooms? Willed to a descendant as the nucleus of a numismatic display? Fit object for historical numismatics, who now possesses them, where are York, Windsor, Kent, Gloucester?

Later that summer, sitting on the edge of my cot in the rustic cabin, our sleeping quarters, behind the Lazy Bar Grill, I pondered a full-page photograph in already fading sepia rotogravure of their Majesties leaning over the rail of the *Empress of Britain*, waving their hands, as the quayside band played "Will Ye No' Come Back Again?" in that gesture of faked Scottishness which so desperately offends the sense of later generations. Noo, laddie, noo, they didna' come back again, they had ither things to do, ye ken.

I paid scant attention to the figures of King and consort,

studying instead the enormous funnels of the great and unhandy *Empress*, at that time one of the largest passenger liners afloat, built in Scotland, naturally, sold to the CPR at a price widely open to review. Never a profit-maker, not a handsome vessel, her career ended in flames, two years after that storied day. The *Empress* carried King and consort to their homeland; the most protracted Royal Visit of modern times drew to a close. Jobbers with stocks of bunting left on their hands, with piles of cardboard paired medallions bearing royal likenesses stacked in lofts, hoped for some further occasion to rally local patriotism. Parades. That's what they needed, parades. Flags. Love of King and Country. It's King or chaos.

We had had to follow the progress of the royal couple at a distance; their itinerary had not brought them to Jackson's Point, although a connecting branchline ran, and still runs, north from the city, CN trackage that gains the Lake Simcoe shore at Pefferlaw, then runs around the east side of the lake through Beaverton and Brechin. I wonder which of the great gangster railway-promoters built that little spur, so strongly reminiscent of the line to Mariposa immortalized in the final chapter of *Sunshine Sketches*, perhaps the very line, perhaps not. An alternative route circled the other shore of the lake, passing through Orillia, usually accepted as the original of Leacock's little town, standing in the same relation as Cabourg to Balbec.

"P'tit train va loin," says the proverb. The little train to Pefferlaw and Beaverton, worth thinking about for some moments perhaps, is one among many tiny, wandering single-track railways that bubble along like creeks and brooks northward from the great railhead at Toronto, the carrying-place.

We used to read in the old grey geography book, which gave figures from the 1931 census, that Toronto wasn't so much an industrial centre—a role filled by grimy Hamilton—as a warehouse and merchandising centre, and a focal point for distribution—an implicit comparison with Chicago that forces itself more and more on observers as time passes. When I was eight, nine, ten years old, I wondered how Toronto could be the rail centre it was cracked up to be when southern Ontario lay so far away from the course of the transcontinental railways. The existence of the many tiny rural railways north of the city is explained by this circumstance; the city is both advantageously and disadvantageously located, depending on how you consider it. Its advantages are rooted solidly in its lakefront situation between the mouths of the Humber and the Don, across the relatively small Lake Ontario from the immensely populous northeastern United States. If you think of southern Ontario as a wedge driven into the northeastern US from the north, rather than as a part of Canada, it becomes clear that this much-blessed wedge is geographically a part of the States, rather than of Canada. The hoary arguments between Liberals and Conservatives about the tariff, fought out so vigorously in Ontario to this day, stem very largely from Toronto's ambiguously American site. Toronto wants to have it both ways, naturally. Who doesn't? So the city impinges by its port on shipping patterns all over the Great Lakes. It's a port city like Cleveland, Conneaut, Ashtabula, Toledo, Chicago.

And then the little rail lines like the "train to Mariposa" link the city with the Canadian north and west. Every afternoon the train for the west leaves Montréal at five PM and arches north and west through Ottawa toward the Manitoba border and Winnipeg, leaving Toronto several hundred miles to one side. But every day the trains from Toronto that connect with the CN or CP main line start north to catch the transcontinental. Toronto asserts its double nature daily.

If *Sunshine Sketches of a Little Town* is what I think it is, one of the two or three books at the nerve-centre of Canadian life, then it's no accident that its author, a political scientist by profession, made the central Canadian political question surface in the book's next-to-last chapter. A member of a delegation says to Josh Smith: "Mr. Smith, I'm an old Free

Trader." And Smith, the Conservative candidate but willing to reflect all opinions says: "Put 'er there. So'm I."

A member of a more orthodox Conservative group, putting a question about the tariff, gets this reply: "I'll put her up so darned high they won't never get her down again." And then we get this delightful exchange in an interview: "Mr. Smith . . . we'd like to get your views on the effect of the proposed reduction of the differential duties."

"By gosh, Pete . . . you can search me. Have a cigar."

"What do you think, Mr. Smith, would be the result of lowering the *ad valorem* British preference and admitting American goods at a reciprocal rate?"

"It's a corker, ain't it? What'll you take, lager or domestic?"

Naturally Mr. Smith is elected on the Conversative platform, a protectionist platform, because he can be seen to be willing to compromise it where necessary, a fairly Canadian attitude. His election opponent, John Henry Bagshaw, must now take his way in retirement toward "that country from whose bourne no traveller returns." And Leacock notes that, "he was understood to be referring to the United States."

Sunshine Sketches is about as Canadian as you can get. Its author was born in England and came here as a baby; his two masters were an English writer and an American: Dickens and Mark Twain. His choice of subject matter and form are, or were, essentially Canadian. The book is a pastoral idyll treated satirically, one of the major literary kinds, perhaps the most appropriate choice of genre in the earlier stage of our history. Nowadays what is wanted is an epic—this is clear enough—with comic interludes but no satiric ones. The heads of our novelists and poets, Murray Sansfoy, Alcide Beaulieu, turn again and again toward Louis Riel, Brébeuf, Almighty Voice, when they might better taken a good look at the figure of the locomotive engineer. Maybe Sir William Van Horne is our Achilles, an

epic condition foreseen by Leacock in his Homeric parody
from *Behind the Beyond:*

> Then there came rushing to the shock of war
> Mr. McNicoll of the CPR
> He wore suspenders, and about his throat,
> High rose the collar of a sealskin coat. . . .
> Thus in the Stock Exchange he burst in view,
> Leaped to a post, and shouted, "92."

The little railways that tie Toronto to the hinterland and to
the main line as it crosses Northern Ontario look like a
tenuous spiderweb on the map of the province. They show
how goods were shipped from Toronto before the highway
network evolved. The King and Queen could have come to
Jackson's Point, or anyway very near it, on a line that runs
north from Toronto through Leaside, where it divides. One
spur runs through the towns along Yonge Street as far as
Richmond Hill, and then northeast, bypassing Newmarket
and Sharon by a mile or two, to Mount Albert and on to Pefferlaw, Beaverton, Uptergrove, Atherley, and finally to
Orillia/Mariposa.

The eastern spur runs through Uxbridge to Lindsay, and
opens up the Kawartha Lakes.

On the western shore of Lake Simcoe there's another CN
right-of-way that comes north from West Toronto through
Maple and King City and Newmarket to Barrie, round the
lake, once again terminating at Orillia. Either of these might
be Leacock's *"p'tit train"* but I prefer to identify it with the
train to Pefferlaw and Beaverton, because that was my little
train too. All through June and July of that curiously
chopped-off summer, usually on Monday or Tuesday of any
given week, my father would pile us in the car, us three kids,
leaving my mother, the chef and the waitresses to look after
the Lazy Bay. I wondered why we had so many waitresses on
duty all the time; there was a problem in arranging a roster

of six girls who came in at rotating intervals. The restaurant was open from seven in the morning until long after midnight. As a rule, one of the town policemen, the one who was on the wagon, would pass an hour in the place around one AM, when my dad would check the register tape and take off a balance for the day, put $20 in silver and small bills in the lower drawer, and write up his bank deposit for the next morning. Then he would turn off the electric sign and the policeman, Tom Walton, would say goodnight.

Charlie Lee, the chef, lived in the restaurant in a small room off the kitchen. He usually took Monday off, and Tuesday till the late afternoon. He never began work till the late forenoon. My parents looked after the cookery when Charlie was off, and not badly either. By the middle of July, Amanda Louise and I could make marketable toast, orange juice, milkshakes, and so on, and we used to fill in as short-order staff. My father did the different kinds of hamburger, cheeseburger, baconburger, and my mother handled the occasional order for steaks and chops when the chef was off. On the whole we could manage to prepare the food among ourselves.

But we did have to employ several waitresses, and their salaries, though not high, were a heavy charge on the business. The Lazy Bay Grill was a surprisingly large room, which could seat close to a hundred diners at a counter with fourteen stools, four big booth-type tables seating six each, ranged along the large front windows, another ten tables for four distributed around the open middle floor space in the room with a rack of magazines and books in the middle facing the door, and finally two small rows, at the back, of booths for two, five booths to a row, along the side and back walls. Adding this up, I see that it comes altogether to 98 persons, and my recollection is that the licence framed on the wall behind the soda fountain, next to the hatchway through to the kitchen, stated that occupancy by more than a hundred and ten was unlawful; these seating arrangements were well planned and well within the law. There were fire exits at either end of the building, and a pair of large double doors facing out onto the highway, that is, toward the west, and there was a further exit through the kitchen. The customers' washrooms were around at the north end of the building past the soda fountain and cigarette counter; the large kitchen was directly behind these counters and there were two serving hatchways for smaller meals to be handed through. It was a well designed layout, the arrangement of the tables allowed three waitresses to handle them at all but peak hours. One girl looked after the ''A'' station (my fathers' nomenclature), comprising the six large booths at the front, which for various reasons were the most used—they got the most sunlight and had an agreeable view of the main street, and a side street that ran down below high-arching trees toward the lake.

A second girl looked after the ''B'' station, the ten tables for four that stood out on the floor, and a third was responsible for the ten small booths in the back; the least experienced or least willing girl handled this ''C'' station. When business was at a peak, the two larger stations were too much for a single waitress to handle. At these times Amanda Louise and I used to work as busboys, removing dirty dishes and setting up fresh serviettes, silverware and glassware, wiping off the tables, straightening the chairs, sweeping. Even so, during occasional real rushes, my parents would don starched white coats to pitch in and take orders. Often my mother acted as a species of lady *maître d'hôtel* on Friday and Saturday nights, greeting customers at the door and assigning tables. I will never forget one marvellous night when there was actually a lineup of parties waiting for the big front tables, and Marianne Keogh, our best waitress, was sweating so hard under her arms that she had to change her pretty, lime-green uniform twice in the course of the evening. We all pitched in; we all had a hell of an exciting time; it was marvellously educational, and we gave full value for money.

To give really excellent, quick service required this sizeable staff. My father never managed to arrange the waitresses' time so that he didn't have to pay six full-time salaries. He wasn't being miserly. He'd have been glad, as he kept saying rather plangently, to create six good jobs for waitresses. Jobs were still hard to find in towns like Jackson's Point, in the summer of 1939. ''Practical capitalism,'' my father would say musingly. He had too active a conscience, and it hurt him. It hurt him all his life. While he worried about running the restaurant efficiently, it puzzled him to wonder how to serve everybody neatly and competently, and at the same time not have the girls sitting around idle half the time.

He liked most of the six girls very much, including one who was a bit of a muddler, regularly mixing up orders and annoying people she was serving. It was very characteristic of both my parents to try to help her as much as they could—her name was Romola Kechechemaun—by giving her extra time on duty and paying her a little more than she actually earned. If there had been any question of reducing the staff, Romola would have been the last girl they'd have let go, because they felt concerned about her, and wanted to help her become independent.

But the place couldn't support six full-time waitresses working daytime and evening shifts. From around noon through two PM, from Wednesday through Sunday, there was usually enough work to keep three girls hopping, but not nearly enough to occupy them fully from ten till six. Dad didn't mind this; he used to say that no job should require a worker to give it his full productivity for the entire eight hours of a shift. On the other hand, he felt it reasonable to hope for peak output from the girls for a third to a half of the shift. My recollection suggests that they came in a bit after ten, spent the next couple of hours idling around their tables, not doing very much at all, then worked pretty briskly through the noon-hour rush down to about two o'clock. After that, the restaurant lost money having them around because the stretch from two through five was very quiet; I could have handled most of the business we did myself, and I was nine years old.

At 5:15 the night girls arrived, in clean uniforms and well rested, ready to work. My father didn't want tired and edgy people waiting on the dinnertime trade. He made a point of arranging things so that at least two of his most efficient waitresses were available then, especially on the weekend. He allowed Romola Kechechemaun to work the evening shifts too, apparently hoping that the experience would allow her to learn the business, which it did. Her work improved steadily all through the early summer. Where she used to spill soup on people in late May and early June, by the big July weekend she was showing signs of some aptitude for the work.

I believe that Dad had some idea in the back of his mind about helping Romola learn how to manage a restaurant, do the food ordering and budgeting, hire staff and all the rest of it, but the project never matured. We weren't in the business long enough, and Romola could read and write, and spell some, but not really adequately, and her arithmetic was shaky. I doubt that she could have mastered the training.

My father was an incorrigible teacher. For the rest of his life, no matter what other enterprises temporarily engaged his attention, he was always trying to help people to better themselves by education or training, either administered by himself or paid for by him, often when he had little enough money to spare. He was a genuine *academic* in the great Greek tradition, who believed passionately that education improved people civilly and morally. He thought of politics as an extension of personal education. He used to buy easy books of arithmetic, and spellers, and would ask Romola to sit down with him for half an hour in the mid-afternoon, to work on small practical exercises. He'd get her to help him add the current supplier's invoices, things like that. Eventually she became a bit suspicious, fearing that he would get work out of her that she wasn't being paid for. Dad was quite equal to forestalling this suspicion. He'd pay her something extra for adding up the invoices or making entries in a daybook.

"Matt, when you're trying to help somebody," he told

me one evening when the restaurant was empty, "you've got to be careful not to let them know. People hate being helped; it makes them feel inferior. I think the way to do it is to make them feel they're helping you."

"Is that why you always ask Romola if she can spare a minute?"

He widened his eyes. "You're a good observer. Sure, that's why. She's dropped out of school, you know. I don't think she got past the fifth grade, and that means it will always be hard for her to get jobs. But if she had some solid experience here with us . . . I don't know . . . maybe it would give her a bit of a skill, like a trade. I could give her a strong letter of recommendation."

"But she isn't a good waitress, is she?"

"She isn't right at this moment, but she could be. She could be almost as good as Marianne."

I laughed at that. It was common knowledge that Marianne, far and away our best waitress, a recent high-school graduate from Sutton, who hoped to go to university in the fall, had a bit of a crush on Dad. I said, "You like Marianne, don't you, Dad?"

"I certainly do, and I like Romola."

"As much as Marianne?"

"No."

"But you do more for Romola."

He stopped stacking cartons of Gold Flake and Millbank cigarettes, straightened up, and looked at me. "I don't want to bore you, Matt, but I'll tell you something that's hard to understand and pretty disagreeable. Some people are naturally likeable; some people are neither one nor the other; some are naturally unlikeable. It doesn't seem to have much to do with whether they're *good* or not. You can be likeable—attractive—without being good, and the other way around. Marianne, as it happens, is attractive, *and* good. Romola isn't terribly likeable, on a first look, and she isn't really terribly good either. There may be some connection, but I'm not sure what it is. She could be good—it's within her power, if you see what I mean—even if she can't be naturally attractive. I'm getting mixed up. What I mean is that some of our personal qualities are in our own hands, and others aren't. The thing to do is to work on the ones that are controllable. If Romola learned how to run a small restaurant very well, she might have a much more contented life than otherwise, and it *is* possible. It's something she really could *do*, whereas no amount of wishing will make her extremely attractive, and no amount of lipstick either.''

"I don't like the sound of all that."

"Neither do I," said my father, "and perhaps I'm wrong. Think it over."

He had no capacity to dogmatize.

He and my mother struggled with their consciences for some time, finally deciding to guarantee their six girls a full week's pay whether the restaurant was busy enough to keep them working or not. This small staff of six was in its way a paradigm of a typical working force, showing in miniature the same kinds of worker that management identifies in larger groups. Some of the girls had special days when they did, or didn't, want to work. Some wanted to put in as much time as they could; some wanted to do the absolute minimum in order to pick up a full week's pay. But this last group wasn't composed wholly of the lazy or incompetent. Two of the girls who wanted to work minimal hours were in the middle of blazing love affairs, and wanted most of their time free for that reason. All the requirements of these six had to be taken into account when my mother made up the weekly work-schedule and explained it to them on Monday morning. This was also payday for the girls; they would drift into the restaurant around ten in the morning, all six, and sit around one of the big tables in the window, chattering away like starlings in early spring, with my mother in their midst handing out their pay envelopes. In most ways my parents were model employers, who got very favourable reactions from their workers. In the whole of that summer, only two of them quit, in either case for understandable personal reasons, and by that stage in the season there was no point in replacing them. So the six whom I remember so clearly from that distant point in the past really were our whole serving-staff.

These six were: Ruthie Battaglia, Gloria Kirchner, Joan Keating, Tommie Hibbert, whose real name was Thomasina, the only Thomasina I've ever known, Romola Kecheche-maun and Marianne Keogh. They made a remarkably striated work-force. Sometimes Amanda Louise, now twelve years old, and almost as big as Ruthie Battaglia, would slip on one of Ruthie's uniforms and fill in through lunch hour if one of the girls was temporarily off work. But that group of six was the first and last body of employees that my father ever had anything to do with. He used to say that hiring peo-ple was a richly human and Christian act, but that firing was inconceivable. Sometimes he would leer at himself comically in a shaving mirror that hung in the kitchen, practising his firing technique.

"How would you do it?" he would demand. "What do you say? Would you wait, for example, until Christmas Eve? Do you inundate them with abuse, or do you simply snarl, 'You're through here. Pick up your time at the front office.' "

As he grew older my father's sense of comic parody ri-pened and invaded his everyday conversation, He was able to keep it out of much of his writing, although from time to time the text of *Property and Value* gives the impression that certain other philosophers are being parodied by an ex-cessive gravity of tone.

He said that he couldn't and wouldn't ever fire anybody and acted on that declaration. "Judge not," he would pro-claim, "lest ye be judged."

Ruthie Battaglia was the daughter of the man next door who ran a large, flourishing fruit store. A high-school girl, thin, dark, very pale, given to sudden and apparently uncon-trollable fits of laughter at things my father said to her, Ruthie was as sweet and agreeable a teen-aged girl as you could imagine. Her father was proud of her first job, and sent a lot of business our way.

Gloria Kirchner was the only misfit in the group. She didn't really want to work in return for her pay, sometimes failed to call in when she intended to miss a shift, did the minimum. My father used to wonder what it was about him and my mother that offended Gloria. He worried about her, tried to be nice to her, arranged special, easy, work-schedules for her. Poor old Gloria. She was probably in her late twenties. Unmarried. Not at all bad-looking either. Not much schooling. We never found out what was troubling her.

But everybody on the shores of Lake Simcoe knew what was troubling Joan Keating and Tommie Hibbert, who were conducting the two incendiary love-affairs I've mentioned. In addition to being in this happy or unhappy state, they were best friends from the Sutton high school, a year behind Marianne Keogh. Their boyfriends were often underfoot in the Lazy Bay, a classically comic pair of late teen-agers, one of whom owned a car of sorts and the other a power launch. These two conveyances were the setting for the girls' amatory escapades, which were the cause of much mirth in the village.

Romola Kechechemaun, as I have said, was in some ways my parents' favourite, not because of her good looks, though she was rather good-looking in an unusual way, nor because of her skill at work, but because of the interest they took in her as somebody who had had an unlucky start in life, few opportunities and a not very promising outlook. She was about twenty, and had left school at twelve. She was an Ojibway girl from the reservation lands on Georgina Island, which lies in the southeast corner of the lake. Her father, Ed Kechechemaun, her brothers and two sisters, were often seen around the Point and the large boys' camp operated by the Christian Brothers, which lay a mile south of town along the shore. Sometimes the girls worked in the kitchen at the camp, or as maids at the Lakeview Hotel. Ed Kechechemaun was prepared to do any guiding that might turn up, but as Lake Simcoe was no longer taken very seriously as an angler's paradise, there wasn't much guiding for him to do.

His wife stayed on the reserve. I never saw her, but Romola, her brothers and their dad were familiar figures around the Lazy Bay. Later on, people told my father that he'd been a fool to be so friendly with this family; they were said to be no good, drunken, dirty, all the stereotypes that used to be trotted out against various Indian groups. None of the Kechechemaun family that I met was any of these things. None was what is called "shiftless" either. They all found it hard to get regular work, but everybody in Canada found that hard in the thirties. My father especially liked Ed Kechechemaun and one of his sons, Timmy, and used to spend long stretches of the afternoon listening to them, in an empty booth. When Romola came on duty, she used to shoo her father and brothers out of the place, as if she were slightly ashamed of them. I don't think she really was. I think she found it hard to believe that my father took them seriously.

It seems to me amazing as I look back how persistent those damned stereotypes are. Lazy. Idle. Shiftless. Drunken. Dirty. Untrustworthy. All these qualities used to be attributed to the Kechechemauns without any supporting evidence that I know of. My father would say, "These are good people who haven't been treated right." I think that about sums up his views. He worked hard to help Romola to a chance in life, and tried to avoid condescending to her or acting as if he were doing her favours.

The girl my parents liked best, and most appreciated, was the industrious, pretty, almost beautiful Marianne Keogh, who was going on to the University of Toronto in the fall. She was working as many hours as possible all summer to save money toward her fees and living expenses. My father still had many academic connections, and there was some question of his writing letters of recommendation to various admissions-officers and residence-staff, on Marianne's behalf. She was a tall, graceful girl, strong, able to work through an extra shift without apparent fatigue or complaint. Amanda admired her. Tony was a favourite with her. Personally I found her a bit too schoolmistressy, too good to be true, and far too much addicted to one popular song. "Music Maestro Please," often played that summer, after being a big hit the year before. Marianne used to feed small change into the Wurlitzer and play that number over and over, humming it to herself while she looked after her tables (very competently, I must admit). Once, late in the afternoon, tired of listening to "Music Maestro Please" for the fifth time, I pushed the little button at the side of the machine that interrupted the record. Marianne was working hard; the evening rush was starting to come. She may have been feeling tired and cross without showing it; unluckily for me she glanced up and caught me at the Wurlitzer. "Why, you bad little boy!" she exclaimed. She came over, seized me firmly by the arms and shoulders and propelled me toward a vacant table in the middle of the room, right in the middle of all the customers.

Marianne had several younger brothers and sisters whom she used to look after in the evenings, and what she did next betrayed her experience as a substitute mother. She sat on an empty chair, briskly turned me face down across her lap, pulled down my short trousers and my underpants, and spanked me efficiently, thoroughly, very hard, for what seemed an hour but was really about five minutes.

At first I thought she was only teasing. When she half-undressed me in front of all those people, I started to struggle and kick, but she had her left arm wound tightly around my waist, positioning me. Before a blow landed, I thought that even a grown-up girl really wouldn't be able to hurt me much, but with the first solid impact of her open palm on my naked flesh I was sadly astonished. I hadn't expected that it could sting so much. A dozen spanks reduced me to floods of embarrassing, babyish tears. The worst thing was the noise it made, a sharp, loud whack whack whack. I thought everybody in Jackson's Point must know Matt Goderich was getting a spanking, and I cried hard, mostly from pain but also in part from humiliation and shamed feelings.

I begged her to stop. "Oh please, Marianne, I'll be good, I'm sorry." My pleading made not the slightest difference to her. She went right on, perfectly calmly, with what she was doing, until she was certain she'd made a strong impression on me. When she was good and ready, she stopped, adjusted my pants methodically, stood me on my feet still in floods of smarting tears, then walked composedly back to her station, where she picked up her order pad and went on as if nothing had happened. I guess in her view nothing much had.

But I wished the earth would open and devour me. I swallowed hard several times, tried to stop crying and couldn't, then fled through the kitchen and backyard to our sleeping cabin, where I threw myself face down on my cot and wept stormily for a quarter of an hour or more, from crazily confused feelings of rage, humiliation, hate and at the same time passionate adoring love for the girl who had chastised me so severely and exposed me to such degradation. After a while my sobbing stopped. I stood up, undressed and examined myself in the mirror. No permanent injury had been inflicted, though my poor bum was a bright pink. I swore that I would even the score. I would ask my dad to fire her. But even while raging to myself and rubbing my smarting buttocks, I knew that my parents wouldn't pay any attention to a demand for Marianne's dismissal.

This was the first time in my life that I felt, and even partly understood, how raging hatred can mingle with intense attraction. Standing alone in the bedroom, I imagined that I could never face my family again, so great had been this loss of personal dignity, so ridiculous my humiliation. What would Gloria Kirchner say? She would giggle at me, and say I got what was coming to me. I hated those big girls. I'd get even! When I grew up, I would go looking for Marianne Keogh and do the same to her, with everybody looking! I'd get my revenge. Meantime, how was I going to face everybody?

I saw that I would just have to swallow my pride and face them out, that's all there was to it. I wasn't going to let my young life come to an end because I'd been publicly spanked. I knew even then that there are far worse things in life than temporary embarrassment. I came out of the cabin for supper with as cheerful a face as I could manage, and one of the best things about that summer was that nobody, not Charlie Lee, not Tony nor Amanda nor my mother and father, said a word to me about the incident.

Gloria Kirchner was on duty that night. After supper, passing through the kitchen on some errand, she saw me, came over and patted me roughly on the shoulder. "Don't you mind," she said, rather obliquely. "You're a good kid." I was flabbergasted.

Next morning I was stiff and sore, and I remembered the occurrence vividly for a long time. I managed to make friends with Marianne too, and followed her around like a puppy during the rest of our stay at the Point. Sometimes I courted her indignation in the half-conscious hope that she might punish me again, perhaps less publicly. I think she understood my partially exhibited need. She certainly never contemplated doing anything about it. For Marianne, once was enough. About a week later, I said to her, "You know, Marianne, that's the first time anybody ever did anything like that to me."

She knew what I was referring to. "About time!" she said.

Enraged and humbled, and perversely enchanted as I felt at the time, I see that she was right. I owe to her brisk, unemotional chastisement a total readjustment of my understanding of girls and women, of how they act and how they possess themselves. Up till then, I'd had pretty much the view of women most boys and young men learn from an ordinary Canadian upbringing. I exempted my mother and sister and Mme. Archambault from the judgment, but the ordinary run of women and girls seemed to me remote, barely comprehended beings, imperfectly human, never to be taken really seriously, to be mistreated casually at need or when convenient. Jakie Forbes and Eddie Reilly and I would push girls aside with contumely when encountered on the playground, and though I might burn with obscure impulses at the age of six for Letty Millen or Mrs. Bannon, and at seven for Bea Skaithe, these were merely moony narcissistic projections of conflicts inside me.

Was I the only small boy ever to have been civilized by an incidental spanking? Up till the moment I found myself powerless across Marianne's lap at the age of nine, a boy to whom unpleasant things were being done against his expressed will by a much more powerful woman, I'd taken it for granted that women couldn't exert real physical force. They simply weren't strong enough, I imagined. Any boy, of any size, just because he was a boy and would be a man, could beat up on any girl. A good little man would always beat a good big woman.

Plenty of men and boys still retain, instinctively and unhesitatingly, a notion of their inherent, qualitative, superiority in kind. My lucky/unlucky encounter with the heavy hand of Marianne freed me from that element of masculinist folly. I learned with pain and tears that a woman could overmaster my will and treat me as a thing, an object to be taken up and set down as she pleased. Very fortunately for me, this happened at an age when I could buffer the shock rationally, and recover from the pain without psychological damage.

I mean that I wasn't turned into a habitual and obsessive masochist by the incident, even though I already had strong concealed wishes to be babied—the classical masochistic infantilism. As Marianne said, it was about time. My mother, always cool in affect, and low-key in her treatment of the maternal attitudes, had never put a hand on me in the way of punishment, and, what is more important, almost never in the way of a caress.

I know that she sometimes caressed my father, and with deep passion. Once or twice I saw her do this. I have seen her respond to his caress in a way that tranformed her from the collected, reflective, witty, rather sexless person that she seemed to me, into a blushing, ardent girl. But that was outside my power of identification, naturally enough. I see now that my parents loved one another with more than comic intensity. I say comic because their life together was the reverse of tragic, or rather, superseded tragedy. It was lived at a level far beyond the essentially trivial categories of tragic and comic.

Marianne was the first, as it turned out the only woman who ever punished me physically in a serious and humiliating way. After I became devoted to her, because she'd been the one to show me that women had power and would use it decisively, I acquired attitudes to women and to sex that I think humanized and civilized me. I would no longer rest content to have the experience of half the human race closed to me. I think now that there is an enormous, untapped, reservoir among men of acute interest in women's feelings—not simply interest in them as sexual respondents, but as subjects, living persons.

Most men, I think, would like to know at first hand how it feels to be a woman, and I expect the reverse is true, as the myth of Tiresias suggests. Now and then I've asked men, whose intelligence and intimate care for women I respect, whether they've ever tried on their girl's clothes: a skirt, a pair of shoes, pantie-hose, a slip. . . .

Most of these men have shuffled their feet, then answered yes, a bit sheepishly. And of the no-sayers, a surprising number have mumbled to me a bit later, "You know, about my girl's dresses . . . I remember now . . . once or twice, just to see, I did try on a . . ." whatever it was. I've done this myself: modelled a dress, high-heeled shoes, a girdle and bra, before a mirror and before my wife, to shouts of her charmed, delighted laughter. This isn't transvestism, fetishism, an impairment of sex, or anything at all like it. It's an exhilarated, delightful awareness of our *likeness* to women, our shared humanity, community of sex. It involves a playful curiosity that dissipates unspoken misunderstanding between men and women by drawing it to the surface. Certainly men are stimulated by women's clothes: they are meant to be. The clothes are colourful, sensuously charming in their look and feel. They smell nice; they are immensely evocative of some aspects of femininity, but aspects that are not unmasculine: love of perfume and silk. "She" and "her" are for most men two of the most communicative words in the language, they mean so much.

Power is always involved in human communion, no matter how we may wish to abdicate it, no matter how we struggle against objectifying others. My father decided on principle not to fire anybody, but he had the power to do so, knew that he had it, consciously fled from it. In the conduct of a large business, this policy would have issued in the collapse of the enterprise, the ruin of all the employees. The understanding of power, and its just use, was the philosophical enquiry that stirred him deepest. His first book, *The Place of Conceptual Thought in Ethical Judgments*, contains a long passage on the parental relationship, in which he denies that the parent has a property interest of any kind in his offspring:

In common speech a parent is said to "have" children. A young mother "has a baby." A public man is described as "having four children." Many societies codify the parent's property right in the child, requiring an abductor to compensate the parent for economic loss. The sale of adoptable infants is still common; the very young and the newborn are from time to time murdered in ways which make it unmistakeable that they have been considered by their parents as portable property. It is clear that the imputed ownership of children by parent springs from the greater age and cunning of the latter, and from the greater physical and mental force the adult can exert. Parenthood is so often an occasion for physical coercion; the father who refuses to punish his child physically may end by maiming him emotionally, for there is arguably a need in some children for the physical illustration of their parents' displeasure or discomfort. Coercive power and ownership are from the earliest times connected, often identified. Let us consider the indentification.

He is led from this discussion into an an analysis of the metaphysics of ethics, especially of the ethical relation between two free persons. Usually, but not always, my father's thinking was expressible in the terms of Christian theology and metaphysics, without distortion. I'm not sure that his analysis of free human interaction was thus expressible. He seems in a number of places to deny the possibility of responsibility for sin, though not of responsibility for the consequences of our acts. He seems to have thought that sin, in the terms of Christian orthodoxy, was such a serious matter that the human will was not equal to its malignance. He had a certain intuition of what might be called the heroism of evil—seeming to argue that genuine sin requires a superhuman will—the tendency toward a doctrine of Satanic agency is clear. Like all great romantics he was fascinated by the theology of the Fall.

Otherwise in his ethical theory he was a fairly regular neo-Kantian. His thinking was sinuous though, and subtle and passionate. Maybe his Kantianism was superficial. In any case it gave him an early awareness of the wickedness of using free persons as objects having the status of material things, and no more. He used no person like a thing, if he could help it, and to do this was obliged to put in brackets, as it were, his coercive power, almost his persuasive power. He didn't go so far as to refuse to use objects as objects. He wouldn't apologize to the salt and pepper shakers for taking them up and putting them down. But he could never have taken me up and set me down as Marianne Keogh did. I learned infinitely more from him than from Marianne, but I learned *one* thing from her that he couldn't have taught me, that physical punishment and personal humiliation can change one's course of life. The whole network of values is perplexing.

On those free Mondays, while the girls were sitting

around the Lazy Bay, giggling and being intolerably girlish together, my father would take me and Tony and sometimes Amanda, and drive in the Durant over through Sutton to the way-station for the reception of goods by rail, which were usually consigned to Pefferlaw, occasionally to Beaverton, though that meant a slightly longer trip. Once or twice a fellow named Art Comstock, whose family owned the big local resort hotel, the Lakeview, with nine-hole attached golf course, came along with us for the ride. He was the first out-and-out neurotic I ever met, the youngest of four sons, for long a mother's boy, now past the end of his mother's patience. He was effectively unemployable, could neither find nor hold a job. Sometimes he washed and re-enamelled golf balls for resale in the tiny pro shop at the hotel golf course. He had entered the Lazy Bay out of curiosity, one evening at the end of May, recognized a receptive listener in my father, and attached himself to him.

He would take a drink. On one drive to Pefferlaw to collect the Blue Ribbon shipment, he turned to stare at Tony and me as we squabbled in the back seat. "That's a nice pair of kidneys you've got there," he remarked to Dad. This unexpected remark became proverbial in the family, though my mother considered it in questionable taste. I can see Art Comstock now, the first really disappointed and destroyed man I'd ever encountered knowingly—for I knew as soon as he appeared on the scene that his mainspring had broken—with his perpetual half-befuddled, discontented smirk. His family was rich. Art and his brothers had gone to Upper Canada College in Toronto; there were relatives in widely separated parts of Ontario: in London, in Stoverville and, I think, in Collingwood. Art couldn't get his hands on any family money, one of his major sources of discontent.

I was rather afraid of him; he used to persuade my father to accompany him into beverage rooms, while we sat in the back seat of the car for an hour in the heat. Dad would appear from time to time with cones for us, then soft drinks "to wash your cones down" and to expiate his offence, as he considered it, in leaving us alone. He'd nod apologetically toward the hotel door and indicate silently that Art was feeling misused and unhappy, that he felt responsible for him, that we must forbear to say an unkind word. And this was all true, blindingly visible. He did feel responsible, acted on the feeling. He drank sparingly, as a social gesture, and much enjoyed a chilled glass of beer on a hot summer day, never more than one.

"The relish is in the anticipation," he said to me once, while looking with pleasure at a tall, full, seidel, down the sides of which foam and beer ran onto a glass-topped table. This was much later in our lives. "I could look at it for hours, thinking, 'here I am, drinking a cold beer. This is me, drinking this beer, enjoying it.' Seeing myself doing it. Or going bowling, or at the stock-car races."

"I wonder why the actual taste is never equal to the pleasure of anticipation?" I said, grinning.

"You're parodying your old father," he said.

"I know."

"Remember the fate of the sons of Noah."

"Yes," I said, "I will. But I'm not mocking you."

"Parody is but a step from mockery," he said sententiously.

"Why then you're the greatest mocker of all, you *pasticheur sans restreint*."

He took up the glass and swallowed hugely. "You're right. It isn't the same."

In his case pleasure, reflection and valuation were fatally intermingled. He used to look after Art Comstock and worry about him, a man he'd known three months. When they finally emerged from the taproom in the old, white-painted hotel in Beaverton, rubbing their mouths in very masculine fashion, Art would be talking confidentially in Dad's ear as if they had been friends from the cradle. He was trying to talk Dad into acquiring an interest in Elsie's Tearoom, a luncheonette in Sutton operated by a woman confederate of his.

My father said, "No, Art, no, I don't want to build up a chain."

"But you could order from Blue Ribbon for both places at once. It would cut your work in half."

"More likely double it. Come on, let's go over and see what Blue Ribbon has for us today."

He coaxed the old car into second gear and we rolled noisily off to the tiny railway station, stopping beside the freight shed painted in the familiar dark brown-red of Canadian National buildings from coast to coast. A man appeared pushing a small, two-wheeled wagon. In those days, the powerful fork-lift truck wasn't to be found in way-stations.

"Gotcher stuff stacked right in here, Andy," said this man, smiling broadly. "Hello, Art, gonna give us a hand? Hello, boys." This was directed at Tony and me as we stepped squinting into the sunlight. "Comes to twelve cartons, Andy. How you gonna get that in there?"

Dad stepped round to the back of the car and lowered the spindly luggage-rack. "We'll tie some on here, and some we'll shove in the back seat. I'll leave the boys here for payment."

"Go on," said the freight-agent, "what would I do with them boys? There's no meat on them."

"You can't tell without squeezing them," said my father. He picked Tony up and hugged him, laughing at me over my brother's shoulder. "These are good plump boys."

"We want to come back with you," I said soberly.

"I guess we can manage that," he said. "I'll give the salesman a cheque when he calls, and I'll hang onto you. Let's see. Four on the back, the tea and coffee, four small ones inside, that's the spices, essences and flavours, cocoa powder and some other stuff. And the four flattish ones we'll tie on the top. Got it all figured out."

He and the agent and us two boys loaded the car, while Art Comstock wandered around in the sunshine, blowing fuzz off dandelions and admiring the King Billy butterflies and the occasional cabbage-moth that lurched past. When we had crammed the car full, and Dad had signed the agent's book of bills, we took time out to snoop around the station premises, the main rail line, the sidings, and some boxcars standing idle up lengths of rusty trackage; the usual branch-line litter of rolling stock, an old wheel-sharpening car up at the end of a spur, a work-gang bunk car, three heavy old handcars. My sense of identification with railway-men sharpened and deepened. I began to hear the ringing of bells, the creaking of ancient gates at the level crossing 200 yards away.

"That'll be the second eighteen," said my father and he was right. About matters like the various sections of freight trains he was invariably right, never seemed to forget anything. "They made her up overnight and she left Toronto at 8:54."

The agent happened to be standing right alongside of him when he was telling us this. "By God, Andy, you ought to be a railwayman," he said, "where in the world did you get that?"

"You told me yourself, Windy, the first time I came by."

"Yeah, but you remembered."

"I thought it was interesting," my father said, turning to look at the little train as it moved slowly into the yard. "She's got a bum bearing, and her pistons need packing, but that's a fine locomotive, that's no yard engine. Number 6916." He waved a cordial greeting to the engineer, who waved back with equal cordiality, smiling at us boys.

"Time we went home for lunch and unpacked this shipment," said Dad, "before those girls eat us out of house and home." This was a favourite phrase. "House and home," he repeated, "eight of them."

"Six," said Tony.

"Eight counting your mother and sister. And Charlie wants his spices for tomorrow. Tony, you can sit on Art's lap for the ride home."

"No," said Tony, "I'll squeeze in with Matt." We

crowded together in the back seat of the hot and stuffy car.

"Are you all right in there?"

"Fine, Dad, fine," I said. The agent stuck his head in the window and said goodbye to us. "No meat on those boys," he said in farewell.

"There's plenty of fat on this one," I told him, indicating Tony, who was bumping around half on and half off my knee, making me feel rather queer; that ice-cream cone and Orange Crush felt obtrusive. "Don't bump," I ordered Tony.

"I'll be quiet," he said happily, and we rolled away. We could see Windy, the agent, waving as we turned down the dirt sideroad, oily and brown-black, pools of rejected crankcase oil lying tarry here and there. We passed an abandoned 1930 Chevrolet, drove out of Beaverton and away home. As Dad drove into our side driveway he said to Art, "You can walk from here, eh?"

Art said, "I suppose. It's under a mile."

It was about three eighths of a mile down the road to the Lakeview. He set off, and we didn't see him again for some time. All the girls appeared on the sidewalk at once. They helped us unload the shipment and store it.

"The Acme Dairy came while you were gone," said my mother over lunch, "and I took ten two-and-a-halfs. Is that about right? With what we have in the cabinet, that should last us till Friday. I got four vanilla, two strawberry, two chocolate, one maple walnut . . . "

"Good," we all said together.

" . . . and one special."

"What's the special this month?"

"Rum and raisin."

We all made gagging noises in ensemble.

"How do they think of these things?" said Dad.

"It's all right," said my mother. We were lolling over a long lunch at a table in the kitchen near the big sinks. She got to her feet to answer a call from the restaurant for counter service. "Brother Luke called from the camp, and ordered a can of ice cream for the moonlight hike tonight. He said he'd be glad to have rum and raisin; in fact he seemed delighted with it. He wants you to deliver the ice cream to where they're going on the hike. Just a minute, while I take care of this man." She passed through the swinging doors toward the cash register, sold two packages of Du Maurier Filter Tips, and came back unhurriedly.

"Can't we have *any* rum and raisin?" said Tony wickedly.

"You're only asking because you know it's sold," she said smiling. She picked Tony up and set him on her knee for an instant. "Little *bagarreur*," He climbed down and wandered off to clamber around the Battaglias' winter woodpile, which abutted on our backyard. He had some mysterious preoccupation with those logs. I made a mental note to cross-examine him about them.

"Brother Luke said you could drop Matt off at the camp after supper, if he'd like to go along on the hike. Then you could pick him up at nine."

My father said to me, "Would you like that?"

"Yes, but what about Tony and Amanda."

"I'm going bicycling," said Amanda.

"It's too late for Tony," said my mother, "after all the boy is only six."

"But a good six," said Dad. "Right. I'll drop Matt off and find out where they want the ice cream delivered. Maybe I can sell them some sandwiches. Did he say how many are going along?"

"He said it was the Bantams. About 40."

"I wonder if he wants cones."

"He didn't say, but he's expecting to see you later."

"I'll go along right after supper."

I often participated as a day-boy in camp activities. This wasn't one of those wilderness emplacements wholly sunk in totemic practice, inaccurately selected Indian names, week-long, exhausting canoe trips from lake to lake. The Christian Brothers, who ran the place, were mainly Irish-Canadian or Québecois, from Toronto or Montréal, used to the solid comfort of their city residences, by no means voyageurs or experienced backwoodsmen. Their camp was almost exactly 50 miles from Toronto, on the shore of a practically suburban lake, convenient for buses; there was a Gray Coach stop at the entrance. You could make the drive from the city, even on the suicidal three-lane strip of Yonge Street near Aurora, at 50 miles an hour average, if you wanted to push it. There was a gentleman from Detroit, a Mr. Johnson, who always had the newest-model Oldsmobile, who always drove to and from the camp with his wife and two sons crouched terrified in the back seat, at about 90 miles an hour, a speed considered outlandish in that era. Between Jackson's Point and Detroit, for example, there was no mileage, none, of four-lane, divided, controlled-access highway. The Queen Elizabeth Way, just then under construction, running from Toronto around through Hamilton to the Niagara peninsula, and ending at Fort Erie, wasn't a controlled-access roadway. For decades after its opening, dreadful accidents used to occur where various cowpaths wandered across the right of way. It is interesting to reflect that the great and famous Ontario 401, now called the Macdonald-Cartier Freeway, was on the design-boards at this time, would have been begun the next year except for historical accident, and did not call for controlled access.

East of Toronto, near Pickering, a rail line crossed both lanes of the 401 for years, and still does, though it carries no traffic. The earliest overpasses constructed on the freeway are dated 1947; they are tiny little things, the right of way beneath them is constricted, the exit ramps (like those on the Hutchinson River Parkway in Westchester) are frighteningly angled and too short for today's speeds. All those highways derive in their design from the Pennsylvania Turnpike and the Merrit Parkway, the first modern, high-speed, multiple-lane roads in North America, and they in turn derive from investigations made in Germany, and elsewhere in Europe, which led to the construction of the system of *autobahnen*. The revolution in highway design—inseparable from the history of the "modern" movement in art and technology—accompanied the regular increase in performance of the ordinary passenger automobile in the thirties. By 1939 a car like Mr. Johnson's Olds could maintain speeds over 80 indefinitely without danger to the alloys of the engine metal. New highways had to be created, but of course no general program of highway construction could be financed by any modern industrial state for almost a decade following 1939. It's sometimes said by archaeologists that the Interstate Highway System in the United States will stand as the great engineering monument of its culture for centuries to come, in the same way that the Roman roads in Britain, or the transcontinental railways in Canada do. I suppose no other program of public works has been so lavishly endowed in our age, perhaps in recorded history. A society is best judged by the buildings to which it gives its closest artistic attention and the bulk of its funds. In one age, the representative buildings may be pyramids, in another cathedrals, in another the great institutional public buildings, law courts, the Pantheon, the Capitol, in yet another domestic architecture may take the leading place, or industrial buildings, factories. In North America the long-distance highway system has been the most splendid, useful, most-loved of public constructions.

Mr. Johnson of Detroit was a citizen of this culture, and it would seem to us, seeing him arrive in his Oldsmobile, always a brand-new one, always with Goodrich Silvertown tires on it, proof, we knew, against blowouts because of Safety-Seal Innerlock, that he was a kind of demi-god, that he expressed something that was inside us all, a new apprehension of the possibilities of rapid motion between places. His wife was always stunningly carsick. His two sons, Don and Chuck, would be incapable of taking part in camp activities for two days after their arrival because of stomach upset, but Mr. Johnson would have shaved another two minutes off his travel time, door-to-door, from Grosse Pointe to Jackson's Point. I can't envisage his precise route, because those old roads have been superseded, but I suppose he must have taken Highway 2, at that time the main east-west trunk road in Ontario. He'd have had to drive through Windsor, Chatham, London, Woodstock, Brantford—the mind quails at the prospect. And yet people did that, not more than a generation ago, thought it normal, enjoyed it, and towns like Chatham and Woodstock existed in quite a different way around quite different social patterns, than they do today. Around Aurora, on either side of that agreeable village, as it then was, lay stretches of Yonge Street, Ontario 11, that had been redesigned as a *three-lane* highway, a depression-minded compromise between the constriction of two lanes and the great cost of four. Drivers were to keep to the right at all times, using the middle lane for passing only—with predictable results. A more suicidal design for a highway can hardly be imagined. There were the Mr. Johnsons of Detroit and the world, who held resolutely to the middle lane, refusing to yield it under any circumstances, day or night, treating it like a bowling-alley of which the outer lanes were the gutters. Your ordinary man at the wheel, travelling southward toward Toronto, pulling out to pass and confronting Mr. Johnson on his way north, was either transfixed by the sight, continuing to rush forward toward death until the intrepid Detroiter swerved around him and proceeded northward, still cleaving to the middle lane, or else he cut back to the right in front of the car he'd just attempted to pass, often with drastic effect.

There were also the pairs of drivers coming at each other uncertain of their intentions, like over-polite gentlemen trying to avoid one another in a doorway. One driver would wobble to his right; the other would interpret this tentative gesture as a polite one and vacate the middle lane. Then, very close together, they would both resume the centre, to their mutual grave dismay.

Our Durant was never to be found in the middle lane, my father preferring to maintain a leisurely pace, which the rest of us found quite acceptable. We were seldom or never carsick, while the Johnson boys would vomit copiously at the notion of their return trip to Detroit in late August. Their father, an oval-faced, sunburnt, blond man who used to play golf at the Lakeview nine holes on week-ends, sometimes with my father, was in most respects quite sane, even friendly and conversational, and not at all a bad golfer, whereas my father, disciplined and reserved in the driver's seat, was a ragged and satiric player of golf. "Pasture pool," he would chuckle maliciously.

There were many other interesting and noteworthy persons to be seen at this summer camp. Priests. My God! They had priests coming out of the walls. There was an attractive and commodious chapel, a white-painted wooden building with the seating capacity of many a parish church, with a fair-to-goodish portable organ, a handsome wooden high altar screen, two side altars, and two chapel-altars down at the back of the nave. I believe the edifice would hold fully as many as the Beverly Theatre, maybe more. At a guess, I'd estimate seating capacity at 700 to 800—there were three Sunday Masses. The 10:15 was a High Mass, not a solemn High Mass, just a routine High Mass with four altar boys: master, censer, two acolytes. This one drew a big crowd from all over the nearby resort districts, a radius of some fifteen miles. There were other churches in the area, at Pefferlaw, at Keswick, and the camp chapel wasn't a parish church. It was dedicated to St. John Baptist de la Salle, the founder of the Christian Brothers (feast day 15 May) and its plank benches weren't comfortable pews, but it collected together on Sunday mornings the better-off churchgoers from round about. A worshipper often seen at that Mass was Toronto Maple Leaf defenceman Reginald "Red" Horner, then the ranking badman of the NHL. He was racking up impressive totals in penalty minutes in those years, and as he advanced toward the chapel of a Sunday morning across the green campus, his wife's arm in his, two pretty daughters scampering on before, folks would nod in admiring recognition, saying (according to the *idée reçue*, as it were), "Isn't he a lovely husband and father? Just look at those sweet girls. You'd never guess he was so mean on the ice, would you? My goodness."

Another quintessentially Canadian figure was often in residence at the camp, the object of many glamorous tales—of how he had turned up at the camp garden party one year and paid for free entertainment at the fishponds, gambling wheels, horseraces, for the entire crowd for the evening with a hundred-dollar bill off a wad big enough to choke a puma. The founder of the Laura Secord Studios. This was the legendary Senator Frank P. O'Connor of whom boys at camp used to say, in awed undertones: "He has ten million dollars."

I never knew how they arrived at the exact amount; it was always given as ten million, neither more nor less.

He was an extremely handsome man with silvery hair and a noble presence, and certain admirable personal standards, which he put into his manufacture of candy. The word "studio" was his personal choice; it gave the operation a touch of the personal and artistic. I used to imagine the Laura Secord Studios as a place where constant research into the structure of chocolate was carried forward. The familiar oblong box in white and black and gold, with the cameo of Laura Secord on the lid and the photo of her memorial on the side, reinforced this intimation of seriousness, commitment, superb quality. My mother kept her sewing materials in a group of these candy boxes whose white paper covering darkened and yellowed as time passed, becoming part of the array of imaginative properties of my childhood fantasy-life.

Senator O'Connor was also famous as that very rare entity, the owner of a Canadian company with a US subsidiary, the Fanny Farmer candy shops, a chain operating in the American northeast. I have a dim feeling that a generation afterward this relationship was reversed, the American heroine and representative of corporate investment interests acquiring a gradual ascendancy over sweet Laura Secord in the boardroom where she could not have done it in battle at

Lundy's Lane, a remarkable case of corporate symbolism acting out real national economic policy. Laura lorded it over Fanny for a time; in the end Fanny came out on top.

Laura Secord was an ambiguous heroine in any case. A well-known Canadian monologist used to mention that "she afterward remained three days with Lieutenant Fitzgibbon and his men," with a leer and wink that made the lady's sojourn seem widely open to review. Sometime later the forbidding middle-aged person in the cameo who resembled one's sternest aunt was replaced by a fetching young creature, sweeter, less stern, in an off-the-shoulder confection of the period. By the time that modern public-relations image-revision effected this change, Senator O'Connor was in his grave.

Ten million dollars. Well, perhaps. He'd been rich. O'Connor Drive up along Bayview northeast of Lawrence Park was so called from his ownership of real estate in the area. The Senator presented the Christian Brothers with a parcel of this valuable real estate, where they later created a boarding-school annex and residence, attached at a distance to their midtown Toronto high school.

I think of Laura Secords as simply the best candy in the world. Don't preach at me about Swiss or Dutch chocolate, or Italian, or about liqueur bonbons. For freshness, for familiarity, for French crisp or Milton caramels, for buttermallow bars, for French mint, for Kiddie Pops, perhaps most for those Easter eggs with simulated yolk of rich yellow butter-cream, legendary from one year to another in a Canadian childhood, I celebrate our Canadian heroine, placing her above those other claimants to the confectioner's throne. People used to say that you couldn't make a million dollars honestly—a populist slogan of the early decades of this century. I consider the O'Connor ten million very honestly acquired in the manufacture in those arty little black-and-white-curtained studios of the best candy in the world.

Also to be seen at that camp were Father Cantillon, shortest and oldest priest in the Archdiocese, Father A.E.

McQuillen from St. Catharine's but with multitudes of
Toronto relatives, who taught me to act as censer at High
Mass. There was Father Doherty, also a very short priest,
hard to see in the pulpit, famous for having said in a sermon,
"In a little while ye shall see me, and again a little while and
ye shall not see me, for I go to the Father," and then disappearing suddenly by stepping backward, falling or rolling
down the steps and being lost to view, convulsing his be-
holders with unseemly laughter.

"Oh God," said my mother years later, shaking tears
from her eyes, "that was so funny. It happened at Our Lady
of Lourdes. We'd decided to go down to Lourdes for Mass
because Father Regan had held a special collection four
weeks in a row. And there was little Father Doherty speaking
to that text, ". . . and a little while and ye shall see me, and
again a little while and ye shall not see me. . . .' That was
where he tripped backward, and as he disappeared you could
hear 'for I go to the Father.' It was like witnessing a miracle.
Some people thought they had witnessed a miracle. Old
Mrs. Whalen—you remember her, Andrew, her nephew
was a professor of law at the University of Ottawa—thought
a miracle had taken place. She could hear him, but her sight
was dim, and suddenly she couldn't see him any more."

My mother went all helpless with laughter. " 'For I go to
the Father.' "

Legend, legend: family history, national history. I heard
numberless tales of this kind at the camp, whose owners and
operators, those kindly Christian Brothers, were inexpert
businessmen, often easily imposed on. In early July that
summer, there appeared at the gates of the camp—or more
accurately down by the breakwater—a canoeist calling
himself Chief Little Wolf, who beached his craft and strode
to the Camp Director's office. He was paddling across
Canada, he said, and would be glad to address the campers,
for a nominal fee, on his experiences throughout our inland
waterways. You could paddle right the way to the Pacific, he
claimed, with no portage of more than a few miles. His trusty

canoe and paddles, his pack and equipment and photos as
evidence, were all down there by the breakwater for anybody
to examine. The Camp Director, Brother Alexander, a kindly and trustful man of God, arranged an evening appearance
in the large building called the Pavilion, where stage entertainments, sometimes very impressive and elaborate, were
mounted on Saturday nights.

I was at this lecture, brought down from the Point with
Amanda Louise by my mother, who was curious about Indian life and lore. Brother Alexander, who liked our family,
gave us a seat up front beside him. Chief Little Wolf appeared on stage very promptly at 8:15. He had paddles,
blankets, wampum, the whole deal. Pictures of himself on
Lesser Slave Lake. It was all in the last degree circumstan-
tial. He spoke for more than an hour, concluding with an appeal for popular understanding of our red brothers, slightly
Uncle Tom in tone, I remember thinking at the time.
Brother Alexander thanked him warmly for this instructive
lecture, handed h;m an envelope. They shook hands, and the
Chief made some other gestures of thanks and brotherhood,
then stalked to the shore, boarded his canoe and paddled
away into the summer night.

"What did you give him, Brother Alex?" asked my father
afterward.

"$50, worth every cent!"

Two weeks later, driving through Sutton on some local errand, my mother spied an impressive form stretched insens-
ible in the gutter in front of the hotel Beverage Room. This
figure seemed oddly familiar, and on closer inspection proved
to be that of Chief Little Wolf, quite truly an Indian, truly
a chieftain of his tribe. But not really on his way across
Canada by canoe, permanently diverted by the enticements
of civilization—the only drunk Indian anybody in my family
has ever seen.

"Do you think I should mention it at the camp?"

"No, my darling."

"Oh, very well."

I felt pleased to know something that the campers and the Brothers didn't know, and I think I did well to say nothing about the matter till now. My mother was skilful at holding her tongue, particularly around birthdays or Christmas, but I've always burst with secrets.

I knew where we were headed on our moonlight hike long before any of the campers did, that night we walked down the dusty back highway behind the camp. Unpaved, thick with fine white dust which rose from its excellent gravel, it was an easy route to trace under the lovely moonlight, and comforting to little boys out past normal bedtime. The Bantams were the second youngest group of campers, aged ten or eleven. Most of them were a head taller than me, and I felt proud to be striding along in their midst toward a destination unknown to them, though not to me. I hummed loudly to myself in accents that indicated, "I know something that I won't tell," and the other boys grew displeased with me.

"Just because your father's supplying the food."

"If you're so smart, what kind of ice cream are we having?"

Brother Pascal gave me a conspiratorial smile and wink. I smiled back and hummed louder, and managed for once in my life to keep a secret. The Bantams had a pretty good notion of where we were headed anyway; the routes for moonlight hikes were pretty well fixed. We didn't go into woods or brush at night, and stayed off highways on which there was heavy traffic. By the time we'd been strolling along for half an hour, and it had begun to get dark, everybody knew our destination. Walking along at a moderate pace, I gave myself up to the pleasure of thinking that my dad had made a good sale, that maybe business would pick up, as he had been predicting since Victoria Day.

"Once this cold spell moves east, the real summer will start. We'll get the good hot weather and the Point'll be full of cottagers. Then you'll see."

"Rain predicted again for the weekend," my mother would say.

When we got to the creek bend and found my father there sitting in the old Durant with the windows rolled down for maximum coolness, the can of ice cream in one of those funny old refrigerant sacks the ice cream company used to lend us, pockets for dry ice on its sides, I felt a sharp pang of love for him as I walked up. He didn't see me, at first, and the expression on his face was unfamiliar. I couldn't make out what he was thinking. Then he saw me and his face changed; he smiled widely. "So you walked the whole three miles?"

"Course I did."

"I'll drive you home if you like, and any Bantams that are tired."

"I'm not tired."

"No. No. But by the time you've had a swim and something to eat you might start to feel sleepy."

He was right like he almost always was. I had two sandwiches but no ice cream. I traded my cone for the extra sandwich, and I had an Orange Crush, my second of the day. I don't know how he managed it, but my father had managed to keep them cold, with chilly perspiration running down the sides of the bottles.

"Great food, Mr. Goderich," said one of the older Bantams.

They all joined in. "Yes, sir. Nice ice cream. Lots to eat."

There was the swimming and the singing and the wrestling on the dewy grass, and watching the moon move up the sky. Brother Pascal told a ghost story. Two boys cried. It was a story about a black cat sitting on a rotting corpse buried in a hole in a wall. Terrific. I didn't cry. My dad drove me and five of the smaller boys back to the camp. That was on Monday. By Thursday cloud cover had moved in, and on Friday afternoon it was raining hard. It was by now mid-July. Crowds were swarming through the Flushing Meadows site of the New York World's Fair. Magazines were full of the Fair's architectural symbols, the Trylon and Perisphere. My father called it "the Perish-Fear." I didn't know why. In variety stores you could buy little objects resembling the

Trylon and Perisphere, which were actually a small screw and ball-bearing. "Screwball," get it? "The World of Tomorrow" was the theme of the fair. Sometimes that summer I wondered, not very discerningly, not anxiously, what the world of tomorrow would be.

Friday afternoon it rained and rained and our restaurant was empty. Ruthie Battaglia, Gloria Kirchner and Joan Keating sat around a back table, feeding the Wurlitzer and giggling together. Joan was explaining something about her boyfriend and his boat. I didn't quite catch the sense of her remarks, but they must have been hilarious. I sat down on the floor in front of the modest magazine rack which faced the door, flipped through the comic books, all of which I'd read, then reached down a copy of a magazine called *Ken*, which was flourishing at that epoch. It was reputed to be slightly risqué in spots, and while I wasn't precisely forbidden to read it, I was made aware that it was meant for grown-ups. I felt faintly guilty about looking at it, but when my mother glanced at me from behind the cash register and saw what I was reading she made no move to correct me. I read the titles given in the table of contents; they seemed vague, out of focus. One or two of the cartoons arrested my attention for a moment; they seemed silly and ill drawn. Then the magazine fell open near its centre at a full-page illustration that froze my glance. It wasn't an illustration for a story, nor a cartoon exactly. It was raining hard in the picture, just as it was on the main street of Jackson's Point. Looking down the street from the front door, you couldn't see the drugstore a hundred yards south through the downpour.

I crossed my legs and hunched forward over the glossy magazine page to examine it more closely. It showed a muddy, shellhole-pocked battlefield of the Great War, dark, brown and grey, with a low horizon-line, posts and strings of barbed-wire jutting up along the horizon, under a heavy rain. There was a huge crater in the foreground, earth tumbled up in heaps around its sides, soldiers' bodies barely visible in mud. A desolate scene.

Above the shellhole in the foreground rose two terrifying ghostly figures that occupied most of the middle of the page. They were shrouded in misty drapery, just as ghosts are conventionally depicted. These ghastly foggy draperies hung in thick folds from cadaverous bony shoulders. At least one of the figures held a rifle to which a bayonet was affixed, its point forming one of the most vivid details against the dripping sky. The heads of the two spectres were simply skulls whose eye-sockets were cavernous holes. On these skulls were set tilted metal helmets of the kind worn by British and Canadian soldiers in the trenches. The eyes were infernal, deep-black, riveting the attention.

At the bottom of the page, the caption read, "Do you remember what we saved Europe for?"

I sat transfixed on the floor, listening to the heavy rain on the roof of the one-storey building. Somehow the falling rain created the strong impression that the building, and I myself, were in the picture on the magazine page. The same rain fell on the dreadful pitted scene and its attendant spectres as was falling on me. I pondered the picture in all its sorrowful aspects as deeply as my years and the limits of my imagination would allow. The 1914–18 War. I knew nothing about it from direct experience. Neither of my parents had been directly involved in it, my father having been barely into his teens when it began, and again barely old enough to enlist when it ended. My mother had been effectively a child in 1914, not much older than I was now, not quite as old as my sister. Really a child, not much more capable than I of understanding what a war was, much less a war of those terrible dimensions.

My father would probably not in any case have enlisted, even if he'd been old enough. His pacifist and socialist convictions, he used to say, had formed themselves in his mind as soon as he was old enough to reflect seriously, certainly before he was out of his teens. He could tell many tales about the Great War, most of them concerned with its correct historical interpretation—whether it had been an imperialist war, a trade war, an ideological struggle, the death throes of nineteenth-century culture and the European monarchies, or all these things and more. He thought of the aftermath of the Great War as almost the first human opportunity to found a lasting peace. He was an ardent supporter of the aims of the League of Nations from the moment of its inception, had in fact been a member of a model League of Nations, a kind of debating forum, while still an undergraduate at Dalhousie during the period of the Peace Conference . . . had founded that model society and carried the notion along with him to Toronto in 1922 when, fresh from his MA year in philosophy, which finished at McGill that spring, he had begun his career as a precocious lecturer in his subject at University College, U of T.

It sounds all too Canadian to say this, perversely comic, but my father met my mother at a meeting of the Society for the League of Nations, which he organized in Toronto in the fall of 1922. My mother wasn't a close student of world politics, but she was a sprightly, lively, clever girl who didn't mind sitting through meetings in which young men somewhat older than she spoke at length about the Hall of Mirrors, "open covenants openly arrived at," Senator Lodge, Colonel House, Clemenceau, Arthur Balfour and other matters of which she came gradually to take in the sense. By the time she'd known Dad six months, she was his—and the peaceful world comity's—forever. They were married in 1925, taking no League of Nations Pamphlets along on their honeymoon. Internationally minded, yes. Stuffy, no.

They had common memories of the second decade of the century, Canada's century, it will be remembered, and a common hatred for the War. That is too mild a way of putting it. They detested all war and the very notion of war, my father from rooted principle and my mother at first in admiring emulation of her husband, later from principle. It amazes me to meditate on how very strongly that damned bloody murderous war was lodged in the minds and emotions of adults, and quite young adults like my uncle Philip, when I came into the world in 1930. I began to hear wounded, agonized recollections of the War—always spoken of as if it had quotation marks around it, "the War," like that—as soon as I could understand human speech, say in 1931. By then it was perilously clear how all the social wrongs of the decade of my infancy, now concluding as I sat cross-legged on the floor of the Lazy Bay Grill, were birthed out of "the War." My uncle Philip's collection of the *Boy's Own Annual*, which ran from 1916 to 1927, was filled with pictures of tanks, trenches, Boy Scouts acting as couriers for the infantry, bicycle brigades, Spads, Sopwith Camels, Field-Marshal Haig (most untalented of strategists) and waddling, slow old battleships with barbettes and ram bows and names like *Black Prince*, *Collingwood*, *Indefatigable*, *Inflexible*, *Indomitable*; these last three were battle-cruisers, I believe. The *Boy's Own Annual* was replete with accounts of Jutland and of the dashing heroism (with never a critical word) of Sir David Beatty, in command of the battle-cruiser squadron.

If you were a fan of the pulp magazines, you could read *Air Aces*, *Thrilling Flying*, *Amazing Air Stories*, *Sky Squadron* and a dozen other mags, each carrying four to six tales of air combat in the rickety biplanes and triplanes of "the War." All the paraphernalia of "It's forty kilometres of hell between here and Caudron, sir!" Or, "God, it's murder to send the lad up in a crate like that!" Or, "Willoughby's gone west, sir. He went down in flames over Gondebec." How it comes flooding in.

There were the stories of Canadian participation: of Billy Bishop and his VC, and Roy Brown, slayer of Richtofen, of Sir Sam Hughes and the Ross rifle, of the Ypres salient, the Somme, Vimy Ridge, Passchendaele. The flu epidemic of 1919, when they called off the hockey playoffs, and "Bad Joe" Hall died of the rampant disease. Not too many stories circulated freely in Ontario of certain matters that went forward in Québec, which I never knew much about until 30 years later. In Québec, as everywhere else for two decades after 1918, nightmarish memories of what happened during "the War" were swirling and boiling just below the surface of life. Farm labourers desperately hiding from recruiters, under haystacks and in barn lofts. Rejection of the legality of a draft. The attitude to that senseless, hideous conflict, on the part of most Québecois, my father often said, was the sanest he knew of—disgust and repulsion, and hatred of its protracted idiocy.

"I missed it by a year," he would say, laughing strangely. "Another year and they'd have jailed me for a conchie." It had been the transformation of the European social system after 1914 that caused the depression, the break-up of the old international monetary system built around the gold standard, the disastrous German inflation of the early twenties, the crushing demand for reparations from the Allies. All those complex international problems that I was weaned on: the Polish access to the Baltic, the Sudetenland, the Ruhr, Gdynia, Danzig, Anschluss, Lebensraum. All came out of "the War."

It was, for example, a stupid and unteachable British military officer, who by some accident had commanded Canadian troops before Vimy Ridge, who refused to take the advice of a Canadian Prime Minister and grant a dissolution of Parliament, which precipitated the constitutional crisis of 1926 and 1927 and intensified the wish of the inner circle of the Liberal party to find more and more means of developing Canadian autonomy, and continental links with the US, to the chagrin of the Conservatives, whose fantasies and needs remained chained to "the mother country." When R.B. Bennett was thrown out of office in the "King or chaos" election that angered my father so deeply, in 1935, he departed to live in the UK with these words on his lips: "It's grand to be going home."

He had been Prime Minister of Canada, but now he was going home. This person later accepted a peerage under the style, "Viscount Bennett of Calgary," an act quite illegal under Canadian law, titles of nobility here being under rigorous interdiction. It's hard to see how a man could conceive such an act, then carry it out. How can you violate the law of a nation, even one you've quitted in high spirits, then choose a place-name from that nation as your title, when to do so is against the law in the country whose place-name you select? It takes a complex conscience to do that, but I suppose R.B. Bennett had that sort of conscience. To be Prime Minister of Canada, you have to have a complex conscience, so that what is vilely guilty in one light is modestly ennobling—to the extent of a viscountcy, ambiguous patent—in other light, in darkness. I don't for a moment propose the naïve and simple-minded Bennett as at all a complex thinker or intelligence; he had multiple loyalties and judgments, that's all. King, now, was a different article. He had complex loyalties; most of them were toward himself, then his cronies, then his party. He had the complex mentality too. Not a fine intelligence nor a generous one, sympathies neither large nor fluent. But multiple, multiple.

When Viscount Byng refused to grant the required dissolution, King must have thought, "O Lord, thou hast delivered mine enemy into my hands." In that crisis his enemy was the vice-regal prerogative. A year later, he might be found defending such prerogative to (apparently) his last breath. What are we to make of this confrontation between honest, foolish, incompetent World War General and King, humble colonial first minister. If we find in literature a likeness to King, it is surely the image of Uriah Heep, the 'umble servitor, oh, wery 'umble. Ah, yes. The humility of the taciturn boa-constrictor. I can think of no politcal character more interesting than King's. Others—almost any others—are more honest; hundreds of thousands are more truthful. Some more energetic, a few more philosophical. None approaches King in cunning, in policy, in obscurity of motive. Take a letter from his nickname and you're left with "wily," and this is surely appropriate. The author of *Industry and Humanity* (a title admired by my father for its conciseness and imitated by him in *Property and Value*) developed by degrees into a coiling serpent of cross-hatched strokes of

motive and policy. Confronted by him, the footling Byng
must have felt himself in the position of the yokel hunting for
the pea in the old shell game. "The hand, my dear Viscount,
the hand is quicker than the eye. Where is the little fellow?
Ah, yaasss." If the speech requires the tones of the immortal
Fields to make it humanly credible, this isn't accidental. I
think always of W.C. Fields when I think of Mackenzie
King.

It's hard to tell whether Fields is a subtle and refined
parodist of King and his tribe, or whether King is a coarse-
grained, lesser W.C. Fields. When we recollect that the
comedian possessed small savings-bank accounts in every
quarter of the globe, getaway money in the event of his being
unmasked, the policy reminds us overwhelmingly of Prime
Minister William Lyon Mackenzie King. Yet he too, King,
had been a rebel in his time, at the very same University
College in which my father passed sixteen years, a progressively more disenchanted presence. When I see these
names lined out:

Viscount Bennett
Mackenzie King
Viscount Byng

I'm uneasily aware that there is a found poem concealed in
the six words. An earlier noble Byng, unlucky Augustan admiral, was shot as an example to his men. One senses
elements in the Byngs of the world undesirable in a viceroy,
in a dog-catcher, come to that. But Viscount Byng had been
in command at sanguinary Vimy Ridge. Makes you think,
that does.

51,000 Canadian men lost their lives in "the War," which
is a dreadful total, though distant from the terrifying
numbers of French losses—an entire generation of young
fathers-to-be—an enfeeblement of the nerve of a great nation
for 50 years. But 51,000 young men, in a nation whose
population approached ten million in the nineteen-thirties,
was a quite sufficient blood-letting. It amazes me, thinking

back, how readily those spectral figures in the magazine drawing sank into my imagination, my soul, so that I can see that page now, four decades later, as if I were nine years old sitting on the floor on a rainy summer afternoon. They belong in my imagination, those ghosts; a place had been moulded, prepared for them, as the placenta is dressed for the child in the womb before ovulation occurs. The terror, horror, murder, hate, fear, spill of intestine on rusted wire, separation of parts of bodies by screaming metal shards all were lodged there. I associate the sound "Byng" with the sound "bang." Most Canadians of a certain age would make the same link.

When our complex, wily, serpentine, constricting, King-and-no-king outmanoeuvred this proponent of the Big Bang, Canadian soldiers felt loyalties so mixed as to be purely Canadian. Vets and sweats may have felt a sentimental movement of the heart on behalf of the retired general, now so wrongly situated, given his talents, though they retained misgivings about his tactics below the Ridge. Many had fought under him, a man's good reason for following him again, though it be into a hail of machine-gun fire. But not a fully human reason. All women reject it.

The Big Byng Bang. The Vimy Ridge memorial to the Canadian dead still stands in place. There is a pleasant avenue in Montréal called de Vimy. And similarly named streets elswhere, I don't doubt. "The War" was the 1914–18 horror, and they don't have wars like that anymore.

My mother crossed from the counter and looked over my shoulder to see what had so preoccupied me. "Oh, so that's it. It's a scary picture, Matt, but it's only a picture."

"Is that what it's like?"

"What what's like?"

"The war. Dying. Getting shot and gassed and going down in flames." I looked at the picture again; it was mighty impressive.

"I don't know what it's like and I hope you never do," she said. "I don't want to know."

I stood up, feeling stiffness in my knees from long cross-legged squatting. It was very damp, outside and in; we did no business at such times. My mother took me by the hand and we walked to the pair of screen doors facing the street. Flecks of rain wetted us as we came near the opening; there was a semi-circular wet area extending inward from the threshold for several feet. My mother rubbed at the wet floor with her shoe soles, made as if to go for a mop.

"I'll get one," I said. I brought my mother the mop from the kitchen, then stood and watched as she moved it carefully and evenly back and forth over the wooden floor. As the water sank into it, the grain of the pine floorboards was revealed clearly; its complicated geometrical pattern, extremely subtle in the mathematics of its curves, caught my eye and I stared at it admiringly. Being of God in the universe. That floor was kept immaculate; the mop turned up no dustballs, no mud, just rainwater. The rain came heavier. A 1936 Buick came wetly up the street, a doctor's car, dark blue paint gleaming. New York plate. Probably campers' parents. I concentrated on the Buick, trying to influence the passengers into stopping for a snack. But it was the wrong time of day, too late. Rainwater streamed in cascades from the eaves.

Gloria Kirchner detached herself from the giggling little band in the shadowy recesses of the long room and came over to look out. I smelt the Evening in Paris cologne she wore, heavy in the humid air. She offered us each a wintergreen Life-Saver.

"It's a bugger, isn't it?"

The Buick slithered up the street without stopping.

"It is indeed," said my mother, laughing ruefully. "Tell me, Gloria, is it always this rainy at the lake?"

Gloria made an oblique, uninformative answer; she was that kind of person, one of the first people I knew who made me aware that character isn't all of a piece, that unexpected behaviour is to be expected from lots of folks. She had tried in her inarticulate way to comfort me, after my run-in with Marianne, but most of the time was rather unpleasant to me. She seemed to like Tony. Tony rather liked her.

"I don't know what you can like about that old Gloria," I'd say.

"She's not so bad," he would answer mysteriously. "I showed her the kittens."

"What, before you showed me?"

"Well, yes."

I felt betrayed, and by my own brother. He'd been spending long periods of every afternoon in the backyard near our sleeping cabin, climbing around on a huge pile of stacked firewood that belonged to Mr. Battaglia of the fruit store next door. It was used in winter to feed an enormous old iron-and-brass stove, which stood in the very centre of the fruit store. In summer the woodpile lay undisturbed in the backlot, slowly settling in on itself and almost solidifying from its own weight. Little tunnels and hidey-holes formed along the length of the stack, which was a good twenty feet long and five feet high. From some angles you could peer into it, and see almost the whole length of the pile. It was like a magic castle. I can see how it would have charmed Tony, story-teller by nature. From our very first May afternoons that summer, he passed his leisure time examining the woodpile, telling himself tales about magic beings who inhabited it.

One sultry afternoon as he was lying on his stomach at the forward end of the stack, looking along one of the spaced-out tunnels between the logs, he was astonished to see a small, indeed a tiny living creature appear around a corner inside the pile, approach him, then put out a pink tongue so small as to be invisible to all but the keenest observer and lick his—Tony's—nose. Despite its minuteness, this pink tongue, he said later, was rough like a fine-grained sandpaper.

"What did you do?"

"I rolled off the pile and a log fell on me."

"We never heard you cry."

"I didn't cry. I was excited."

"What was this thing? Tell!"

He'd pulled away a couple of smaller pieces of wood to

enlarge the hole he'd been looking through, then applied his face to the widened opening. A miniature cat was sitting just inside, deliberately washing its face. A kitten with dark brownish-grey fur mixed, he thought, with orange. It stared at him, put out an almost invisible tongue once more, made a quiet sound.

"Meow," Tony said in reply, "meow, meow." Then he got excited, "MEOW MEOW MEOW. Come here you!"

The animal disappeared suddenly, and he pushed his skull as tightly into the aperture as it would fit. It was dark down the tunnel through the woodpile, but his sight got accustomed to the darkness and suddenly he realized that the interior of the woodpile was alive with felines.

"It was exactly like *Millions of Cats*," he said, "there seemed to be millions of cats in there, all very small, all different colours. Oh, and two great big ones."

He said nothing about this to anybody for days; he felt that there was a wonderful unspoiled quality about these mysterious beings, as long as he was the only one who knew they were there—like a private enchantment, his and only his. When he and I and Amanda Louise passed back and forth from our sleeping quarters to the kitchen, Tony would gaze at the woodpile and hug to himself the awareness that we had no idea of the life inside it.

He trained some of the kittens to come to him, smuggling saucers of milk out of the kitchen. He found a place on the other side of the woodpile behind Battaglia's store, where he could crouch unseen on an old butter-box and feed his pets. Of course what had happened was simply that the fruit store mouser had made a home for one of his wives out back and their offspring, playful, half-wild little things, were growing up beside civilization but not really in it. Tony was the first human being who ever fed them, I suppose, and he developed an extraordinary love for the little animals. When he had to leave them, early in August, he cried in a way he'd never cried before. He was desolated with grief, for a long time inconsolable.

None of us was happy to leave Jackson's Point, but the break had to be made sooner or later. The restaurant could not be made to pay under the weather conditions of that summer. In another year, on the other side of the street, perhaps even in the same location, a similar operation might have succeeded. Dad declared for years afterward that midweek business rose steadily, the longer we hung on. Tom Walton, the abstemious policeman, had started to bring friends around in the late evenings. The Brothers at the camp often mentioned our place to campers' parents who were passing through the village. My father was diligent, in no way inefficient or irresponsible in the management of the Lazy Bay, except perhaps in the one particular of carrying too much staff. But that salary item plus the lousy weather did him in.

"I never saw anything like the summer of '39," he'd say, for decades afterward. "Clouds would break on Monday morning; on Monday afternoon the sky would be an empurpled vault." The poetic diction was accompanied by a rueful grin. "A cloudless and empurpled vault, cerulean streaked with azure and occasional ultramarine. Not a trace of nimbus nor strato-cumulus nor even cirrus. Tuesday would be set fair; by Wednesday the radio would mention prospective heatwave. The good weather was like the socialist vote, prominent when not needed. Thursdays it would cloud over and the wind would be high overnight. At Friday breakfast heavy rain would fall and we would feel cosy and happy, in out of the rain. On Friday afternoon the downpour would be steady, continuing through Sunday midnight. Ten weekends in a row. I've never known a summer to tie it."

It's impossible to judge such circumstances. I saw the rain, every weekend. I know those rainfalls occurred. My maxim, "you make your own luck," fails in the face of fact. My father was no fool; his judgment was sound; his prices were fair and his food was good, and efficiently served. And he went out of business in ten weeks, because it rained on every weekend from Victoria Day till Civic Holiday, on the first Monday of August. He lost all the money he'd put into the place, and all of Grandpa Goderich's investment. It's much to my grandfather's credit, and Miss Nancy Carroll's credit, that they never spoke a word of reproach to him about the vanished investment, which amounted to almost $4000 of their money. My grandfather never even said that he'd told my father so, and the effort to refrain must have cost him something.

The whole family except for my mother, who was in Toronto on business, the four remaining waitresses, Charie Lee, and nobody else at all, were sitting around in the Lazy Bay eating their heads off on the evening of Monday, 7 August, Civic Holiday—what the English call the August Bank Holiday. We were closing permanently that night. There hadn't been more than a handful of customers during two days of torrential rains. Suddenly the handle of the front doors was rattled. We all looked at each other. Surely this couldn't be a customer; it was getting on for ten PM. But it was a customer, in fact two customers.

Tom Walton, dressed in his policeman suit, and Art Comstock in his usual nondescript attire, both men soaked through. It was some time before any of us realized that they were handcuffed together, a fact that was revealed when Art Comstock raised his arm to drink a hot cup of coffee.

"Why are you going around like that?" said Amanda Louise.

"I'm under arrest, actually," said Art Comstock.

"He's my prisoner. I'm guarding him," said Tom Walton with justifiable pride, "but we're both so damned wet we thought we'd get something to warm us up before we drive over to the jail; the hotplate isn't working in the cell. I've never had so many people wait on me. I'm sorry you're closing up."

"Never mind about that. Tell us what happened."

"Well it looks like Art here got a little bit annoyed with his daddy and mummy, didn't you, Art? Anyways he went and set fire to the Lakeview and burned her right to the ground.''

We all wanted to ask the same question. It was Dad who spoke first.

''In this rain. How did he get it started?''

5

No motor vehicles were allowed on the island at that time excepting the fire-engine stationed at the foot of the main drag, perpetually polished and petted by shift after shift of firemen and, if I remember right, an old Chevrolet stake truck used by men at the Filtration Plant to carry trash around for disposal. It was necessary to have a bicycle and my father, who couldn't afford to buy five, compromised on the purchase of a single, full-sized, girl's bike, which he and my mother and Amanda Louise managed easily and which I could ride if I didn't sit down. When perched on the worn saddle, I couldn't quite extend my leg far enough to accomplish a full circuit of the pedals; that was in mid-August 1939. My brother couldn't ride this bike at all, a fact of which he complained without interruption during that month.

My father said, "When we get our furniture out of storage, when we can lay our hands on things, you can have Matt's old sidewalk bike, Tony. It should be just right for you now."

"I'd like one of my own."

"I know you would, my dear son, I know. And when I can manage it, you'll have one, the best I can find."

They would smile at each other with rich and pure affection, and I would reflect deep at the back of my mind that I was almost certain I was my mother's favourite.

A bicycle, a bike. We had to have one straightaway, the

old Durant being parked—it looked like a terminal situation—on the lot in front of the mainland ferry docks. In summer there was no practicable way to bring a car across; this was in any case forbidden. In a later winter, crazy Buster Fremont drove a 1937 Ford coupé across the ice in the bay, appearing on the main drag quite suddenly late one Friday night, drunk but abundantly capable of eluding Constable MacFie, who had only his bicycle on which to give chase. One of the memorable manhunts of island history then ensued. The Ford had an eerily defective horn with humanoid accents that emitted a despairing clamour as the constable approached, then receded into woodland or along frozen lakeside. The scene resembled something from ancient Russian folktale, with the Ford as wounded boar, us boys as pack of yelping hounds, PC MacFie as Stenka Razin, possibly Ilya Mourametz. I had been a passenger in the car when it crossed the frozen bay, a fact that mercifully never came to my parents' attention.

In that troubled August though, no freeze threatened. The main drag was thick with bicyclists, although technically you were supposed to walk your bike along its crowded length between Lakeshore Road and the bridge down by Long Pond. This was an unenforceable by-law, there being far too many cyclists for the two-man police force to make an attempt to supervise them. We got our bicycle from a bike-rental across the road from the hotel; it was in quite decent condition, only a little old, the paint darkened and chipped. I can place it in the history of contemporary style by noting that the rear mudguard was pierced along either edge by a series of small holes, by now clogged with successive repaintings. Only persons of advanced age will guess why. At an earlier epoch, a series of taut strings had been threaded through these holes to keep ladies' ankle-length skirts from draping themselves over the wheel in such a way as to be wound up in the hub or caught in the coaster braking mechanism. It wasn't a new bike, but it was reliable and cheap, eight dollars. My father put new tires and tubes on it and had the vendor lubricate it, tighten everything up, and adjust the brakes. We got a lot of use out of that old wheel. There was a neat little wicker basket attached to the handle-bars, in which I used to stow a lunch and disappear for the best part of a day.

When we'd been on the island for a week and I'd mastered the art of riding this bike without quite sitting, I began what became a fixed habit on days when I wasn't helping my parents settle in at the hotel. I'd beg sandwiches from my mother, announce more or less casually that I'd be using the bicycle for the afternoon, and before anybody could register a blocking motion I'd scoot out the door to where the tall old two-wheeler was leaning in one of the stands that lined the street. Nobody ever bothered to lock up his wheel on the island. Cycling was known by all residents to be a basic condition of life there; only some depraved outlander would ever have stolen a bicycle—there'd have been the problem of getting it back to town on the ferry.

Now and then somebody would borrow a bicycle without asking the owner, ride it from, say, the Centre Island ferry docks to the Lakeview and leave it there in the stand outside the hotel. This wasn't considered theft, more a species of comradely trust in one another. Something of the sort is now in vogue in the Netherlands where bicycles rather than automobiles are the staple conveyance in the inner cities, with bicycle paths set aside for their use only.

I would pedal gingerly along the main drag toward Lakeshore, keeping an eye open for Mr. MacFie, who would once in a way tell a juvenile cyclist to walk his wheel. The shore once gained, right by the big bath-house, I would ride easier, turning east for the run along the lakefront, pass 320 Lakeshore (later on our winter residence), past Clandeboye Avenue where Bill and Ian MacLeish lived, past Chippewa and at length up a slight rise a mile east of the main drag onto genuine wooden boardwalk, the wooden roadway that formed the eastern stretch of Lakeshore Road, connecting Centre Island and Ward's Island.

Sooner or later the historian of Toronto will have to confront the necessity of explaining that the three islands (so-called) across the bay, Centre Island, Ward's Island and Hanlan's Point, aren't wholly and distinctly and in every respect separate. They are three in one, a point often brought forward by little Father Doherty (''and again a little while and ye shall not see me, for I go to the Father'') when he used to celebrate Mass at St. Rita's church on the island, corner of Mohawk and Iroquois.

''For you see, my dear good Catholic people, the Blessed Trinity are like these islands in this, that they are three in one, each retaining a distinct person, yet united in the Divine Nature.''

I could see as a boy that the illustration wasn't really adequate to explain the Trinitarian mystery, but Father Doherty had a point all the same. It was difficult to say where Centre Island ended and Ward's began. Was it at the board-walk? At Chippewa? At Clandeboye, Hooper or Oriole? In the same way, did Gibraltar Point mark the border of Centre Island and Hanlan's Point, or did it not? These matters used to amuse my father.

The geography is simple enough. What are called the Toronto Islands are really a low sand spit formed by the curve of the shore of Lake Ontario, the feed of water and mud into Toronto Bay from the Don and Humber rivers, and the prevailing winds and movements of water along the shore. This spit juts westward from what is now called Cherry Beach, and was deliberately severed by dredging in the nineteenth century, to form the Eastern Gap. At the other end of the spit there was a natural entrance to the harbour through the Western Gap, the entrance still used by commercial shipping bound for the inner harbour.

This low, sandy, curving, finger-shaped peninsula is not a single land-mass; there are eleven tiny islands clustered around the curve of the main forefinger: Olympic Island, Mugg's Island, Donut Island, Forestry Island, then down toward the east Algonquin Island, Snake Island, three or four nameless ones, eleven in all. But the well known names,

266

Ward's, Centre, Hanlan's, all refer to a single formation, the main island around which the little ones are fitted in by the underwater movements of sand. Ward's, Centre, Hanlan's are Trinitarian, triune, and though the National Harbour Commission, under whose jurisdiction the island falls, may have charts showing precise boundaries, few or none of the residents knew exactly where those lines were drawn. If you started east from Centre, you moved by degrees into the feelings of Ward's. The same if you went west. Hanlan's wasn't like either more easterly community—for that of course is what they were, three very distinct communities rather than three islands.

Anyway the Eastern Gap was man-made, the sole justification for the isolated distinction of these three communities, much as the English Channel insulates Britain as England, Scotland, Wales. And just as the Channel Tunnel project has for over a century excited fear among certain islanders that their cherished distancing from European affairs might be destroyed, so the slow filling-in of the Eastern Gap by movement of wind and water has sometimes threatened to allow the Toronto Islands to revert to what they were when Colonel Simcoe and his lady arrived on the scene from Niagara-on-the-Lake—a mere peninsula without the splendid isolating channel to protect, distance, distinguish.

At different times since 1858, the Eastern Gap has been useable by ship traffic. Then again at other times it has been closed, silted-up and dangerous to traverse. It used to seem that a single entry to the thriving Toronto harbour, from the point of view of a port engineer, was the most economical means of directing ship traffic around the bay to this or that berth. I always doubted that, and considered it, even as a boy, a mistake to allow the Eastern Gap to fall into disuse. Half a century after that epoch, experience has begun to confirm my infant judgment. Far far out beyond the primordial cement pier, there now extends a system of moles, roadstead, harbour entries and lights, which create an immense new harbour, more easterly than the Gap, a vision of Toronto trade for centuries to come, a transformation of my old

Gap, superseding the inner harbour at whose eastern end, in the late nineteen-thirties, lay most of the berths, including those later used in ocean trade, after the coming of the St. Lawrence Seaway. The old turning basin still lies up a narrow channel at the extreme east end of the bay. In the thirties, huge piles of coal and the gassy smell of oil-storage tanks dominated the Cherry Beach area of the mainland, just across the Gap from Ward's. You could smell that rather nasty smell on most days, especially on damp, humid or foggy days, when it hung heavy over the area from the Gap to Ashbridge's Bay.

We had a standing joke about Ashbridge's Bay, shared by island youngsters, by children of the Beach district too, to the effect that you could walk across Ashbridge's Bay because it was so clotted with excrement. There was some truth in this in those days, in the mid-thirties, when the Toronto beaches first began to display notice-boards suggesting that these waters were unhealthy—the first time any of us ever heard the word "pollution." The last time the waters of the eastern-most Great Lakes, Erie and Ontario, were substantially unpolluted was the year 1931, when I was a baby, when you could still catch whitefish off Centre Island. I have this date on scientific authority, as also the assurance that this unpolluted condition can be recreated, the destruction of the healthy purity of the lakes arrested and turned around by a change in industrial habits. The filthy, dung-laden waters of Ashbridge's Bay, Hamilton Bay, even, God help us, Toronto Bay, can be made safe again for swimming, for marine life, just as the waters of the Thames at London now allow marsh fowl, and various species of fish unseen near London for two generations, to breed and be observed in places where they might be supposed to be gone forever. In 1971 the principal water intake from the Thames for the Battersea power station was choked with the bodies of fish, an amazing and unpredictable occurrence. The Thames now teems. What has been done there will be done, is being done, on the Great Lakes.

Aboriginal fault can be corrected, atoned for. The lakes

will regain their pristine purity probably around 1980. In the end, the pollution will have lasted for half a century.

But in the thirties you could walk across Ashbridge's Bay on the ordure that flowed into it, or so the tale ran among boys my age. Certainly sewage disposal and the control of industrial waste weren't perfectly understood or directed at that epoch; the smell that was wafted across the Eastern Gap from Cherry Beach, gassy, oily, stinking, was doubtless a compound of the effluvia of coal, fuel oil and almost raw sewage—the sole unpleasant element in my childish view of that romantic region.

Until the visionary creation of the new outer harbour, the water passage through the Gap was ill maintained, often not maintained at all. The silt that seems a permanent element of the geography of the shoreline around Toronto almost filled the passage in. For perhaps twenty years through the nineteen-fifties and nineteen-sixties it was useable only by small boats, which took away from its romance. I've watched ship traffic all over the northern half of the globe: the facilities of Rotterdam, the greatest port in the world, of Antwerp, Hamburg, Bremen and London and Liverpool. Cardiff, the Firth of Forth, the approaches to New York. The crescent of the Mississippi at New Orleans, the riverside at Savannah. No port has been so much my darling as the port of Toronto. Twice in my life at widely separated intervals I've been told by shipmasters that the port of Toronto is the most efficient and agreeable on the Lakes, the cleanest, best managed, served by the best corps of longshoremen, an aspect of Toronto life not much appreciated by its citizens. Think of all the ports from Québec and Montréal to Duluth and Superior. Think of Thunder Bay, Chicago, Sault Ste. Marie, Hibbing, Bay City, Milwaukee, Toledo, Sarnia, Detroit, Cleveland, Ashtabula, Oswego, dozens, perhaps hundreds of them.

The coming of the Seaway changed all the patterns of shipping on the Lakes, and closed my old Eastern Gap for decades. At no time could the deep-draught ocean vessels

operated by Fjell, Poseidon, Hapag-Lloyd, have made the
bay through that silted passage. Only the Western Gap
allowed it, so the shallower passage fell into disuse.

In the thirties, what a difference! The smaller lake vessels,
and particularly the passenger steamers, used to circulate in
and out of the Eastern Gap at every hour of the day or night.
Their names made a kind of poem in my infant ears:

Britamolube
Britamoco
Britamolene
Britamoil
Britamette

These names are collapsed-portmanteau words such as
James Joyce might have inserted direct and unaltered in *Fin-
negans Wake*. They contain the following lexicon: British,
American, oil, company, lube, lene, ette (feminine ending
suggestive of cute girl).

Britamette was the cutest, smallest, most female-looking, of
the five tankers in the British American Oil Company fleet,
which used to call regularly at the oil-storage tanks near
Cherry Beach; she was a chunky, chubby small vessel of
around 850 tons' displacement, not much more than the size
of one of the river coasters of the St. Lawrence estuary.
She and her sisters must have been engaged in a sizeable
trade though, because they were in and out of the harbour all
the time. I used to read a column in the *Telegram* that was
first called "Along the Waterfront" and later simply
"Waterfront." At the top of the column was a picture of the
CSL upper laker *Lemoyne*, at that time the longest ship of
Canadian registry on the Lakes. In this column there was
careful coverage of all harbour news, and at the bottom a list
of arrivals and clearances in which the names of the five
British American tankers appeared several times weekly.
Where were they coming from, where were they going? My
guess is that they were coming from the refineries to the

Toronto storage site, then later on reloading in Toronto and carrying petroleum products off for redistribution. In watching the comings and goings of these small tankers, when I was nine, I was witnessing another testimony to the city's function as a distributing centre. *Britamette* was too small a ship for practical use as bulk carrier; she functioned mainly as a carrier-away of the product from the storage site. You might see the little tanker berthed in smaller ports like Stoverville or Kingston, pumping supplies of fuel-oil into local storage tanks. I remember seeing her coasting along the lakeshore near Port Hope, and identifying her correctly when I was seven or eight.

"There's the *Britamette*," I suddenly hollered, breaking a studious silence as our family drove through town on Highway 2, making my father swerve slightly at the unexpected outcry. It was late Saturday afternoon; we were off on some protracted excursion begun the previous evening.

"You don't use the definite article before the name of a ship," said my father moodily. "You just say, 'There's *Britamette*,' as if she were a person."

My mother stirred in the back seat. "Tell me, Andrew, if a ship has a man's name, like *Prince George*, is it still 'she'?"

"Yes," said my father. "I can't explain that."

"There's *Britamette*," I said loudly, as we drove past the single small dock area of the port.

"He's quite right, you know," said Dad. "She's coming in here. Let's stop and watch." He slowed the car and turned off the highway, driving down a sloping lane toward some wharves and moorings where the little tanker was now slowly approaching her berth., We sat there in the cool car for half an hour while lake breezes played through the windows, while the dockers moored the tanker, connected her pumping lines and began unloading. The unmistakeable Cherry Beach smell of thick oil drifted over to us and we all nodded in recognition.

When we were children we used to be taken for Sunday automobile rides, sometimes into the country to places like

Agincourt, Stouffville, Langstaffe, Rouge Hills, Maple, Port Credit, Brampton—and sometimes down to the docks. Those were the regular options. I'm not certain which was the more popular; perhaps they were equal. I think now, in maturity, of Proust and of his narrator's weekend choice of excursion from Combray along the Guermantes' path, or alternatively along the way to Swann's house, and of how the narrator discovered much later in life that the two ways finally united themselves into a single meaning.

I see as in a moral vision that our weekend excurions had the same range of implication. "Down to the docks" led deeper and deeper into city life, into the essential Toronto of pickup and delivery and redistribution of wealth into parceled-out units in small tankers. "Into the country" uncovered our supportive hinterland, the recoverable past of Upper Canada. Those little rail lines leading to the back country were the city's landward life-lines, as the lake freighters travelled those across the water. Toronto living was distinguished by topography as much as by anything else, that slow, gradual, very lovely slope of the land up from the commodious and easily accessible harbour with protective sand spit and twin rivermouths. King Street was low, Queen Street only less low, then the graceful slope began to show itself, up to Bloor, rising again at "the Hill" and thenceforward all the way to the height of land above Newmarket, in a mounded rounded swelling rise which, more than anything, reminds us of the adorable curve of a pregnant woman's belly.

From the high point of this sweet sexual swell the ancient portage dropped away to Lake Simcoe, to the sites of Atherley and Orillia and Lake Couchiching, and the Severn portage over past Severn Falls to Honey Harbour, Victoria Harbour, finally Georgian Bay and the continental water route westward. Chief Little Wolf was a mythmaker, no doubt, and hadn't perhaps travelled the watercourse his imagination had discerned. But he was quite right in placing these swift-streaming courses at the heart of his imagined life. Likewise for the Chief, for all of us, a course could be made out through the Kawarthas past Fenelon Falls, Lindsay, Peterborough, down the Otonabee through Rice Lake, then along the gorgeous Trent River to its mouth at the west end of the Bay of Quinte, a magnificent sheltered inland waterway whose furthest reaches allow traffic almost to Kingston, where the St. Lawrence begins.

Heroes and heroines of much of Canadian life take their sources on these waters. Al Purdy lives in country surrounded by the Bay of Quinte and Lake Ontario. Bobby Hull comes from Point Anne, right out on Quinte. The great novelist Margaret Laurence has a very private retreat on the banks of the Otonabee. Canada has more fresh water than *all the rest of the world*, more lakes than there are anywhere else. The ways of Guermantes and Swann, imaginatively recast in Ontarian terms, are the ways "into the country," "down by the docks."

For all of recorded North American history, Toronto has been "the Carrying Place." That narrow forefinger of sand curving out from Ashbridge's Bay and Cherry Beach, cut off from the mainland by the Eastern Gap—those two trickling streams now dirtied, damned, nearly destroyed, our Don and Humber—this excrement-laden bay, these polluted beaches, are the scenes of aboriginal commerce unimaginably ancient. Before historical time begins in North America the carrying place was and is. When I mounted our tall old family bicycle those long calm days in August 1939 and wheeled shakily and tentatively eastward toward the Gap, I was beginning to grasp at—to sense myself in tune with—a system of living predating the Bronze Age, extending back perhaps to the Palaeolithic. Lakes and rivers, glaciers, ice, melting water: Rideau system, Trent system, Niagara, Huron, Superior, Georgian Bay, Kawartha, Simcoe, Couchiching, Severn Don Humber, oh blue Ontario's shore the old Ontario strand the cottage on the Otonabee, the cottage at the lake. That is all of us.

Our Guermantes go "into the country" and our narrator

goes "down to the docks" where he studies *Britamette, Coalfax, Fernie, Renvoyle,* and on one dreaming summer night at the corner of Carlton and Yonge sees sky light up and runs to the docks to see the wooden *Noronic* burn to the waterline at her moorings, her passengers dying asleep in the flaming hull. I saw that. And long before I saw the paddle-steamer *Kingston* sail out the Eastern Gap on a softly serene Saturday afternoon bound for Rochester and Kingston and finally Prescott, where her passengers would trans-ship into *Rapids Prince* and proceed through great turbulence toward Montréal and the lower river. I'd wobble along the boardwalk for three quarters of an hour, sometimes trying to hitch my crotch up over the saddle, resting myself and stretching my legs as far down as I could on every sprocket-turn. Maybe the reaching downward would make me grow. Often I would see off to starboard, well out front, a tall spreading smudge of smoke that indicated a ship just below the horizon. This could mean a race between us, I pedalling as fast as I could on my unhandy conveyance to reach the longish cement pier or mole that formed the west side of the Gap before the ship came in.

Once arrived in Ward's Island territory, the boardwalk narrowed, began to show signs of neglect. Grass sprouted between the boards, which here and there were badly splintered. Low trees bent over the driveway, which narrowed as it drew near the waterside; you passed an old lavatory-bathhouse up a cement walk, and various red-painted iron railings, emerging suddenly onto the wide concrete runway formed by the man-made pier that walled the gap, in all perhaps a quarter of a mile long, perhaps slightly less. On the opposite side of the Gap, at the extreme south, lakeside end of the correspondent pier, stood a tall wooden structure with a light on top marking the entrance to the channel. A foghorn was housed here, and I well remember its doleful BBBBEEEEEUUUUHH mooing out of heavy greyness on certain venturesome Saturdays out along this slippery walkway.

If it was a bright day I would bicycle out to the extreme
end of the pier, flattering myself at my intrepidity and my
balance, then as now generally firm, sometimes shaken
slightly by circumstance. Sometimes I wobbled needlessly
near the edge, always the west side of the cement well away
from the channel. I wouldn't have minded falling into the
drink even on a bicycle, as long as there was no risk of being
run down by one of the ships (as Edie Codrington nearly
was, years later off Stoverville), which seemed immense as
they passed, great swell of bow wave running high against
the walls of the Gap, there cresting, then receding with a
deep hollow behind the leading swell, then the rusted sides of
the vessel, most often high out of the water, for many ships
were arriving to load. If there were no ship near, I generally
rode north to the mainland end of the pier to watch for
passenger steamers quitting their berths at the foot of Bay
Street, near the ferry docks. Four regularly scheduled excursion boats departed from there: the *Kingston* which ran across
to Rochester, then down to Kingston and the river, not quite
the only paddle-wheeler still to be seen in Toronto Bay.
There were still two paddle-wheel ferries in service at that
date, *Bluebell* and *Trillium*, last of their line. But the *Kingston*
was the only paddle steamer still sailing a regular run across
the lake, an impressive, oddly shaped ship vaguely suggestive of Mark Twain's Mississippi traffic, with three
straight tall narrow stacks and many decks. I associate her
with the *Mariposa Belle*, about which you could say the same
thing you said about the *Lusitania*. Both were big steamers.

I don't know whether the *Kingston* was built by Harland
and Wolff of Belfast or not, but she and the *Mariposa Belle*
and various ocean greyhounds like the *Lusitania, Aquitania,
Mauretania, Olympic, Titanic* (always described as "ill-fated,"
the *ill-fated Titanic*) were all balled up in my head in those distant days, the multiple smokestacks causing this confusion. I
thought a big steamer ought to have at least three stacks
placed amidships, and was always displeased at the tendency
of smokestacks on lake boats to be located right aft where, in
my view, they had no business to be.

The *Kingston* wasn't so ill-fated as the *Titanic*, thank God, but at least one death occurred after an accident on board of her. Some years after I first saw her pass through the Gap bound for Rochester, two kids in their late teens, a boy and his girlfriend, were fooling around on the boat deck late at night, seven miles off Rochester. It isn't certain just what happened; they made their way in the darkness around behind one of the ship's boats where there was no rail, and went over in the dark. The young man was brought on board half-drowned and scared to death; the girl drowned. These kids were almost exactly my own age. The image of the girl lost in darkness on the wide lake, crying out for the lifeboat's crew and not being heard, was dreadfully pressing.

Other excursion boats were seen from the Gap, getting up steam. I'd stand as far along on the bay side as I could get and stare for an uninterrupted twenty minutes at the stacks and rigging of the *Cayuga* motionless in early morning preparing for her run. I could spot at once the alteration in position that meant she had let go her lines and would shortly emerge from her berth. She would come out stern first, around in front of the ferry docks, always slowly and carefully, giving the tubby ferries a wide berth. Then her bows would come round and she would proceed eastward quickly, picking up speed; she had a graceful movement through the water, the *Cayuga*. I'd say swanlike if the comparison didn't seem affected. I'll say it anyway because the likeness was genuine; her swift movement toward the entrance to the Gap seemed effortless, powerful, precisely swanlike. Soon I could make out movement on her upper decks, hear the sounds made by joyful excursionists. She would swing in past me, moving quickly now, and I would mount the family wheel and rush along the pier beside the ship, but I couldn't keep up. By the time I'd got to the other end, the *Cayuga* would be past the pierhead, moving due south, a course she always held for several minutes until she passed a buoy well out from the shore, indicating deep enough water for her to alter course to starboard and make for Niagara-on-the-Lake.

By then I'd be seated smugly with my back propped against

a wooden upright on which were hung lifesaving implements· and a notice about safety regulations. I'd have a lunch. The bicycle would be on its side behind me, wheel spinning idly with an almost inaudible hum—we kept it well oiled. There'd be sandwiches and a bottle of cream soda or orange, at that time my favourites. The cream soda used to foam in the most delightful pink froth; the liquid was poisonously, cheaply sweet, but when shaken it looked wonderful.

I could make my abundant lunch last for well over an hour as I watched the *Cayuga* drop below the horizon, smoke streaming away behind her. In that time other ships would have passed along the rim of the clear sky, some heading for the Western Gap, others proceeding toward Hamilton, while some few came straight toward me. It was endlessly fascinating to spot the very first faint smudge low down on the line made by the merge of water and sky, to try and guess the ship's heading from the gradually modifying position of the smoke. In ten minutes it was possible to tell whether she was heading toward me. Then the game of identification began. Sitting out there day after day I came to know many ships by their silhouettes or other personal characteristics. Some made more smoke than others; some carried special self-unloading conveyor systems on deck; length varied relative to beam; amount of freeboard showing, arrangement of the deck-houses, frequency of call at the port of Toronto. I absorbed all these things without really thinking about them, assimilating them into the permanent set of my imagination and thereby enriching my whole life.

When the *Cayuga* had vanished and even her smoke was nothing more than a faint discolouration away off to the southwest, I might discern another equally faint dot in that direction, which grew and grew at what seemed then an amazing pace. This was *Northumberland* coming from Port Dalhousie—in my memory the swiftest and handsomest of these passenger vessels. Legend had it that *Northumberland* had been built in Prince Edward Island, then made a series of voyages to England during "the War." This seemed unlikely; the shape of her hull was more suggestive of idle sunshine excursions to the amusement park at Port

Dalhousie than of the rigours of the North Atlantic, rock-bound Cape Race, treacherous Sable Island, then the open sea, ice, fog. She was faster than *Cayuga* by some two or three knots, and seemed to race along like one of the early torpedo-boat-destroyers from the beginning of the century. Her hull and upperworks were painted a smooth grey, picked out in accents of black. In misty or rainy weather she was a ghostly figure, making little sound as she slid toward the Gap. I recall mornings when all was still except the small sound of the water breaking around the pierhead, when visibility was poor and a fine drizzle settled on my bare neck and arms as I sat gazing out across the lake, peering into the haze. Then, swimming swiftly like an elegant dolphin, *Northumberland* might materialize from the mist, going like mad for the Gap and her berth across the bay. At such times I could believe in her as wartime troopship, evader of submarines and surface raiders because of her speed. And yet, I believe, she wasn't an unusually fast ship. There was a peculiar authority about her pace; she seemed to plunge forward as she neared the pierhead, inclined to pitch rather than roll. There was nothing tubby or graceless about *Northumberland* as there was about her companion vessel, *Dalhousie City*, last and least of the four excursion steamers that made Toronto their home port.

Sometimes there would be a whole morning and afternoon when no ship traversed the Gap. On such a day I'd find myself fighting off sleep, out there at the very end of the city. Very occasionally another boy or an inquisitive adult might stroll out along the long walkway to see what held my attention. They would pad quietly up behind me, but I could always sense their coming.

I never spoke, never could have expressed the charm that place held for me, the solitude, the unending motion of the water.

La mer, la mer, toujours recommencée.

The gulls turning in the clear light. I didn't intend to tell anybody what I felt when I was out there. We only had the one bicycle, so I always went alone. What my sister did when she had the bike I have no means of guessing—perhaps making friends with other girls, like the truly striking Ina-Mae Rae. Accidental circumstance gave me those endlessly protracted mornings and afternoons in August 1939—a strange month in which to find an unchanging image of tranquillity, but there it was.

I used to fancy myself as the attendant spirit of the place, in my own way as ghostly a figure as the gliding silent misty *Northumberland*. Impalpable hulls were frequent then. If I squinted hard and concentrated, on a good day, I could just barely spy, away away off down the east, the old steamer *Toronto*, long ago retired from lake service, at her final berth at the mouth of Ashbridge's Bay. I had been out at the end of the pier several times before I brought myself to believe that I really did see a ship down there that didn't move, was always in the same place as if on a painted bay. The vision had a definitely spiritualistic tone, as if some medium had conjured up the old boat.

Later in the day the lifesaving stand would begin to seem mighty hard against my backbone, and I'd stand and stretch and go home. I'd get back to the main drag around 4:15, and would walk the bicycle down the street; this was the hour when people arrived home from their day in the city, when groceries were bought, dates made for the evening. In among the day-trippers were the folks who lived on the island all summer, and the much smaller number of true islanders who lived here the year round, a community maintaining a tenuous existence in the ocean composed of the two larger groups. It took time to become accepted as a true islander. A summer's residence wasn't enough, or even two or three. Twenty summers might qualify you but the real ticket of admission was winter residence, going to primary school there, riding the *Ned Hanlan* or the *Geary* from the Filtration Plant on frozen winter mornings to work or school in the city, playing euchre or rummy in the small smoke-filled cabin below the waterline in the bow and hearing the ice crashing against the plating, arriving at the John Street tugboat dock to walk along the frigid quayside to the streetcar stop at the foot of York Street, that was to be a true initiate, something of a participant in extremely esoteric rites.

This was my first encounter with multiple social groups existing inside one another like, I almost said, the rings in the trunk of a tree, but that metaphor is better suited to the occasion on which I've already used it, the psychological growth and increasing self-awareness of the normally introspective child. The three—perhaps more than three—distinct communities that dwelt on the island didn't so much form concentric rings with the winter residents the hardwood core, as parallel streaks of colouring like the veining in marble, or again perhaps like the coexistent strands in coaxial cable. I think the likeness to the veins in marble is closest, taking the summer day-trippers who came for picnics as forming the mass of the block, the summer residents at either of the big hotels, the Lakeview (now under the management of Andy and Isabelle Goderich) or Whitehalls', who came for periods of up to two months, as a strongly marked wide vein in the block, the May-to-September residents as various narrower streaks of crystal colour, and the few hundred year-round denizens of the place as an attenuated, wandering, barely traceable thin line or vein indicating a radical flaw in the mass. If a monumental sculpture were shaped from this hypothetical block and subjected to grave shock, it would fall open along the seam defined by this last, most tenuous vein.

The winter islanders weren't like anybody else, dear God no. I came to be able to pick them out of any crowd, partly because of their eccentricities of clothing, partly because of their accents. Mainly because of the rich gleam of lunacy shaded and almost hidden in their long-lashed eyes. Those long lashes were a mutation achieved in at most two generations by decades of gazing in sun-glare at the ice along Lakeshore. Perhaps I only imagine this at a generation's remove, but Denny Denton, Tom and Gerry Cawkell, Bobby Weisman and his family, even the lissome and unpredictable

Ina-Mae Rae, all seemed to me to have profoundly shaded eyes, lashes protecting them in downward glance from the arctic sunlight of a morning's walk to the Filtration Plant to catch the *Ned Hanlan*.

The owners of the Lakeview Hotel, first contacted by my mother during our final two weeks at Jackson's Point, when she had suddenly absented herself from the kitchen of the Lazy Bay Grill and returned to the city "on business," as my father said, were a lady and gentleman called Si and Lila Trousdell. They had two children somewhat older than us. I suppose Ramona Trousdell was in high school by that time; she was old enough to have a more or less steady boyfriend, who was planning to become an engineer. Ramona must have been sixteen. Her brother Clifford occasionally played with me but was really too old for me to cope with, not quite as old as Amanda Louise, and not the sort of boy she'd have selected for an associate—if Monty McNally is the archetype of the category. Clifford was an in-and-outer, term familiar in the usages of professional sport. Sometimes he was friendliness itself; he always made a good impression on adults. Even my father was at first very favourably impressed by Clifford Trousdell.

"I can put up with a lot in return for fundamental good manners," he said in this connection, during our first week at the Lakeview, plainly referring to young Clifford.

But Clifford couldn't sustain an even pace, was capable of sudden deviation into questionable behaviour. He smoked cigarettes and wasn't above petty theft from the coffee shop operated by his own family. I've never understood the motive that causes you to steal, as it were, from yourself, a form of behaviour often met with. It seems to imply an extraordinary capacity for self-deceit, and yet it is regular, almost indeed a norm. Clifford would sneak behind the counter and steal packs of gum. Juicy Fruit was his favourite—no ambiguous reference is intended—when his parents would gladly have given him all the gum he desired. A strange youth, alternately attractive and friendly and deceitfully malicious.

Si and Lila, as they urged us to address them (I never managed that, and my mother couldn't either), had inherited the Lakeview Hotel from Mr. Trousdell's great uncle, one of the pioneers of the island community, who had caused the rambling, barnlike structure to be erected sometime around the year 1904. I suppose Uncle Trousdell—the Trousdells always referred to him so—was around 60 at the dawn of the new century, which would put his young manhood back to the time of Confederation.

We have such a foreshortened history.

Uncle Trousdell may even had had something to do with cutting the Eastern Gap—the original definition of the island as an island. His masterwork in a long and successful life was the Lakeview Hotel, whose main mass abutting on the main drag, including an enormous verandah at front and sides, a lobby of really impressive size, a suite of owner's apartments at the back of the ground floor and a large restaurant and coffee-shop beside them, was the first stage in a species of serial construction. Above this frontal mass rose two storeys of resort-hotel rooms and suites with the long, galleried balconies characteristic of the lakeside hotel in Ontario, a partition separating portions of 'the galleries for the individual rooms, each of which had a doorway leading to the fresh air. As a rule, the partitions were only a couple of feet high, amounting to low railings, over which one could easily climb. I think that this arrangement was dictated by fire-safety regulations, because the iron ladders down the flanks of the hotel, which served as fire-escapes, could only be reached by passing along the balconies, hurdling successive low obstacles. In any serious fire, the interior corridors would have been impassable from the moment the fire began.

Some rooms still contained the red fire-bucket full of sand, with FIRE stencilled on the side of the bucket in bright yellow. A few rooms even had the length of thick rope tightly knotted to a ring in the wall below the windowsill, down which the escaper was supposed to make his way in the event of fire. I never heard of anybody using these ropes as fire-

282

escapes. Clifford Trousdell and I, in our madder moments, used to shinny down them from second-floor rooms in a game that was forbidden, but hard to prevent.

Successive additions at back and sides had enlarged the hotel to grotesquely swollen proportions. I would estimate that there were as many as 120 indidivudal rooms of all shapes and sizes in that crazy building, as it stood in August 1939. Naturally the hotel was never filled at the most flourishing times of the later thirties, although for a brief time in the previous decade, around the era of my parents' courtship (which had largely been enacted at the island), the Lakeview had sometimes been filled to overflowing with resident vacationers. It must have been around 1924 that the amenities were added at the sides and back of the hotel, and the addition to the main building at the rear. Where this addition joined the main structure, on every floor, there was a short flight of two or three stairs. The addition, indeed the main building, had been erected on infirm footings; this was understandable, for the island was virtually all sand. It was next to impossible to dig a cellar in such a location. In fact few buildings there had any kind of basement. Heating was apt to be supplied by oil-burning space heaters or by Franklin stoves. The Lakeview was uninhabitable in winter except for certain special areas, which had been insulated and supplied with outsize heating equipment.

Many island residents held that the Lakeview was settling, sinking into the sand that supported it. From the irregularity in the pitch of its interior corridors, especially on the higher floors, and from the tortured appearance of some of the plank siding on the rear wing, I'd say that this was so. No architect, no trained engineer had participated in its planning. Few or none of the buildings on the island had been raised by construction experts. All the dwellings were rickety, though many were of great size, some rather handsome, some the property of quite rich people. The great catch in construction—the element that gave these buildings their endearingly flimsy and impermanent character, was the fact that the land on which they stood didn't belong to the persons who owned the buildings, but to the federal office administering harbour lands. I believe that many of the buildings stood on land that had been leased for 99 years. No doubt the authorities had long-term plans for the place, which made building anything likely to stand for more than a century superfluous. All these buildings disappeared one after another in the nineteen-sixties, excepting only a tiny enclave of a hundred cottages on Ward's Island. Now nothing remains to indicate where the Lakeview stood, or Whitehalls' Hotel, with its charming adjacent bowling green, or English's Boathouse. All are gone.

To one side of the Lakeview there used to be a miniature golf course, to the other, a pair of badminton courts. Toward the rear, on the lake side, was a flower garden with table and awnings, where English-style tea could be had in the late afternoons. This is all gone.

I didn't know, when we moved there from Jackson's Point in August, that my parents had already had considerable, rather charming experience of island life, but this was so. The whole tone of life as carried on at Centre Island in the summers had changed, and changed again, from one decade to another, much as life has altered everywhere as the century proceeds. In my time, much of what went on there had a strong flavour of the *déclassé*, the raffish, a much more than faintly disreputable air.

My father would say, "Anybody who lives on the island permanently is either drunk or hiding out." Then one of us would always ask him which was his case, since neither alternative as proposed seemed quite appropriate. He would then quote a renowned English satirist not known to me at that time, Evelyn Waugh. "I have been in it long enough," he would intone, "to know that no-one enters the profession of the schoolmaster unless for some very good reason, which he is anxious to conceal."

This libel on the teaching profession for some reason appealed to him forcibly.

"We don't know what you mean."

"I will probably have to do some teaching again, in the

not-too-distant future." When he'd left the university, he'd broken with formal education in his own mind, and hoped never to teach in a formal academy again, unless perhaps in the kind of "freeschool" that evolved 35 years later. Now and then he and my mother would talk over the possibility of starting an experimental infants' school, making use of material drawn from the Montessori experiments, some theories of Piaget, and new notions of their own adapted to Canadian conditions. My father must have been among the very first educators in Canada to evolve a practicable approach to primary education in the light of the work of Piaget and Maria Montessori. He was the the first person I ever heard mention them—that would have been as early as 1935 or 1936. When we were living on the island at the end of the thirties, he often proposed to my mother that they open their own school for the island infants and "pre-schoolers," to prepare them for primary education in the orthodox graded school then in existence on the island.

The basis of my father's view of education was highly classical and abstract, at the same time highly experimental and practical. He thought, for example, that the central human act was that of knowing by means of our intelligence. He placed emotive activity somewhat below this. Sexual action he set in a lower place still, though an extremely high place by his reckoning, beside practical science and applied art. That sounds as if he followed some absurd form of ranking the claims of the various kinds of behaviour. This isn't what I want to imply. He believed in a modified form of faculty-psychology, that's all, and believed that the intellect is prior to the will, logically, and in experience.

"We are to know, love and serve God. Notice the order of priority," he would exclaim.

His idea of education aimed at perfection of the intelligence, by rather surprising means. He considered that there was a great element of intelligence in the activity of the senses, especially in the pre-logical activity of children's imaginations and art.

"I don't see that all intelligent activity has to be logical," he often said, influenced there by Piaget. "I think babies are mighty intelligent." He did a lot of work with us when we were babies and pre-school children, with oddly shaped coloured blocks, never turning our play with them into a lesson, simply watching what we built with them, which shapes we found unhandy, which attractive. I often wonder why he took so long to see that I could judge and enjoy the niceties of physical form in a very precocious way, though I could not create it. It might be that he wasn't looking for extraordinary behaviour in us, but for what he expected to be normal. He understood readily that there was a sensuous and imaginative aspect to spelling, for example, the look of words and of printed letters.

His two main ideas, that behaviour was always intelligent, though not always logical, and that sensory activity could be and usually was full of intelligence, seemed radical when applied to primary education. When the application was made, they turned out to be correct, eminently reasonable. I suspect that he got the idea that one could act entirely reasonably, but yet not perfectly logically, from Newman.

"Logical inference is for theoretical physics, and for pure mathematics," he used to say. "It has very little to do with the business of life, of getting through the night, a different kind of inference altogether, full of feeling, emotion, instinct. Look at the way young children play together."

He was fascinated by the group decisions made by kids at the age of three or four—their idea of law, of justice or fairness, how they arrived at agreement.

"That's prefectly human choosing," he would say. "It isn't pre-human or sub-human. A four-year-old man or woman isn't one bit the less a man or woman. It's a mistake to think children aren't reasonable. It's true they don't philosophise, but that's not to say they don't think. What does inference consist of anyway? Preparation for choice? The analysis of concepts? What about contemplative action?"

When he reached this point we all used to go out of the room. There was nothing forbidding or comic about his behaviour; it was just that whatever it was that he was doing, we couldn't do it with him, or help him when he was in that state. He wasn't inaccessible, or at all unsociable. Thought is an inward action, I suppose, best accomplished in solitude, anyway hard to get through in groups.

When he'd established to his satisfaction that reasoning wasn't purely theoretical and axiological in form, that it was streaked through with every modality of feeling and image, he would then argue that the sensuous manifold is inseparable from thought, that thinking must always be full of sensation, that the body thinks.

"Certainly the body thinks," he said. "I think with my toes quite a lot of the time. When punting on the Isis. I expect Mozart thought with his ears. Music is a perfect example of sensory thought. There is no musical intelligence except as embodied in beautiful sound."

I remember those puzzling building blocks, and the way he used to watch us laughing as we fooled around with them.

Amanda Louise was a venturesome architect. She built tall towers, which then served as piers for bridges; she always built bridges, with seat cushions and steamer rugs.

I was useless at vertical construction, but excellent at making roads with my blocks. And railway rights-of-way.

Tony always built dwellings of various kinds, from huts to skyscrapers. I don't know what inferences my father made from what we built. I'm sure he saw early on that of the three of us Amanda had the greatest capacity for engineering and design. I've often wondered why she didn't choose engineering as a profession. I suppose sexual taboo pure and simple kept her out; she'd have been a superb engineer.

Anything I built with the blocks had a weird and straggling quality, unpredictable and ill-formed, but interesting.

Tony was the stylist. His means were always the most elegant, pared-down, understated. What he built would stand up strongly over slender support. Tony would build cardhouses of extraordinary airiness and extensiveness of design. He was the only child I've ever seen who could build them up to six or seven storeys. The supply of cards around the Lakeview lobby was virtually inexhaustible, but he didn't use an excessive number of them and was early able to judge how high his construction might rise, consistent with the demands of style, elegance and supply of materials.

Watching this sort of architectural goings-on caused my father to stress children's art in his idea of education, with many important and careful distinctions made explicit, at a time when very different currents of opinion dominated Canadian primary schòoling. But it was above all his conviction that men need—before anything else—to speak the truth in all things that supported, founded, his approach to children's schooling

"Nothing is so warping as lying, nothing so harmful to the person. We need to know. The more we understand, the more human we are, the more ourselves."

He dismissed the idea that education is first of all training for socially approved conduct, and knew that the forms of children's activity are rooted in their wish to know, and to be free. He saw that unless free inquiry was open before children they couldn't hope to acquire knowledge, discover truth. He was a permissive teacher but not a licentious one, and hoped always to form in our minds the foundations of inference, in free intelligent behaviour before the age at which logical capacity emerges. Free, full and varied sensory experience was the rich soil out of which the tree of wisdom would ascend.

When his experiment in the restaurant business came to an end, he was perfectly ready to take on the direction of the services of the Lakeview Hotel, giving my mother the principal say in its administration, and really acting as her subordinate. They both realized after the first couple of months at the Lazy Bay that she had more talent in this line than he did. So she left Jackson's Point toward the end of July, when they'd definitely decided to close down before they ran really into debt with their suppliers—a serious and pressing danger. They had about run through their money, as well as the $4000 invested in the business by Grandpa Goderich. We were now poor. My parents' savings and the residue of my father's last payments from the university were all gone. When they talked about opening a kindergarten, it was partly because little capital would be required. But they had no capital at all.

Back in Toronto in late July, my mother remembered her happy courtship fifteen years before: afternoons in canoes, with mandolins, along Long Pond, near "the Aquatic," in 1922, 1923, 1924. Young men in striped blazers. Some in Norfolk jackets with loose belts in the back. She pondered employment possibilities for married couples with children—few enough at any time—and decided that she and Andrew had learned enough about restaurants to work for somebody else, as a team of managers. Happening to be running through want-ad columns, she noticed an advertisement for a manager capable of taking over a large resort hotel. She had doubts, even qualms, but she wasn't a timid woman. When she noticed the address, Lakeview Hotel, Centre Island, it seemed like an omen, because of there being a Lakeview Hotel at Jackson's Point.

At that time, there were Lakeview Hotels in every summer resort in Ontario, just about. There can't have been another name in more frequent use, unless perhaps the Queen's, or the King's. Maybe the Pines, but I doubt it. Even now I'll bet there are more Lakeview Hotels than any other kind in this country, which is reasonable enough. All Canada is the Lake District, a situation to cause in a new Wordsworth complex intimations of natural inspiration.

She caught a two-o'clock ferry to the island and almost trotted to the Lakeview, anxious to locate the opportunity she envisaged. She found Mr. and Mrs. Trousdell sitting discontentedly in the small office at the front of the owner's suite, rather an agreeable room, cosy, with one of those doors that divides in half, so that you can swing open the top part, while the bottom forms a counter or, in this instance, a registration desk, complete with fat register, faulty pens, bell to signal an absent room-clerk.

To the Trousdells, the Lakeview was an albatross or white elephant, something they got their livelihood from, with infinite inconvenience. They didn't much like Centre Island, finding it deficient in gentility, in decline. They wished they were somewhere else most of the time. Somewhere like Forest Hill, a modish municipality surrounded by suburban Toronto. Or Palm Springs. Actually they weren't enormously rich, but they weren't as ridiculous as that makes them sound; they were simply in the acutely annoying position of having a large amount of money—money enough to make them moderately rich—tied up in an investment from which the capital couldn't easily be extracted. No buyers—at least none wholly sane—ever presented themselves for the Lakeview Hotel, not after 1929 anyway. There it stood, enormous, quite a moneymaker at certain seasons, all their capital on the hoof, as if they'd tied it all up in a champion bull, say, or some other investment with specialized appeal and qualified resale value.

Every summer for a generation Si and Lila and eventually Ramona and Clifford had come reluctantly to the island in April to begin preparing the hotel for the season. They didn't have to do all the work themselves. The operation made enough money through each summer to pay for paint and paper, floor-polish, renovation of a certan number of rooms annually, supplies for the restaurant and coffee-shop, without any problems at all. The embarrassment of the Trousdells wasn't financial but social. They felt lowered in class by the connection. They didn't really like the owner's suite, which was damp.

They couldn't figure any way to get their money out.

When my mother hove in view, they looked her over with care and found the prospect good. She was a university graduate. She was quietly attractive, and spoke beautiful English. They'd never heard of my father or his loud indictment of the Ontario university system, or his radicalism, as it then seemed. They had in mind a kind of superior head waitress to keep an eye on the coffee-shop, but when my mother put it to them that they really needed a husband-and-wife team to take over the day-to-day running of the hotel, leaving them free for long-range planning and high-level policy-making, they were persuaded almost at once. My mother had a remarkable, dangerous gift for noticing chinks in armour.

"You probably have plenty of spare accommodation upstairs," she said breezily.

This was a better-than-fair conjecture. The hotel was about one third full that month and even at that was making money. Taxes were low.

"We could find something. Three children, you said?"

"A girl and two boys. Amanda Louise, Matthew and Tony."

It has often seemed to me that my parents made an only ostensibly neutral choice of Christian names for their kids. When I notice them, repeated in a row as I've put them down, I notice most their strongly upper-class tone. Amanda. Tony. Like characters in a drawing-room comedy by, most likely, Noel Coward. This makes me think again of my mother's strange regard for English fiction and drama of the period between the wars, of a not terribly high quality. It wasn't exactly a vulgar taste, and she could laugh at herself for it. Still, there it was: Amanda, Matthew, Tony. The Trousdell children were called Ramona and Clifford. One name came from a song popular when the child was born; my father used to hum it absently when Ramona Trousdell came under his eye. The name of Clifford ran in the Trousdell connection, may even have been the given name of the legendary Uncle Trousdell who built the Lakeview Hotel. If that is so, poor Clifford probably had to bear a load of ambiguous feeling about his name on his parents' part, which might have influenced his often erratic behaviour. I believe that the name Clifford was in the beginning a family name like Nelson or Harvey or Stanley, perverted to use as given name because of the greatness of some individual Clifford, but who? What great Clifford authorized, for example, the bestowal of his name upon poor Clifford Trousdell, who didn't in the least resemble a Clifford? He looked like a Joe or Pete or even a Matthew, like the rest of us.

They had funny names, those Trousdells. Ramona, Clifford, Lila. And Si. Actually a shortening of Silas. Mr. Trousdell was the only man named Silas I've ever met. He was not in any way like his name, not a gawky New Englander slapping worn britches and ejaculating, "Wa'al, by jiminy, I swan." He was a smooth man, all over, smoothly brushed hair ascending in shining auburn waves from an unlined forehead. He favoured suits, with vests, of smooth hard material in dark shades of brown and green. One didn't often see a green suit in those days, but Si Trousdell wore them. Not a simple man. I think he really hated the old Lakeview.

He started speaking to my mother quite slowly, thinking his words over, glancing at his wife now and then. "We were looking for a lady to run the coffee-shop, but actually if you both came into it we might arrange for you to run the hotel completely, from day to day, and we could give you any information you needed. Any help. Whatever you want to know, see? Lila and I don't really feel that we belong in this line of work. We inherited the hotel and we run it out of our feeling of responsibility. I figure as it stands now—and you can't tell about prices; they say there's going to be a war and that will send prices sky high—at today's prices, now, this minute, I estimate the Lakeview is worth $200,000, maybe $250,000. In any given year, after all operating expenses, Mrs. Trousdell and I can figure on a net profit of over $12,000, from six to seven per cent on $200,000. That's at today's prices, mind you. If a war comes and living accommodation gets scarce, we think we may winterize part of the hotel and operate the year round, and the earnings would double. Tell you what, if you and . . . what did you say your husband's name was again?"

"Andy."

"Well, suppose you and Andy came here in the beginning of August, say, you'd have the remainder of the summer to get to know the building. It has its little peculiarities; parts of it at the back are next to impossible to heat. In summer that's all right, but we couldn't use the rear wing through the winter. We intend to close it off completely, seal it right off. Then we'll install space heaters in every corridor, and we'll have to decide how to heat the individual rooms. We really do plan seriously to try and stay open this fall, starting with the coffee-shop. It's already useable in winter; it's insulated and heated, and there's extra heat from the kitchen ovens. It might be real cosy in December. We'll stock it up. You say you've been running your own place, Mrs. Goderich. Now tell me, if you would, why you're giving it up."

My mother said, "We lost all our money. The weather was wet every weekend."

"It sure was. It rained here too, right up till last Saturday. Of course the Lakeview has been here for many, many years. It would take more than one wet season to knock us out, wouldn't it, Lila?"

His wife gave a horrific grin. "You said it."

"The Lakeview's been here for 35 years, Mrs. Goderich, and looks to be here a while longer. Why not come in with Andy the beginning of August. Bring the kids. Settle in good. If we all get along, we'll leave you in full charge after Labour Day. At the end of November we can all sit down and see what we can do to work up some income from the place through the winter. I think you said three children?"

"That's right."

"Well, we can assign you a nice family suite, three connecting rooms at the front of the main building, directly over the kitchen and the coffee-shop. There are connecting doors, and we can help you to arrange them into two bedrooms and a sitting-room. The bedrooms have washstands. I'm sorry to say that none of the rooms at the Lakeview have private bathrooms, but there's a bathroom just at the end of that corridor, two or three doors from your apartment. We can arrange things so you have a private toilet and shower. The hotel is getting kind of old and we've never cared to install complete new fixtures. But we'll take care of you. We'll have PRIVATE lettered on the door, and give our other roomers notice of the change. I can't show you those exact rooms today because they're occupied, you know. But I can show you ones nearby that are furnished about the same. In the winter your rooms would be easy to heat. One of the stovepipes runs up through the floor of your sitting-room. We'll connect a stove to it, for your apartment, and you'll be snug. Real snug."

This was only partly correct, though not an intentional deception. In succeeding winters our sitting-room was indeed comfortably warm, but the bedrooms grew colder proportionately to their distance from the stove. The front bedroom—the kid's room—was really cold. We used to heat bricks in the big kitchen oven downstairs, then wrap them in flannel and set them on the small stove in our living-room to keep hot till we went to bed. Just before retiring we'd shoot the bricks down between the flannel sheets, and the beds would be entrancingly hot despite the cold air outside. Our parents gave us the colder outer room, not because they wished to keep the warmer one for themselves, but because they stayed up much later than we did, and didn't want to have to keep passing through our room while we were asleep; the standard hotel-room door to the corridor in both bedrooms was locked shut and weather-stripped against drafts during the winter. It was like living in a beleaguered city.

"It all sounds wonderful," said my mother, impressed by Mr. Trousdell's volubility and openness, with good reason. He was an ingenuous man, sometimes faintly condescending to people he considered his financial inferiors, excessively uxorious, foolishly indulgent to his children. But he was also perfectly honest and truthful. He told my mother, that first day, that he hoped eventually that she and "Andy" might join him in ownership, then finally be able to buy him out of the business.

"I don't think so, Mr. Trousdell," said my mother. "We

couldn't ever raise the capital—you said $200,000 or more."

"There are banks, Mrs. Goderich," he carrolled happily, "and that's what banks are for. I want you to consider that you and your husband are in business for yourselves. If you can show a good return on the operation, we'll work it out."

After some brief discussion of salary terms for a husband-wife team, which was concluded quite generously, everything considered, my mother reached an agreement with the Trousdells. Room accommodation, all meals for the family, and a joint salary of $125 a month for my parents was the outcome of the negotiations. Mr. Trousdell seriously imagined that he might someday sell his $200,000 hotel to a married couple with three children, who earned $125 a month and their keep! If the whole truth is to be made clear, it appears that he was more than a little taken with my mother, who retained her fresh, girlish slenderness of appearance way on into middle age. Two decades after Tony was born, she still seemed slim and fragile and young. A dangerous woman, my mother. It wasn't that you couldn't trust her; she was devoted to the truth, and truthfulness, pursued the one, practised the other. She could sometimes be silent, when speech would have uttered an offensive truth. My father often used to quote her description of a friend of their university days, a distinguished bore.

"Taciturn. Almost morose," said my mother.

"And then there was that aborted exchange with Enid Ivings at the UC Ball," my father would murmur reminiscently. "There had been some girlish tiff."

This phrase made my mother laugh immoderately.

"Some girlish tiff, yes. And Enid Ivings said to your mother, 'Do you think I'm a fool?' "

"What did Mum say?"

"She didn't say a thing."

When my mother reported back to Jackson's Point, by long-distance, the generous offer made by Mr. Trousdell, my father was suffused by one of those rare moments of insight amounting almost to prophecy.

"I see a new Lakeview rising from the ashes of the old," he said over the phone, on that dank Tuesday afternoon. "Like the fabulous phoenix that consumes itself on its own pyre, the fortunes of the Goderiches, now utterly burnt up in Jackson's Point, will raise themselves from ashes at Centre Island and there be restored."

"Oh, Andy."

"How extraordinary that we should go from Lakeview to Lakeview."

"Andrew! This call is costing us money."

"I'll write to the suppliers tonight, Ishy. I'll announce closing and give the girls notice. Would there be a job for Marianne at the Lakeview, do you think?"

"I suppose so. Would she want to come?"

So their decision wasn't a snap decision; they'd known for weeks that they were under-capitalized—fit situation for ardent socialists. Marianne had broached the possibility of living with us and doing some housework to help pay her living costs while she went to university. They made this decision to close down on Tuesday, the first of August. The Lazy Bay Grill closed its doors forever on the wet night of the ensuing civic holiday, Monday, 7 August, after Dad shooed Tom Walton and his prisoner out the door, on their way "over to jail." Art Comstock served two years and seven months in the penitentiary for his act of arson. Out of the ashes of the old Lakeview—literal ashes—island residence and a new view of the lake might bring restoration.

I had mixed feelings, riding to Toronto in the back seat of the Durant next day, while Tony sat on Marianne's knee in front next to Dad. We took a longish time over the trip. The car was overloaded; my father was exercising what care he could for the springs. He was at no time a fast driver. We arrived at the Ferry Docks fatigued, sweaty and overheated, all but Marianne who seemed disturbingly cool and composed while my father arranged for a week's parking in the ferry dock lot, then went off to arrange to have the masses of baggage attached to the car carried to the Long Pond freight dock by the TTC freight service. It was around 4:15 when we finally caught the *Bluebell* and rode across the bay. I think all of us, Amanda Louise who grew more and more silent as she surveyed Marianne and my father, Tony who was exhausted, my father who had just seen several thousand dollars washed away by a summer's rain, even Marianne who had never been away from home, certainly I myself, all felt daunted and faintly fearful as we floated along on the old paddle ferry. Halfway across we passed the *Trillium* returning from Centre Island. The two ferries saluted one another in mid-bay with siren-blasts. I thought Tony was going to hurl himself overboard, his reaction was so spontaneous, surprised, terrified. He'd never heard the ferry hoot at all, let alone at such close quarters. We were all a bit taken aback; silence grew oppressive as we now came in sight of the dock.

Happily, though, we spotted my mother immediately, standing at the exit with one of the kids who used to carry baggage on a coaster wagon. This boy, Bobby Weisman, was the first friend I made on the island as we walked up from the docks together, our smaller pieces of hand luggage balanced on his wagon.

"What do you get for a load like this?"

Bobby looked at me slyly, a look he got from his father, who had been out of work for most of the decade. "Dime. Quarter. Depends on the customer."

"What do you think he'll give you?" I nodded at my dad.

Bobby changed hands on the Eatonia wagon handle, sneaking a peek at Dad, who was carrying Tony and talking a mile a minute to Amanda Louise, Marianne and my mother.

"50¢," he spat out succinctly. He had it right on the nose.

His wagon was loaded down with two large suitcases and an old club-bag, a really good one that had been a graduation present to my father from one of his multitudes of Nova Scotia uncles. The rest of our huge load of personal belongings was coming across on the heavy old green TTC freight launch, which could come right the length of Long Pond to

the freight dock below the bridge, at the foot of the drag.
This was where bulk shipments were received for the grocers
and butchers and the branch of Merrill's Drugstore that
stood across the street from the Lakeview. Finding Miss
Clarkson and Mr. Halifax clerking in the drugstore on the
main drag, which they did every summer as a working holiday from the parent store on Summerhill, was the first instance I recollect of those circling recurrences of friendship or
merely acquaintance that crowd in on one, the older he
becomes. When we got settled in at the hotel, which my
father referred to tiresomely often as "the phoenix," we
found our three rooms surprisingly large and comfortable,
having the charm of unfamiliarity in addition to their
gracious proportions. All three rooms gave on the long
balcony running the length of the south side of the building.
The rooms connected. The one nearest the stairway was
definitely a sitting-room, not a bedroom. It had a
mantelpiece with a mirror over it, bookshelves and other fittings. With some waterproofing, this suite was later made
extremely liveable.

That week we made great strides toward becoming true
islanders. We bought our bicycle, and for some reason
the man who ran the bike rental gave us a very good buy.
Since then I've often wondered why he did. I suspect that
like Mr. Trousdell the bicycle man found my mother far
from unattractive. She and Amanda Louise were on the
scene when my father concluded the bargain, and the bike
man kept eying my mother, offering to give her lessons in
bicycling.

"Oh, I know how. I had a bicycle when I lived here
before."

"You lived here before?"

"Off and on for parts of three summers, before I was married."

"I thought I knew your face," said the bike man eagerly,
and he practically gave us the bike. It never hurts to have
that personal connection.

The day we arrived, right after supper (hot chicken sand-

wiches, wax beans, bran muffins), we all went across the
street to the drugstore for ice cream, and there in starched
white jackets stood Ruth Clarkson and her colleague, dis-
pensing drugs, cosmetics, orange ice cream and Campana's
Italian Balm, with all their accustomed aplomb. Happy re-
union! We felt that we had come home, and when Mr.
Halifax and Miss Clarkson had recovered from their puzzled
surprise at learning that my mother and father were now
running the Lakeview, they too expressed similar feelings,
promising to come over to the coffee-shop when we had it in
full swing to enjoy an evening meal with us.

"My, that gave me a lift, when I recognized them. I'd
been feeling at a loss," said my mother.

Dad eyed her incredulously. "Taciturn, almost morose,"
he said, grinning. "When were you ever at a loss? Ishy. My
darling Ishy." He kissed her right there on the street. We all
stood around and goggled. Miss Clarkson smiled approvingly
from the doorway of Merrill's.

When we'd been at the Lakeview for a week, it was like
we'd always been there. I kept bumping into people I knew
in the city, on the drag, over for a picnic usually. It was fun
to tell them that I now belonged here, could go behind the
counter in the Lakeview Coffee-Shop any time I felt like it,
to make my own milkshakes. The following Saturday afternoon, I even saw Adam Sinclair trot by in pursuit of one of
his aunts. I was with Bobby Weisman at the time. Tom and
Gerry Cawkell were there too, a pair of tough kids in the Eddie Reilly mould. They gazed attentively after Adam
Sinclair, and with a single voice ejaculated, "Fucking fruit."

Something told me to keep my acquaintance with Adam to
myself.

Tom and Gerry were older than us, themselves separated
by about sixteen months. Tom must have been all of fourteen, Gerry twelve and a half. They had a sister, Doreen,
aged ten. The family had established some obscure claim on
Mr. and Mrs. Trousdell, some special dependent status,
though not quite like that of the old family retainership ex-

erted over the wealthy Lowther family of Rosedale by the Sinclairs, Cloughs and Farquhars, uncles, cousins, brothers and sisters of poor old Adam. The Cawkells were—I almost said sturdy—obstinate proletarian Torontonians and old-line islanders. Fringe people. Discriminated against by society in many ways; suspected of that crime supposed by the middle class to be worse than rape or murder: shiftlessness. I used to hear this or that lady summer resident of Whitehalls' Hotel—the more upper middle class of the two local hostelries—describe Tom and Gerry and their parents as "shiftless," and I wondered what it meant. I still do. What does it mean, to be shiftless? Once upon a time, a shift meant a petticoat, a slip or similar undergarment. Serving-maids in bad movies modelled after *Tom Jones* were always being discovered in their shifts, nipples thrusting through sheer stuffs in engaging style. I don't think "shiftless" derives from that source; probably comes from the other sense of shift, "to move around or deplace oneself from point to point," as we might say, "Shift yourself over here, buddy!"

To be shiftless wasn't to be without a petticoat, but to be unable or reluctant to be able to move from here to there, with a view to regular earnings. Shiftless people wouldn't get out of their own way to progress in life.

I've never met anybody like that. All the people I've known have been shifting themselves constantly from here to there, trying to make a living. I envy those who aren't. I wish to God I were shiftless, instead of incessantly moving forward from point to point, in order to arrive . . . where? Those good ladies of Whitehalls' were ready to stigmatize the Cawkells as shiftless, while secretly, perhaps, admiring and envying their ability to stay in one place, like big stones stuck in soft mud. But this sticking in mud was illusory. Like all the poor people I've known, at the different times in my life when I've been poor, the Cawkells were full of plans to move ahead. Far from accepting their situation, they came constantly to Mr. Trousdell with visionary schemes for getting along. Mr. Cawkell, ostensibly a handyman, was the unhandiest man you ever saw, his thumb and his hammer inseparable.

But God, he was a trier! I never saw him but he was carrying something, usually a length of either pipe or plank, from one spot to another. Both families, the Weismans and the Cawkells, had their being in the equivocal recesses toward the rear of the Lakeview, on the ground floor—Weismans to the north, Cawkells to the south—in extensive, semi-subterranean lodgements connected with a range of sheds, former chicken-runs, collapsed fruitstands, aborted additions to the main mass of the hotel. The father of neither family had had a steady job during the thirties, but in neither case was this because of pure and simple indolence. To attribute their bouts of occasional idleness to unmitigated sloth would be to commit a libel against human nature. Mr. Cawkell, as I've suggested, was ceaselessly in motion, leading a strangely nomadic life in very constricted circumstances, forever moving through the chilly corridors and galleries of the less rentable parts of the hotel, making a pipe-fitting here, accidentally breaking a plumbing fixture there. He could make a poorish job of anything in the line of carpentry, plumbing, wiring, the semi-skilled aspects of minor construction work.

He didn't of course belong to a trades-union, and had picked up what he knew about these trades in a haphazard, hit-and-miss way, and this incomplete command of any *métier* was what spoiled his life. He just didn't know enough about what he was trying to do to make more than an indifferent success of it. I don't know what education he'd had, but it probably didn't go beyond fourth or fifth grade. Tom and Gerry both intended to leave school as soon as they could "get their papers," as the phrase went. That meant the age of sixteen, when formal permission to leave school and go to work could be obtained; absence prior to that age was truancy, which could land a child in a detention home if long continued.

I seem to recall that in cases of extraordinary family hardship a child younger than sixteen could "get his papers" but

I never personally knew anybody under sixteen who was legally working full time. I knew lots of poor kids—was one myself—who stayed out of school intermittently to work at full-time jobs, at the beginning or end of the school year, or around Christmas. If you were Tom Cawkell's age, and poor like us, you'd have had a least one full-time stint, perhaps begun during the summer and held late into November in covert defiance of the anti-child-labour laws.

This practicable covert defiance was of great benefit to poor families, and to immoral employers as well, who would often hire a boy to do work beyond his strength at fourteen or younger, because they could get away with paying him much less than a grown man. The first job I ever had, in the few years when our family was feeling the sharp bite of genuine poverty, paid $7 for a full week's work, when I was twelve years old, which would have been the summer of 1942.

This was admittedly not a man's work. It was the delivery boy's job at a chain-store grocery on the main drag, involving the use of a huge, heavy old black-painted delivery wheel, with one of those fixed carriers up front and a smaller wheel than normal underneath it. 30 years after, one could see fleets of similar bicyles struggling through the winter slush of Montréal, pedalled by grown men, often Italian immigrants, but in 1942 such work wasn't considered a man's work except in its fatiguing and boring aspect. I was never paid any overtime, and I remember weeks when I put in five solid nine-hour days plus Saturday till noon for my $7, working bloody hard on weekdays from eight till six, with an hour for lunch.

I never held a full-time job for very long during my schooling. My education, far from being interrupted, was proceeding at an intense pitch of concentration at this time. My father would never have let me try to hold a job and skip a lot of school. This was a class attitude that didn't desert him just because we hadn't any money. But Tom Cawkell would be registered in the seventh or eighth grade of the island primary school from September to June, and from time to time even put in a fleeting appearance at the back of the classroom; but the teachers knew, and all the kids knew, that he was working down at the TTC freight dock most of the time; we just figured that as normal.

Class. Class. Class. We hadn't been on the island ten days before I began to feel myself assimilating new class attitudes, those of the kids of the chronically unemployed working-class poor. I don't mean to misrepresent myself or my family, and I persist in believing that the social classes in Canada, even at the end of the nineteen-thirties, were far from the inflexible barriers to mobility of a feudal system. You can go up or down. The proof of this is my almost immediate identification with the Cawkells and Weismans.

I felt like a poor kid. I had a worn blue Melton-cloth windbreaker, frayed around the buttonholes like a poor kid's. I played endless games of Relievo, which stretched from one end of Centre Island to the other, in the company of other poor kids. I felt that the children whose parents owned the old-fashioned summer mansions that fronted on Lakeshore were from a different part of life. Bea Skaithe seemed unimaginably distant. I wondered whether I'd ever really spoken to her.

Our sense of social relationship is just like that, full of personal fantasies compounded of pride or shame and simple feelings of security and belonging. Reading over my feelings at this distance, I can see that they were only partly founded on matters of real economic substance. Feeling like a poor kid was not, for Amanda and me and Tony, a matter of having any less money. It was mainly our unfamiliar location. We didn't have a house anymore and it seemed as if we would never live in a one-family house, all together again. Our rooms seemed agreeable enough, but not the badge of the middle level of society; they had an impermanent, anonymous feel to them. Status was involved in all kinds of behaviour, your diet, your choice of colour in clothes.

Bobby Weisman looked poorly fed. I don't mean undernourished. I mean that he was eating the wrong kind of cheap food, few fresh vegetables and a lot of carbohydrates. For the same money the Weismans spent on his food, he could have had an infinitely more nutritious diet. His colour was pasty, his teeth already in a state of chronic decay. He didn't keep himself clean. Signs of status. I had no objection to dirty clothes, and after a week on the island was always as dirty as Bobby or Tom, glad to be so because it made me feel I belonged to the gang. But I always ate better than Bob.

This whole question is so bloody difficult! The class-breaker for us was partly change in environment but mostly our sense that our father was no longer in the heaven of the university. Class. Class. The artist and the historian will always think of class in wholly different ways from those of the sociologist or economist, because they see the reality of life as lived in concrete particular detail, rather than as abstract schema. The great radical analyst of class in our century has been Mao, who has understood social life as the great novelist does, not as an economist or sociologist.

When we are moved from one set of circumstances to another our egos are involved, our sense of the deference due us from those beneath, and the deference we owe to those above. Is there any society where the metaphor of "above and below" doesn't obtain? Where is the social climber not found? The great political radicals have one after another turned out to be social climbers who, finding themselves at the top of the heap, were pleased to look down on those beneath. How naturally and easily we speak of the underdog, the social climber, manners that are beneath us, the relation of inferior and superior, of rank, elevation, of what is degrading.

Why did I address the great storekeeper's grandson as "sir"? Why did I feel that Bea Skaithe was above me, and what did the feeling mean? I could have reached out and touched her when we were young children in Rosedale. In the intervening years our paths have often crossed, at first on a level, then with a tilt unfavourable to poor Bea. When we went to live in the Lakeview, I felt set down, far down, in social rank, but didn't mind, like it, loved those guys: Bobby, Gerry, Tom, Denny Denton, Baz Babineau those girls, including Ina-Mae Rae, all those floating people who comprised the ambiguous island population. Since then I might be said to have risen in life, but I know that the spatial metaphor doesn't fit my feelings or my social being. I am the same man I always was. Nobody's inferior; nobody's superior. I am a Canadian man, a worker, a teacher. I've been a labourer, may be again, and don't understand what I'm talking about, but feel with Mao that no society can tolerate class-warfare, that the conventional pieties of class-warfare are profoundly wrong, that the middle class (if indeed there is such a thing) and the workers and the members of *apparats* and the artists, and all women, must be preserved into the social whole.

To exclude one fifth of society from the community, to allege that the middle class must be extirpated, is bad Maoism, bad radicalism. The classical Marxist insists that the middle class must wither away, and allows no autonomy to the artist, and ends in totalitarianism. The genius of Mao shows itself precisely in his autonomous *art*. He treats society like a George Eliot, a Balzac, a Dickens, will not amputate healthy limbs on ideological grounds, loves even—perhaps most of all—the bourgeois virtues: steadiness, prudence, thrift, survival.

I'm not a bourgeois, not a worker, not an abused and disenchanted woman nor an artist. I'm an art historian, a connoisseur, of all beings, to the conventional socialist, the most useless. My father was a radical socialist theorist who willingly gave up a safe niche in the educational *apparat* to become a server of food, and later a wandering teacher of the mediaeval kind, and he never repudiated me for becoming an art historian. In the heaven on earth of the new commonwealth, he would declare, the art historian too will find his place, for art exists and is exceedingly high in social utility (but this was said smilingly) and will therefore have its historians in any case.

The blue Melton-cloth windbreakers we wore, from Eaton's Annex, smelled badly. Their blue dye was cheap and ran easily and the flowing pigment smelt of questionable chemicals. Our hair grew long and dirty. Some of us smoked. We used the curt expletives of the street boy. We were a bunch of tough fucking kids that you didn't mess around with. Does this sound like the opening chapters of *Studs Lonigan*? The resemblance is intentional, for in that novel, an explicitly socialist analysis of class structures in urban Chicago early in our century, the young man who is the central character is often spoken of as if he were purely and simply a tough street-urchin. That is part of Farrell's art, for Studs isn't that at all, and it passes belief how often the fact is overlooked. Studs Lonigan's father is a prosperous house-painting contractor who in the year 1916 is worth close to $100,000, owns apartment properties and looks on his life as richly satisfying. The identification of Studs as a poor boy of the streets is wrong as far as his economic background goes, right where his *habits* and conception of himself are concerned. He hangs around pool halls, uses the conventional language of the gutter, sometimes sleeps there when he has had too much bad liquor.

My father was a professor and professional philosopher, later on an elected representative of the people. I was a "worker" and a poor kid for one absurdly truncated period of my life, from first to last less than a decade, and I'm open to the same misinterpretation as young Lonigan. I mean that I can't be classed. I can't be classed! I resist it! Indeed I will not allow it, and the analyst who says baldly, "All hangers-on around the arts, and all artists, have the illusion that they belong to no class," states a half-truth at best.

Was Stalin a worker to start with? He was like hell. He was a career party-functionary. Was Hitler a worker? He was a declassified man on the fringe of the arts—painting and watercolour—and a house painter like Studs Lonigan, a temporary soldier who only briefly contemplated a life in the post-war army, a floating unemployed urban nomad, finally the co-founder of a small local political party—almost a petit-bourgeois of politics. In the cases of Stalin and Hitler, political party was the vehicle of a ruthless consuming political ambition, and a thrust upward toward supreme power, amounting to profound, dreadful disturbance of character.

The tool of Stalin's pre-eminence in power was precisely his control of the party organization. The case was first of all the same with Hitler, and continued so until he managed to establish an uneasy alliance with German industry and militarism after the Reichstag fire, when political illegitimacy was rampant in Germany. From 1934 onward, political legality played no part in Nazi imperialism. The burning of the Reichstag was the sacramental sign of the destruction of rational politics in central Europe. Totalitarianism was born anew in its modern form. Class was swallowed up in the monolith of the state, in Germany as in the USSR, and the historical antagonism between Russia and Germany, which the creation of the Polish buffer in 1919 had done nothing to dissipate, flourished dreadfully from the beginning of the second Five-Year Plan. Against whom was Germany rearming? Against whom was the swift Russian industrial renaissance directed?

We were settling in at the Lakeview the week following the Civic Holiday. We came to the island on 8 August, a Tuesday. On the following Thursday, 10 August, my father said to my mother, "How would you translate 'runner-amok' into German?"

"*Amok-laufer,*" said my mother promptly. "That's a standard term of abuse. I hear it all the time on the shortwave."

"Aha," said my father.

"Who's running amok in Germany?" she said to him.

"Not actually in Germany. In Danzig. In Poland. This is terrible stuff." He'd been running over extracts from the *Börsen Zeitung* quoted that day on the US wire services.

POLAND LOOK OUT. ANSWER TO POLAND,

THE RUNNER-AMOK AGAINST PEACE AND
RIGHT IN EUROPE.

And other things like:

WARSAW THREATENS BOMBARDMENT OF
DANZIG.
POLISH IMPERIALISM THREATENS EUROPEAN
HARMONY.

"I like that," my father said sorrowfully. "the im-
perialistic sabre-rattling of the sheep, which threatens the
tranquillity of the wolf."

UNBELIEVABLE AGITATION OF THE POLISH
ARCHMADNESS.

"Aha, aha," said my mother, pleased to recognize the
phrase, *"Polnischen grossenwahns."*
"It's a completely controlled press," said Dad. "I don't
expect there's any element of a free press left in Germany."
"Will Hitler attack the Poles, do you think?"
"I hope to God he doesn't," said my father. "That might
be the last straw. He's won everywhere else without a fight,
in Prague, in Vienna, in the Ruhr and the Sudetenland, at
Munich. The British and French seem cowed, and aren't
ready for war even if they had the will to fight. The Russians
are the only power keeping Herr Hitler in line."
"Then why does he meddle with Poland? Won't that
alarm Stalin?"
"That's what I don't understand," said Dad. "He can't
mean to risk a general European war with Russia, France
and Britain allied against him. Ever since 1918—well, for a
century before that—the Germans have been terrified of a
war on two fronts. Danzig. Why Danzig? Why the Polish
Corridor? I will say, I always thought the creation of the corridor was a terrible mistake. The Germans resent any parti-

tion of their central land mass; they still claim the part of Schleswig-Holstein that lies in Denmark. I wouldn't have been surprised to see them go after the Danes first—that will doubtless come in time. They wouldn't rest till they got into the Saar, the Sudetenland, on the grounds of the high German population. And Austria, of course. Herr Hitler considers his homeland an integral part of the greater thousand-year Reich. I can see why he yearns after East Prussia, but I can't see how he could risk confronting the Russians. If I were Hitler, I'd do all I could to conciliate them. On the other hand, he may think it useless to negotiate with the USSR.''

''Why is Danzig important anyway? Why does he have to have another Baltic port?''

''Oh hell, it's another leftover from Versailles. The free city of Danzig. The population is 90 percent German. I'm sure the place is completely Nazified by now; there's a Nazi gauleiter on the spot, and the freedom of the Senate has been compromised. Danzig was made a free city when Poland got her independence, so that Poland would have a natural access to the Baltic—Danzig is the only great natural port along that coastline, protected from the open sea, and ice-free except in the most severe winters. I imagined they'd have ceded the city to the Poles at Versailles, if the population hadn't been almost all German. The compromise of a free city hasn't worked; the Poles have nominal control of foreign relations, but the people are German—it's as simple as that. The Poles understood by 1925 that they couldn't really assimilate Danzig, because they went ahead and built Gdynia, which is another kind of compromise. The situation reminds you of Canada.''

By now my father was well into his lecturing stride. It would have been useless for the rest of us to leave the coffee-shop. Even if we'd all gone, he'd have continued this review of Baltic marine politics and geography for himself, muttering to himself quite audibly. Anyway, the whole business was fascinating. I've never forgotten what he said that day.

"I've seen newsreels of Gdynia, and it almost works. It isn't a natural port like Danzig. It's really what a port engineer would call a roadstead, which means a relatively sheltered indentation in a coastline, not a bay or a cove or an estuary. More like a bight. A mere bump in the coastline creating an area of open water calmer than a fully open sea."

He said nothing for a moment, apparently wondering if this was an accurate definition, then resumed.

"The Poles simply moved into a little fishing village and built a range of reinforced concrete moles or piers. You know, Matt, things like the walls along the Eastern Gap."

I nodded sagely. I'd been thinking of the Gap while he talked, guessing that the moles of Gdynia probably looked just like it. Years later I chanced on pictures of the artificial port the Poles had built there between 1925 and 1935, and by golly they did look exactly like the Eastern Gap and certain of the newer structures in the outer harbour of Toronto, or like the concrete arm that shelters the port of Bridgetown in Barbados. Construction like this is fine in temperate weather, but dangerous in heavy seas, the moles as a rule being low in profile, the water in the area shallow. High winds bring seas of terrifying proportions in such conditions, and the docking areas are virtually unprotected. The berths at Gdynia were really unsafe in very bad weather. Nevertheless, the population of the place went from a few hundreds in 1925 to about 100,000 a decade later, when Gdynia was freely spoken of as the hope of Poland.

I have often speculated that the Poles' success with their experiment in artificial berthing at Gdynia may have served as the goad that drove Hitler to attack them. As long as Danzig was absolutely necessary to the health of Polish commerce, the large German population of the city and its attachment to German culture and policy helped to place Poland in a suppliant posture vis-à-vis Berlin. But if Gdynia should supplant Danzig as the main Polish window on the Baltic then the Poles would have freed their commerce from German control and interference. It wasn't really the submission of the large German populace to Polish authority in foreign affairs, or feelings of national and cultural ties to the Danzigers that urged the Nazis to "liberate" them. It was the growing strength of the Polish national state and its commerce, moving ever more rapidly through the new artificial port, that drew the attention of the Nazi leaders.

I'd heard my father mumbling about Gdynia off and on for a year or two, and had imagined that he was talking about gardenias. For a long time after August 1939 I associated the attack on Poland with fluffy pink flowers. Gardenias, Gdynias, why all the fuss. Hitler went right on ranting against what he called a rapacious attack on the commerce of the good Danzigers, this attempt to supplant a centuries-old and natural port activity by a self-willed assault on the open sea by sterile dikes. He had some weird aversion to construction of that kind. "Sterile dikes" was a phrase Herr Hitler loved to apply to the port of Gdynia. Later on he took a special and severe revenge on the citizens of the hopeful new community.

To hear the Nazi chancellor tell the tale, the Poles were menacing the peace of central Europe with their attempt first of all to take over Danzig and oppress the German citizenry, secondly to sap the commerce of this good folk. Danzig and the Polish Corridor must be returned to Germany immediately. East Prussia must be united to the central German geographical mass. Shipping through Polish ports on the Baltic was to be controlled by Nazi officials, and the Polish state reduced to a mere dependency of the Reich. Posen and Upper Silesia were by every dictate (*diktat*) of common sense a contiguous extension of the new Germany and must be politically united to her. At once. At once! AT ONCE!

Undeniably the greatest orator of our age, Herr Hitler was capable of imposing his wishes upon great masses of men by the sheer hypnotic force of the repetition of his demands. My mother, not precisely fluent in German but readily able to follow it, was one of the dictator's earlier North American listeners. She used to travel some distance across North Toronto to the home of friends who possessed an excellent short-wave receiver, to listen to Hitler's addresses at party rallies, and before the Reichstag. For six years now she had heard his growing insistence on the territorial integrity of his central European empire. It might have been even more apparent to her than to my father in what direction the Nazi expansionist policy of *Lebensraum* would lead.

First form a buffering ring around the central German territory by reclaiming lands lost after Versailles: the Ruhr, the Saar, the Sudetenland. Then quell the ambitions of the newly-independent Balkan states: Czechoslovakia, Yugoslavia, Hungary. Repossess the Austrian people and extend the empire to the Alps. Make a friend of the Italian dictator.

This design was clear by 1935, growing clearer and clearer as the next years raced past, as German rearmament proceeded apace, as a navy was built and the Luftwaffe equipped and the Panzer divisions conceived, assembled, exercised in manoeuvres, their tactics and strategy demonstrated in Spain by German military consultants. The union of all of central Europe must be accomplished; the decadent West would be terrified, cowed by this mighty assembly. The French had lost the flower of their manhood in the previous generation; the British were mere cowardly pacifists with an industrial plant rapidly falling into desuetude. The end of the decade would see Germany at peace, impregnable, secure behind a ring of satellites extending from the Pyrenees to the Black Sea. If Denmark refused to restore her German provinces to their rightful owners, why then the pacific Danes would be over-run—as indeed they were—in a day, no more. The estuary of the Rhine, splitting itself into manifold rivercourses as it approached the North Sea, creating the great barge traffic of the Netherlands and the immense port of Rotterdam, would be repossessed instantly, should war break out. If no war came, the Netherlanders, totally dependent on the commerce along the upper waters of the Rhine, could easily be reduced to economic submission. Deprived of their traffic with Germany,

Rotterdam, Amsterdam and Antwerp would wither, whi
Bremen and Hamburg waxed fat.

Herr Hitler seems not to have foreseen that a point would
be reached beyond which this policy could not be carried out
peacefully. My father was constantly asking himself, in the
two weeks that followed our arrival at the Lakeview Hotel,
that is from 8 August to 22 August, what limits the German
Chancellor might set to his adventures.

"Who's to stop him?" he would say to my mother, as he
stood slicing ham for sandwiches in the kitchen of the
Lakeview Coffee-Shop. "What must he do to bring final
resistance? Why is he monkeying with Poland?"

My mother was a closer analyst of the facts of Hitler's
case. "If he controlled Poland, the Balkans and Roumania,
he could maintain himself indefinitely against a sea
blockade."

This claim always vexed my father greatly. "Nonsense.
How could he? He needs rubber! Coal. Iron. Petroleum."

"The petroleum will come from the Black Sea," my
mother said peaceably. "From the Baku fields. As for the
rubber, the German chemists have successfully manufac-
tured synthetics in the laboratory, and are now able to produce them in quantity."

My father's face was a mixture of irritation and delight.
He was intensely proud of my mother's solid good judgment. He used to tell her that she should write for publication, but the notion displeased her, for some reason, and she
never did it. Lila Trousdell and her daughter Ramona, happening to pass through the kitchen, paused and stood listening. It may have been the first time in their lives they'd
heard a woman telling a man something he didn't know.

"Butadiene," said my mother, "in polymerized long-
molecule chains. The scout cars of the Panzer divisions are
equipped with synthetic tires, and have been since the
Spanish campaign."

"Is that so?" said Mrs. Trousdell.

"As for the steel industry, why do you think he moved into the Ruhr?"

A customer shouted for service out at the counter, and my mother wiped breadcrumbs from her hands and went off to serve him.

Ramona smiled coquettishly at Dad, saying, "It's amazing how Mrs. Goderich keeps up with things."

My father said, "Coal. Steel. Rubber. Oil. Electric power. It has a dreadful sound."

This conversation took place around 15 August. That night a Polish soldier was shot on the Danzig frontier, whereupon Polish troops were ordered to open fire on anybody crossing the frontier at night, without challenge.

The next two weeks were drawn out in nightmarish indecision. Everybody thought of war. Adults went around with troubled faces. Mr. Halifax, across the street in the drugstore, was especially alert to world conditions. He had many family connections in England, heard from them constantly and often discussed English unpreparedness with my father. He was fully *au courant* with matters like the ARP, the blackout, barrage balloons, and those other ineffectual measures, so very English, just now going into effect. England, it now appeared, was trying to repair in weeks the sloth and folly of decades, an experiment conducted before and since in her history.

Day followed day when it almost seemed as if the headlines stood unchanged on the front page. Hitler stated terms. The Polish rejected them. The French and English said that they would honour their guarantee of Polish territorial integrity. The name of Sir Neville Henderson was suddenly on everyone's lips, a third-line, untalented FO type, thrust accidentally into a place on the European stage for which he was totally unfitted. Who now remembers Sir Neville Henderson?

There would be a war; there would be a war; there would
not be a war; there would not. . . .

Hitler was feeling uncertain.

Sir Neville Henderson had terrified Herr Hitler by a show
of determination.

There would be another settlement of the sort reached at
Munich.

The western democracies would not accept another
Munich.

What was he waiting for?

What would happen?

Why couldn't they change that headline in the *Star*, for
heaven's sakes?

WAR IMMINENT

WAR THREATENS EUROPE

NAZI ULTIMATUM

CORRIDOR TO DISAPPEAR

In mid-September the rains would start on the central
Polish plain; secondary roads would be impassable by heavy
motorized traffic. Observers thought that Poland might
resist the Nazis throughout the winter, if the attack did not
come before the rains. The obsolete battleship *Schleswig-
Holstein* sailed from Kiel bound for an unknown destination;
she was useless in a naval engagement owing to defects in her
armour, but might serve more than adequately in the bombardment of coastal defences, her eleven-inch guns being
heavier, and capable of firing at longer range, than any
coast-defence artillery in the Baltic theatre:

DALADIER, CHAMBERLAIN TO STAND FIRM

NO SECOND MUNICH SAYS BRITISH MINISTER

"POLES' LAST CHANCE": HITLER

Monday night was a good night at the Lakeview Coffee-
Shop. All tables were taken. Marianne Keogh, who had
taken over most of the waitressing in the coffee-shop, was
speeding back and forth from the kitchen to the tables and
booths, assisted by Amanda Louise, now a really competent
helper. My parents, warm and sweaty, were doing most of

the work in the kitchen. I was in charge of the radio. My father had kept the radio on in the kitchen for days now, chasing news broadcasts around the dial. The names of news reporters who were to be famous for years began to reverberate in our ears: Murrow, Shirer, Kaltenborn, Stoneman, Quentin Reynolds. Dad couldn't get enough news.

At five minutes past six that night, Monday, 21 August, on one of the American network broadcasts we used to pick up from Buffalo, a fugitive voice announced that a trade agreement of some sort was pending between the Soviet Union and the Nazis. Dad was busy making sandwiches at the time. Ham sandwiches. I remember them well. He was laying them on top of each other in a tottering pile. When the news of this proposed trade agreement came over the air he turned sharply and bumped his pile of sandwiches with his elbow. They fell over onto the breadboard. One sandwich fell between his feet.

"What did he say?"

He looked at me with an expression I'd never seen before.

"What did he say?" he repeated.

"He said it was midnight now in Berlin."

"No, no, not that. About Russia and Germany."

"I don't know, Dad. I didn't understand it."

"Just a minute," he said, motioning me to be silent. The voice on the radio said, "And now once again, tonight's news headline. It was announced in Berlin one hour ago, eleven PM Berlin time, that Germany and Russia would conclude a new trade agreement tomorrow. Terms of the agreement were not announced."

Dad took a convulsive step toward me. "Turn it off," he said. He stepped on the sandwich between his feet; he'd spread the butter too thick, and the yellow stuff oozed from between the crushed slices of bread. He looked at his foot, then peeled the spoiled sandwich from his shoe. I'd never seen him look like this before. His world had changed in the instant: the pacific world of socialist theory in which the Soviet Union stood as the principal guarantor against fascist agression, whereas right-wing interests in the "democracies" considered Hitler a welcome bulwark against the terrible threat of socialism.

"It can't be just a trade agreement," said my father his inflamed imagination leading to the correct, awful conclusion. "It'll be a non-intervention treaty. Why? Why?"

This terrible "Why? Why?" reverberated down the next three decades of his life unanswered. Unanswerable now. Stalin must be allowed full responsibility for the agreement with the Nazis. How can this have happened? The political trials now two years behind us could be seen in this new light as ulcers over fearful rottenness; the Stalinist slave camp stood revealed. How could the Russian dictator—for that was what he was by now—how could he have sunk his differences with Adolf Hitler? How? Was he frightened, charmed, mesmerised? Had he no notion that as soon as Hitler had disposed of his enemies in the west he would march on Moscow? How can Stalin have contemplated the armies of the Germans flooding into Poland as they did, virtually without opposition, and expected that a German advance to the east would be long delayed? Stalin did all this, destroying the solidarity of the international left, ruining his credibility among French and British socialists. He astounded the world by this fateful action. The war followed almost at once.

At the beginning of the last week in August, by Thursday, 24 August, it seemed certain that Hitler would cross the Polish border; the only question was one of timing. Envoys circulated tirelessly between the chancelleries. Embassies began to close, to be boarded over. Diplomatic personnel, families with children, began to quit states about to become hostile. When would he go? When?

Still self-possessed, still canny, he waited till the most propitious time, at the beginning of the following weekend, Labour Day weekend as a matter of fact—which might have given any socialist cause for reflection. German troops crossed into Poland about noon on Friday, 1 September.

The last negotiations between France, Britain and Germany were effectively over by eleven o'clock on Sunday morning. Hitler must have considered, among other things, that the effete Western powers would do nothing very much over the long holiday weekend. He was right.

That Sunday seemed like any other quiet Sunday in my life, as I stood beside my father in the large, wet bathroom next to our apartment in the Lakeview. This bathroom had been intended for the use of a couple of dozen lodgers, presumably all male. It had three dripping, steamy shower cubicles, and a fleet of toilet bowls in a separate room at the back, and there were many basins and a row of mirrors in the front room, always covered with mist from the showers. This capacious lavatory had been set aside for our exclusive use—an inconvenience to some neighbouring guests who still from time to time penetrated these precincts in morning disarray.

That peaceful morning, a gorgeous day, the loveliest weekend of the summer, I was standing next to the basin where my father was shaving. It was about eight o'clock Toronto time, that is, one o'clock in London. Two hours before, the melancholy voice of Neville Chamberlain had announced that the United Kingdom was now in a state of war with Germany, "nothing further having been heard in response to our note, from Herr Hitler."

The news hadn't reached us yet. I watched my dad lather up, then manipulate the razor under either ear, along the cheek, carefully beneath his nose and around his mouth. Watching my father shave had been a habit of infancy. I felt obscurely comforted on this quietly menacing Sunday to find myself beside him again. Suddenly my most secret feelings bubbled up.

"If they're going to have a war, they'd better declare it now and get it over with," I said.

My father laid his razor down, resting his hand on the edge of the dripping basin. For a moment he stared at the mirror, lifted his other hand and wiped at it, but it wouldn't come clear. He turned and looked at me, his face changing from moment to moment as I looked at him. It broke up. I saw that he was keeping back tears. He said nothing, but his face went on working and changing. I suddenly saw, dimly at first and then with gathering excitement and clarity, how a single man's life may stand for the lives of many, perhaps in the end for universal life. His sorrow was not just between us. I didn't know what a war was like.

And still we weren't technically at war. Wily Willy King kept us out of it for another week, while the Germans drove across the Polish plain, giving the first terrible demonstration of modern mobile war, what became known in succeeding months as lightning-war, *blitzkrieg.* The *Athenia* was sunk in mid-Atlantic with Canadians on board. Voices on broadcasts from Britain became familiar, as did certain key phrases. "The RAF last night raided the goods-yards at Hamm." Canada didn't go to war, with a formal declaration, until the tenth of the month, when my father's old friend and visitor, Mr. Woodsworth, made a moving declaration of his pacifist faith—my father's faith as well—in the House of Commons, after which Mr. King put through the legal instrument establishing a state of war. A rain of bombs was already falling on Warsaw and the German advance-guard stood at its gates. Off the port of Gdynia, a terrible revenge for the very existence of the place was being enacted by the *Schleswig-Holstein,* her destination now revealed. In the death-struggle of the Polish garrison, eleven-inch projectiles fell upon them, one after another, from the skies, launched by the turrets of the unreachable German ship. Nothing could be done to halt the firing, as the old battleship was anchored in the port of Danzig, launching those terrible high-explosive shells at long range, beyond all posssibility of counterattack. The garrison of Gdynia, the port installations, the new town, were pounded to dust without hope, or defence, or chance of relief. So Gdynia and modern Poland were battered to bits.

On the thirteenth of the month, I said to Tom and Gerry Cawkell, "Hey, your father has a new coat."

Mr. Cawkell had suddenly acquired a thick warm khaki overcoat with brass buttons and a wide collar, the first new overcoat he'd had since the beginnings of the depression a decade earlier. He hadn't had a new suit during that period either; now he was about to acquire a new suit of khaki, a suit of what came to be know as "battle dress." He'd joined the army the day after the formal declaration of war, not so much from patriotic motives as because the army offered him the first steady job he'd ever had, plus the possibility of some training in a trade, training that I believe he later actually received—in field communications, perhaps not very useful training for peacetime. He had simply gone across to the city on the *Bluebell*, walked west from the Ferry Docks a distance of perhaps two miles to the Fork York Armouries where he had been among the first half-dozen to commit themselves irrevocably to a military calling. On that day, the army had had no place to put Mr. Cawkell—just as civilian life had found no place for him—so they simply issued him an army greatcoat as an outward and visible sign of his enlistment, then sent him home to await instructions that were surprisingly slow in coming. He hung around the Lakeview for another three weeks, sporting his beautiful warm coat and receiving congratulations. Around the fifteenth of the month they found a hat for him, or rather a cap, one of those fore-and-aft forage caps with two tiny brass buttons up the front. Eventually he disappeared into the training cadres of the First Canadian Division and was seen no more. Impressed by this issue of free clothing, Mr. Weisman made a series of abortive attempts to join the RCAF, paying call after call to the Coliseum at the Canadian National Exhibition grounds, where the Air Force HQ was located in the former Swine Pavilion. These headquarters revolved around the operation of a place called Manning Pool, which everybody in Toronto thought was called after somebody named Manning, as you might speak of Timothy Eaton Memorial.

Tens of thousands of enlistees passed through the exhibition grounds into various air-force training centres at Trenton, Alliston, and farther afield. Mr. Weisman never made it; he was considered too old at 39. This appealed to my father, a pacifist of precisely the same age.

"I missed the first one," he would say with a weird blend of glumness and hilarity, "and it looks like I'll miss this one too." He never afterward reproached himself with not having served, thought himself very lucky to have missed both wars. I think he was right. I've missed all the wars that have come along in my own life, and haven't on the whole regretted it.

Bobby Weisman's dad finally made it into the army; he'd have preferred a greatcoat in the smart air-force blue, but was ready to settle for anything warm. Those coats were well-made, worth having, you still see them around, on adolescents who don't know what they are, why they are cut that way.

Similar coats began to be visible in many surprising places, on the backs of elderly, long-unemployed men—outside the gates of Manning Pool, at the Fort York Armouries, the University Avenue Armouries and other key strategic locations that might be considered exposed to surprise enemy attack. Toronto apparently abounded in military, or crypto-military emplacements, which Hitler's generals would naturally want to knock out at once. As manpower in the Army was already chronically thin—a complaint from which the Canadian Armed Forces have always suffered—legions of men too old to serve in this war, but with service in the last, were recruited into the Veteran's Guard and given overcoats and Balaclava headgear to resist the rigours of the Toronto autumn. They stood in convincingly military postures on guard around the places I've mentioned and numbers of others, sometimes clutching a weapon, almost always without ammunition.

I first saw a member of the Veterans' Guard on duty, dressed in military greatcoat, Balaclava, tin helmet and bulletless rifle, in strangely depressing circumstances on the desert wastes behind the Filtration Plant, across from

Mugg's Island, heavily guarded so as to insure the purity of Toronto's water supply. Tom and Gerry Cawkell, Bobby Weisman and I had noted the presence of a rickety wooden outbuilding about the size of a privy—which it proved to be— standing or rather leaning off by itself among those scrubby dunes across from Mugg's, in back of Donut Island, visible from Long Pond whenever we passed along the water in an old rowboat borrowed without permission from the Aquatic Club premises. We thought that this little building might easily be removed to some location where we could use it for a clubhouse. We resolved to steal it. Late one October night we got under way in the rowboat, towing behind us a crazed leaky punt that we'd found somewhere. I forget where.

Oh, I don't really forget where. I just don't want to tell where we got it. Anyway around ten o'clock we came stealthily up Long Pond, all four of us sitting in the Aquatic's rowboat. I was in the bow, as the youngest and least strong of the group, marked out as lookout and, most likely, the one to be left behind and caught if anything went wrong. Bobby Weisman sat in the stern, towing the stinky old green punt by a length of wet twine; the damned thing sat so low in the water that it dragged heavily, making Tom and Gerry labour at the oars as they pulled us along. It was about a mile and a half up a long reach to the deserted stretch of humpy sand and stunted beeches and maples behind Donut Island. Past the tennis courts behind the Aquatic, past the closely wooded spot where, a year or two later, the body of Aune Newell was discovered by Denny Denton's father, whose words are worthy to be preserved in this depressing context.

"I was just working along with my pronged stick picking up popsicle wrappers," he told the court. He was a part-time summer employee of the parks department. "When I seen this here stocking hanging from a shrub, I went along into the brush and there she was. When I see that woman's strangled nude body, I knew right then there was something wrong."

We rowed along past the murder spot, not yet identifiable

as such, mind you, but a good place for murder beyond question, eerie in the autumn gloom, which was faintly lit up now and then by searchlights at the Filtration Plant, recently installed as a safeguard against sabotage. We drew nearer and nearer our objective, soon were well into the territory of Hanlan's Point.

Coming inshore past Donut Island and the tiring rowers paused; there was almost no current, and we lay there silently, the dripping oars making the only noise. We eyed the dark silhouette of our objective, the small wooden structure we meant to pilfer for our clubhouse. In the dim light, it leaned precariously over to one side, an insecure toilet facility at best, probably not much used by the Veteran's Guard.

We disembarked, addressing one another in conspiratorial tones, drawing our boats in against the flat, even shore. Rippling water, a faint breeze now beginning, sand, silence. We nipped over to the shack, shoved it over in the direction in which it was already inclined, then all four grabbed at the roof and hauled the structure down the side of the sandbank toward the shore. When we had it at the edge of the water we got a nasty surprise; the Filtration Plant searchlight beam swept overhead and the whole theatre of operations was suffused with an intense brightness. In a second it was extinguished and we all began to wrestle the clubhouse, as we began to call it, onto the punt. It took some doing. We found ourselves sanding first knee-deep, then waist deep, finally in my own case chest-deep in bloody cold water. The only time I'd been in colder water was the day I'd tested my new boots under our clubhouse on the raft at the end of Jean Street.

"I'll have to get home," I said, "or I'll freeze."

"I'll give you my windbreaker in a minute," said Tom. "Come on, dig in hard and you'll warm up."

I shoved. He shoved. We all hauled and pushed and finally we got the clubhouse balanced on the old punt and prepared to cast off. I was in the stern this time, with Bobby, because the drag of the tow obliged us to exert a lot of force if we weren't to lose it.

Tom and Gerry heaved mightily at the oars. In seconds we were out along the wide range of Long Pond. The searchlight beam passed over us again, and as it swung around I saw from my vantage point in the stern a ghastly figure, an apparition that had lately haunted my dreams, one of the ghostly pair in the drawing in *Ken*, which I'd brooded over through that wet afternoon in the Lazy Bay Grill. "Do you remember what we saved Europe for?"

The scene was exactly the same: the dim uneven light mixed with glare and flare of searchlight and God knows what other unearthly illumination. It was the figure of a soldier of the Veteran's Guard, dressed in tin helmet, greatcoat with collar turned up against the damp. His stark outline, alternately flooded over with pallid light and hidden in darkness and silence on that sandy hillocky place, stirred up every fear that hung in my mind about "the War," the trenches, the stink of dead bodies dissolving in shellholes, poison gas, machine-gun fire as you went over the top. . . . One of the old men keeping watch over our water supply, helpless because without strength, or ammunition for his obsolete firearm, a leftover from "the War," everything about him menaced me, terrified me, though I knew he couldn't hurt me at this distance. He was moving across the uneven terrain on patrol, or maybe only looking for the vanished privy. He hadn't seen us, but his shape, the freezing coldness in which I sat, the undeniable fact that the rotten punt was sinking beneath its freight, combined to chill my heart unforgettably.

"Hurry, hurry, hurry," we whispered to the Cawkell brothers. "It's going." And it went. We weren't strong enough to hold the punt up. It filled, hung for an instant immediately below the surface of the reach, then silently entombed itself at the bottom of Long Pond, without a gurgle or bubble to mark the watery grave. Our clubhouse floated off, hanging buoyantly, tantalizingly, for several moments before our amazed stares. Its floor was peculiarly divided; there was an aperture to one side designed to fit over the pit of a latrine, and over this aperture was a plank seat with the conventional two holes. On the other side was ordinary flooring such as we'd expected to see. The clubhouse—we still felt we could easily have redesigned it as such—bobbed slowly up and down. It was getting on for midnight. Slowly the open side dipped down into the waters of Long Pond, which flooded through the interior of the edifice. Lazily, almost peacefully, this stolen prize too was engulfed, disappearing into watery darkness as we gazed. It was a kind of emblem.

Bobby Weisman sat there, mouth agape, staring at me, a piece of twine in his hand, frayed at the end where it had broken off short as the punt sank. "Gone," he whispered.

By now we were well down toward the TTC freight dock. This reminded Tom that he had to be at work in the morning. "We'll ditch the boat at English's, and I'll row it back at lunch time," he said. We made for the centre arch of the bridge, meaning to glide through it and come ashore at the boathouse on the other side. As we approached it, I became aware of the form of a young woman overhead, leaning on the railing of the bridge, gazing suspiciously down. It was Marianne Keogh, and she had spotted me.

"Matt! What are you doing out of bed at this hour? Get out of that and go straight home."

"I'm coming. I'm coming."

"Well, you better come quick," she said. I wondered what she was doing out of bed herself, if it came to that.

"Are you going to let her talk to you like that?" asked Gerry.

"Yes," I said, keeping my thoughts to myself.

I handed Tom his windbreaker, but he paid no attention. He was staring at Marianne, who was coming down to the docks to get me. "A keen piece of ass," he said, to nobody in particular. I hopped out of the boat and trotted past Marianne, evading her outstretched arm.

"Just leaving," I said, with an idiotic grin, intended as a conciliatory move. I scuttled up the main drag. I could hear her footsteps coming along behind.

"Matt Goderich, you're soaking wet. You'll be lucky if you don't die of pneumonia. You get right up to bed this minute."

"Are you going to tell on me?"

We were standing in front of the Lakeview Coffee-Shop by now, and I turned to face her. We stood staring at each other. I felt afraid of her strength, and felt at the same time that I loved her. She smiled at me all of a sudden with a pleasant, surprising sweetness.

"With that father of yours, it wouldn't do a bit of good. Run along to bed before you catch your death." All of a sudden she leaned down and kissed me. I think she meant to kiss my cheek, but it got me on the ear by mistake. She gave me a gentle push, and I darted through the deserted lobby and up to our bedroom. In three minutes I was out of my clothes, which I wrung out in the basin in the corner of the room. I got into bed and began to meditate sleepily on the events of the day. "Do you remember what we saved Europe for?" I thought to myself. I began to feel warm. Tomorrow was Saturday, no school. Why did Marianne kiss me? A shudder passed along my body. Getting warm. There was a war on, all right, all right. Mr. Cawkell died in that war, stepping on a land mine during an exercise in England. Mr. Weisman died at Dieppe, cut almost in half by machine-gun fire as he stepped onto the beach. Morgan Phelan died in the war, and the oldest Silcox boy.

Mostyn McNally burned to death in that war, wireless-operator and air-gunner in a broken Handley-Page Hampden over the Ruhr, one night in October 1940. The aircraft was badly designed and had a nasty way of breaking in half at the first hit; multitudes of young men died so, but Mostyn did it the hard way, caught in the turret, riding the flaming fuselage all the way down. He was nineteen.

For most of us it was the time of the "phony war," of "Roll Out the Barrel" and "We're Going to Hang out the Washing on the Siegfried Line" and the imputed impregnability of the Maginot Line. Troops came out between the doubled row of fortifications along the Franco-German border and played soccer. Sorties and patrols exchanged verbal threats, few bullets. It made for a long fall.